# The
# *Ultimate*
# German
# Shepherd Dog

Edited by **Sheila Rankin**

**HOWELL
BOOK
HOUSE**

**New York**

**HOWELL BOOK HOUSE**
**A Simon & Schuster / Macmillan Company**
**1633 Broadway**
**New York, NY 10019**

MACMILLAN is a registered trademark of Macmillan, Inc.

**Library of Congress Cataloging-in-Publication Data**
The ultimate German shepherd dog / edited by Sheila Rankin
   p.   cm.
   ISBN 0-87605-035-6
   1. German shepherd dog    I. Rankin, Sheila (Sheila M.)
SF429.G37U58   1998
636.737'6--dc21                                                97-46158
                                                                  CIP

Printed in Hong Kong

10 9 8 7 6 5 4 3 2 1

# $C$ONTENTS

# CONTRIBUTORS

**SHEILA RANKIN (Breed Consultant)** purchased her first German Shepherd Dog in 1959, in partnership with the late 'TV' Rankin, and she has been devoted to the breed ever since. Although litters are a rare occurrence, there have been two homebred Champions, Sheracyn Connoisseur and Sheracyn Nevada. Sheila judges at Championship Show level, and judged male GSDs at Crufts in 1996. She is vice-President, Secretary and Show Manager of GSDC Essex, Secretary of the GSD Breed Council, President of the GSD Welfare Fund, and writes the weekly breed notes for *Our Dogs*, one of Britain's leading canine newspapers.

**PERCY ELLIOTT** bred his first litter some 55 years ago and has produced top animals in show and working trials, including many police dogs, and his bloodlines have contributed immensely to the progress of the guide dogs for the blind. He has judged Championship shows since 1951 when he was the youngest Championship show judge in the UK – today he is probably the oldest! He has judged at all the major shows in England and has officiated many times abroad, including Sieger Shows in Denmark and Belgium. Percy was the first Briton to be qualified by the Schaferhund Verein to judge

both in Germany and abroad. He was elected to the German Shepherd Dog League Council in 1960 and is currently President. He was Chairman and Founder member of the Breed Improvement Foundation, and is currently Chairman of the Breed Council Educational Panel and Breed Surveyor. *See Chapter 7: The Breed Standards; Chapter 8: The Judge's View.*

**DAVID HALL** formed his Gayville kennel in the early 1970s, and since then it has gone from strength to strength, being top kennel in 1993, 1994, 1996 and 1997. In 1988 Gayvilles Dixie gained her title and Best of Breed at Crufts, while her brother, Gayvilles Dingo, won his title in New Zealand, as well as being the top GSD in successive years. Cello von Aschera, a top producing male, and Ronni von der Berghutte were then imported from Germany and the result was the top winning GSD Ch. Gayvilles Xera. To date, she has won 20 CCs and 10 Reserve CCs, Top GSD Female 1993 and 1994, and Top Brood 1996 and 1997. Her first litter included Ch. Gaysvilles Nilo (16 CCs, Top GSD 1996 and 1997), Ch. Gayvilles Natalie (9 CCs, Top GSD Female 1996), and Indian Ch. Gayvilles Nemo. *See Chapter 9: The Show German Shepherd Dog.*

**TERRY AND LILY HANNAN** bought their first German Shepherd in 1966 and have been closely involved with the breed ever since. The first Champion they bred was Ch. Jonimay Devil Dick, and his litter brother became Working Trials Ch. Jonimay Drusus. This was the first time in thirty years that a breed Champion and a Working Trials Champion had been produced in the same litter. Drusus went on to win the Kennel Cub Working Trials CC in the PD Stakes – becoming the first GSD to win this award two years in succession. Over the years the Jonimay kennel has produced a number of Champions and Championship Show winners, including the top winning Ch. Jonimany Shannan, from relatively few litters. *See Chapter 3: The German Shepherd Puppy.*

**ALISON JONES BVetMed MRCVS:** Alison qualified as a veterinary surgeon from the Royal Veterinary College, University of London, in 1987. After a short period in research she joined a mixed practice in Gloucestershire where she worked for seven years. During this time Alison developed a keen interest in the use of diet for the management of clinical conditions in both dogs and cats. In 1987 Alison joined Hill's Pet Nutrition where she is now Veterinary Affairs Manager. Alison has had several articles published on various aspects of canine nutrition and is a regular contributor to *Your Dog* magazine where she answers readers questions on canine nutrition.
*See Chapter 4: Diet and Nutrition.*

**DICK LANE BSc (Vet Sci) FRAgS FRCVS:** Dick has worked as a veterinary surgeon in practice for the last thirty-five years. He is a consultant to the Guide Dogs for the Blind Association and chairman of the Board of Trustees of Dogs for the Disabled. He was awarded the Fellowship of the Royal College of Veterinary Surgeons in 1968, and

the Fellowship of the Royal Agricultural Societies in 1993. Other successes include the BSAVA's Dunkin Award in 1977 and the BSAVA's Melton Award in 1987. Dick's literary work includes joint authorship of the *A-Z of Dog Diseases and Health Problems* (published by Ringpress Books in the UK and Howell Book House in the USA), editing *Animal Nursing*, now in its fifth edition, joint editor of *Veterinary Nursing* and joint editor of the *Dictionary of Veterinary Nursing*. He is an occasional contributor to the *New Scientist, Veterinary Times* and *Veterinary Practice. See Chapter 15: Health Care and Chapter 16: Breed Associated Diseases.*

**FRED LANTING** obtained his first German Shepherd Dog in 1947 and became an active breeder and exhibitor in the 1960s, soon becoming well-known even more as a professional handler. His Willow Wood kennel (von Salix prefix/affix) has become almost synonymous with good-looking dogs of working character. Fred is in great demand internationally both as a judge and a lecturer, and is one of only two conformation judges in North and Central America approved by the Schaferhund Verein. His books on the breed, *The Total German Shepherd Dog*, *Canine Hip Dysplasia* and *Canine Orthopedic Problems*, are top sellers. He has been called "the leading non-veterinary authority on hip dysplasia" by directors of the Orthopedic Foundation for Animals. *See Chapter 8: The Judge's View; Chapter 12: The German Shepherd dog in North America.*

**W.E. (Bill) PERRY** is an accountant in public practice, which has included being auditor to the GSD League of Great Britain for almost twenty years. He regards himself as a mere pet owner with a particular interest in the history of the breed in its homeland, especially of working dogs. He has written extensively for GSD publications in the UK.

His original interest in the GSD began while he was on National Service as an instructor in the Royal Army Educational Corps based in Germany in the early 1950s. He has been a member of the SV for many years. *See Chapter 2: Origins of the German Shepherd Dog; Chapter 13: Homeland of the German Shepherd Dog.*

**ERIC ROBERTS** acquired his first German Shepherd Dog when he was sixteen, which he competed and qualified to Championship Test C level. Since those early days, Eric has gone from strength to strength and his famous Callanway dogs have excelled in Obedience, Working Trials and Schutzhund. He started his own breeding programme, and all his dogs are descended from the highly successful El Gaucho of Lazy S (Callan). Among the most successful are Working Trials Ch. Callans Son of Callanway CDex, UDex, WDex PDex, and his son International Schutzhund Ch. Fonzac of Callanway. Eric is a judge in Obedience and Working Trials, and became Britain's first qualified Schutzhund judge. He runs the Callanway Dog Training and Behaviour Counseling School.

**MAX STOKES** is President of the German Shepherd National Council of Australia. He is well-known as a judge, and his Ambala kennel has produced many top winner dogs.

**MALLE MORLEY** is the owner of the prominent Karlrach kennel, and has bred two Gold Medalists at Australian Nationals. *See Chapter 14: The German Shepherd Dog in Australia.*

**BRIAN H. WOOTTON** has been actively involved with the German Shepherd Dog since boyhood when he began handling in the breed ring. In 1957 he registered his first 'Karenville' litter. A keen advocate of the dual-purpose dog, he bred, handled and trained Ch. Karenville Opheilia CDex, a double Crufts CC winner, as well as qualifying a number of dogs at Championship working trials. A UK Championship show judge since 1972, Brian has officiated at major shows in the UK and overseas. He was the first person from Britain to be accepted by the SV as a trainee breed judge, achieving fully accredited status in 1978. Breed Council Breed Surveyor and a member of Education Working Party, Brian has also written *The German Shepherd Dog*, awarded the Diploma of Excellence by the American Dog Writers Association. *See Chapter 11: Best of British.*

**JOHN YOUNG** has a small but select kennel, and his Jonal German Shepherd Dogs have achieved considerable success in the spheres of Show, Obedience and Schutzhund. With over 40 years experience in the breed, John is dedicated to producing sound dogs of excellent temperament. His recent achievements include campaigning Tracelyn Enterprise, Pup of the Year All Breeds, and Cotchees Dipper, Best German Shepherd Puppy 1997. John is Vice Chairman of the German Shepherd Dog Breed Council, and Chairman of the German Shepherd Dog Club of Scotland. *See Chapter 1: Introducing the German Shepherd Dog.*

# 1 INTRODUCING THE GERMAN SHEPHERD DOG

Having thought long and hard, and having carefully considered the environment in which you live, you are now ninety per cent convinced that the German Shepherd Dog is for you. Before making the final decision, let me give you my impression of the GSD as a domestic pet, based on my forty years experience of the breed.

The well-bred GSD is a noble, highly intelligent dog with loyalty second to none. As a puppy he is willing to learn and eager to please. As a companion dog he is a great mimic and will blend into the family unit without fuss or favour. Being of such high intelligence, there comes a point at which he must be given rules to live by, for example the seating and sleeping arrangements. Chairs and beds are for humans, and the floor is for Rover. Ground rules must be established early on in life, otherwise you will find, as I did with my first German Shepherd, that two humans and one Shepherd in the same bed does not equal a good night's sleep.

If, by chance, you are a weak-minded wimp of a person, the roles will be reversed and the Shepherd will impose his ground rules on you. If, on the other hand, you are a highly dogmatic individual whose will is imposed on all and sundry, then you will find the dog unable to reason for himself and he will become withdrawn. As happens when

*The German Shepherd Dog: A breed of intelligence and nobility.*

bringing up a child, the centre road must be taken, allowing the dog to demonstrate his powers of learning. And learn he will! He has a built-in clock and calendar with the ability to anticipate your every move.

An example of this was my very first GSD, who rode shotgun on my lorry as we travelled the length and breadth of the country. I always worked a night shift on Saturdays, leaving the house at 11.00 p.m. At 10.30 p.m., and only on Saturdays, she would appear at my side trailing my jacket. "Come on, Dad, it's time to go" she would be saying. One Saturday night, at the age of 12 years, she did her little trick as usual, but died before I got my jacket on. Yes, there are heartbreaks in owning a dog, but the pleasure and companionship gained more than compensate for them. I have heard it said that the GSD is a one-person dog. Not true. It may be that the dog has a favourite within the family group, but in their absence any other member will do nicely, thank you.

MAINTAINING TYPE

As in all breeds, the GSD has a Breed Standard which is designed – if carefully followed – to ensure not only that the dog retains his noble, well-balanced construction which gives him the mechanism to perform a wide range of gruelling tasks, but that he also has the mental capacity and natural instincts to retain his place as one of the top true working dogs. The GSD should never be bred to highlight any one aspect. For example, let us single out coat. The Standard dictates that white is undesirable, so reputable breeders stay clear of breeding stock which may carry this gene. This has the desired effect of vastly reducing the white population, with the hope of eradicating it completely. However, not all breeders are reputable and they do not breed for the maintenance of the Standard. Rather than breed for the whole dog, they concentrate on

the coat colour to the detriment of the rest of the dog. I see no justification in deliberately breeding against the Standard for fashion or financial gain. Such breeders declare that whites are rare. I live for the day they are declared extinct!

While on the subject of coat we have two main types, normal and long-coated. As previously explained, the GSD is a working dog and the coat plays a significant part in his ability to work in extreme conditions such as mountain rescue, working in deep snow in sub-zero conditions. The normal-coated dog has a dense under-coat for warmth and a top coat which is designed to repel water, with each hair being approximately two inches long. This allows the dog to maintain body heat while performing his duties in wet or cold conditions. The long coat, on the other hand, has little or no under-coat and the top coat is long with a silky texture. Such a coat will, on a wet day, show a distinct parting down the centre of the back, allowing cold and dampness access to the skin and thus reducing body temperature. Also, when working in deep snow, icicles form on the long belly hair, impeding the movement and efficiency of the dog. Definitely not the ideal situation for a working dog.

THE KEEN TRACKER

Because of the wide and varied range of tasks the GSD is expected to perform, they must and do have a keen sense of smell. This is the aspect of the GSD from which I derive most pleasure. The average GSD can be very easily taught to track in a very short space of time and I never cease to be amazed when I watch my dog hit a cold track, then follow a scent and indicate articles en route to his destination.

A good friend and early teacher of mine took this skill to the ultimate, exploiting it for her own devious advantage. She was a keen golfer and always took her old dog, which was an excellent tracker, with her when embarking on a round. While no one objected to the dog wandering round the course, it was banned from the Club House. Now, this was a bit of a problem as my friend enjoyed a wee tipple. Here comes the plot! At some point during the round, she would quietly and discreetly drop an article in the long grass without the dog noticing. On reaching the club house steps, she would command the dog to "Seek". Off the old dog would go, backtracking her mistress's footsteps, while mistress nipped into the bar and had her tipple. The old dog never failed to retrieve the article but with practice she became more and more efficient – resulting in the tipple becoming shorter and shorter. This gives you some idea of the joint fun and

pleasure which can be derived from exploiting one of the natural instincts of the GSD.

### FETCHING AND CARRYING

The GSD is always willing to please, which can be used to man's advantage – or should I say lazy man's advantage. During the early part of our married life, Betty and I lived in the centre of town and, when at home, I would go for the morning paper and breakfast rolls, always accompanied by our young GSD. She loved carrying things, so I gave her a basket which she proudly presented to the shopkeepers for their contribution. By the time she was 18 months she would pick up her basket, trot down the stairs, collect my paper and rolls and return

*Biddable and intelligent, the German Shepherd thrives on mental stimulation.*

*Despite its strong guarding instincts, the well-trained German Shepherd makes an excellent family dog.*

home with her booty all on her own. This is not a remarkable feat for GSDs because they are creatures of habit. Repeat the same enjoyable exercise over and over again and they will very soon perform on their own.

This habit of fetching for praise is quite common. When your dog has been separated from you for a few hours, on hearing your approach he will grab his favourite toy, or failing that, the nearest object, and bound out to see you, offering homage. Beware of painful consequences resulting from such innocent escapades. I once sold a dog to a young couple and, some six months later, was invited to go and see his progress. I was duly driven by the couple to their palatial home and, on the way, they bragged about the intelligence and ability of this dog to anticipate their every move. The wife declared that he knew their next move before they did and I explained that this was probably learned through habit and repetition. As we approached the main door I could hear the excited barking of the dog and, after some scuffles, he came bounding out with his present, sat neatly in front of the young wife and made his presentation. Unfortunately, instead of his favourite toy, he was presenting a pair of scanty unmentionables. Embarrassment reigned. To break the silence I said "See, I told you so, he has learnt by habit. He knows what you normally do next." The words were hardly out of my mouth when the young wife administered such a resounding blow to my face that my teeth fell out! This brought to a painful end my one and only invitation to their upper-class palatial house. All names have been withheld as the husband is now a senior barrister!

## TALENTS AND DUTIES

Built into the well-bred Shepherd are many facets and talents which will stand him in good stead when he is asked to perform one

*The highly trainable German Shepherd is also successful as a guide dog for the blind.*

*Photo courtesy: Guide Dogs for the Blind Association.*

or more of the varied careers ahead of him. Always remember that, from one litter, individual puppies will be dispersed to very different environments, for example, as a police dog, a search and rescue dog, a guide dog, a farm dog and, more importantly, a domestic pet. It is therefore important that you spend time studying the development of your puppy, encouraging that which is desirable and suppressing that which is undesirable.

Once your puppy has completed his initial course of injections and has the all-clear from your vet, he must be gradually exposed to the environment in which he will spend the rest of his life. Routine is very important – regular mealtimes, regular exercise, regular grooming. Expose him to all the sudden, and sometimes frightening, noises experienced in town. Most important, he must be socialised and learn to mix freely with adults and children alike. He must learn it is wrong to be over-possessive with people, toys, food and property.

As far as guarding is concerned, he must

*Photo courtesy: Metropolitan Police.*

realise that his first duty is to warn you of intruders or uninvited guests. That same warning is also directed at the visitor, explaining to him that his best course of action would be to wait there until the bossman cometh. On the bossman's arrival the dog will be given the all-clear, in which case he should accept the newcomer and relax. If no such command is given, he should remain vigilant.

On the subject of food, you are ill-advised to indulge in tidbits unless they are used as a training aid. Food which is available above floor level is taboo. Food at floor level is fair game. He must also learn that other domestic animals are part of the overall plan and should be readily accepted rather than used as an aid to vigorous exercise.

The dog's first year is the most important period of his life. During this time he will learn his place in the pecking order. He will learn that commands are to be obeyed, and *you* must learn that obedience comes mainly through the love and affection that flows between man and dog.

*The working dog par excellence, the German Shepherd has been adopted by police forces worldwide.*

*Photo Courtesy: New York City Police Dept.*

*Do not let your heart rule your head when it comes to choosing a puppy.*
*Photo: Steph Holbrook.*

*With luck, your German Shepherd will prove to be the best friend you ever had.*
*Photo: Steph Holbrook.*

## RESPONSIBLE PURCHASING

If by now you have decided to make that all-important purchase, remember that owning a dog of any breed is a privilege and not a right. He will be dependent on you for the rest of his life, which is a large responsibility. Before you can choose a puppy you must first find a respected breeder. There is only one safe route of purchase, no matter what country you live in, and that is to first contact your National Kennel Club or Breed Council. They, in turn, will give you the name and address of your local Club Secretary who should be able to furnish you with a list of breeders in your area. Before contemplating a purchase, visit the local clubs which participate in the show scene and Working Trials and see what it is all about. Get to know the kennels that produce the dogs which catch your eye and get to know the breeders. They are usually a friendly bunch willing to offer advice. Listen carefully to what is said and form your own opinions. Also, once you have purchased your GSD, your local club will be an excellent source of information regarding the well-being and training of your dog.

Your first contact with a breeder will be by telephone. Satisfy yourself that he or she knows what they are talking about. Ask the following questions:

1. Have you been breeding long?
2. Is this your only litter planned for this year?
3. Can I see the sire and dam?
4. Are they both x-rayed for hip dysplasia?
5. Has the sire been screened for Haemophilia-A?
6. Can I see the certificates?
7. How many puppies were in the litter?
8. Are you retaining any puppies for yourself?
9. At what age do you allow the puppies to go to their new homes?
10. Do you have a sales agreement?
11. Will they be registered with the national Kennel Club?
12. Would you object to an advisor being present during the selection?

The answers should give you some idea of the breeder's experience. In breeders we have the two extremes. At one end of the scale we have the owner of a pet bitch mating her for a once-in-a-lifetime litter and, at the other end, is the puppy farm churning out litter after litter. The size of the kennel is not as important as the care given to the actual breeding and the conditions in which the puppies, and all other dogs within the kennel, are kept. If you are unhappy with the conditions, walk away without even looking at the puppies. Visit as many breeding establishments as possible and see their breeding stock at first hand. A reputable breeder will be only too pleased to allow you to mix with his stock, allowing you to ascertain their soundness of mind and body.

It will also afford you the opportunity to examine the breeding establishment. Is it clean and well-run? Are there too many dogs for the carers and, most important of all, are the dogs clean, healthy and sociable?

It may not be possible to see the sire but it is imperative that you meet the dam in an open situation and not through wire. Her temperament and construction will give you some indication about what to expect from the puppies. If certificates are not available for inspection, proceed no further.

Merely as a point of interest, I find that the best age for puppies to settle into a new home is between six and eight weeks. A sales agreement should be provided and the contents designed to protect the puppy, the buyer and the breeder equally. A copy duly signed by both parties should be retained by the buyer. If the puppy is not to be registered with the national Kennel Club, then this should be reflected in the price. Unregistered puppies should be vastly cheaper and you must ask yourself why they will not be registered. Any reputable breeder will welcome a knowledgeable mediator to inspect the puppies and their environment.

Hopefully you are now about to meet the best friend you ever had.

While you are satisfying yourself as to the suitability of the kennel the breeder is, in turn, evaluating you as a suitable dog owner. There are many reasons why a breeder will reject you as a potential owner. One is if the dog is to be kept in isolation or semi-isolation. Another is if the wife shows an antipathy to GSD ownership; after all, she is the one who will be at home all day with the dog. A breeder will also not like children who appear to be wild and out of control. If the parents cannot control their children then they have little hope of controlling a dog.

I once had a prospective buyer visit my kennel accompanied by his two children. Also in tow was his pal, who also had two children. The party were given a conducted tour of the kennels, meeting and playing with the dogs individually. Eventually we retired indoors for refreshments and the friend who, during the tour, had made vain attempts to impress me with his abundant knowledge of dogs, asked what guarantee I could give as to the nature and character of a puppy when it neared adulthood. I explained that if he bought a puppy it would probably finish up an uncontrolled menace, whereas if the potential buyer owned a dog it would more than likely be a well-behaved asset to the family. The friend immediately asked for an explanation and I was quick to oblige.

During the tour of the kennels the friend's children ran wild, screaming and antagonising the dogs. When indoors, they danced over the furniture, opening doors and drawers – in other words, seriously out of control, showing no respect or heed to their parent. On the other hand, the prospective buyer's children sat quietly on their chairs asking sensible questions about GSDs. The words were hardly out of my mouth when a table went flying, smashing one of my wife's favourite ornaments. The friend was asked (as politely as the situation warranted) to collect his brood and remove himself from my premises, which he did under protest. The prospective buyer returned a few weeks later and purchased a puppy. He kept in touch throughout the dog's life and my prediction was proved correct.

# 2 ORIGINS OF THE GERMAN SHEPHERD DOG

The consensus in scientific circles is that the dog was the first domesticated animal, that it sprang from various subspecies of the wolf, *Canis lupus*, in different parts of the world, and that domestication first took place at least 12,000 years ago. How the first dogs really functioned in human societies is still a matter of speculation, but their usefulness to man no doubt increased with the advent of livestock husbandry and the eventual use of the dog for guarding and driving work. These roles are quite ancient, because current theory holds that, following the domestication of the dog, sheep and goats were domesticated about 9,000 years ago, with cattle and pigs following about a thousand years later. All four livestock animals appear to have been domesticated in the Near East.

Sheep reached central Europe by 5000 BC along the Danube Valley route, though, during the spread of agriculture through the European forest cover, cattle and pigs predominated. However, sheep and goats regained the ascendancy once grazing land became available. The spread of agriculture, together with the increasing importance of livestock husbandry, and the fact that

*Dondar's Gunsmoke returning stragglers to the flock: The German Shepherd Dog was originally used for herding as well as for protection.*

*Photo: Connie Cabanela.*

predators were a far greater peril in Europe than in the Near East, undoubtedly increased the status of herding and protection dogs. Over the ensuing centuries the best of these dogs, on a regional basis, were probably bred together in order to preserve the necessary qualities required in such animals.

Thus it was that recognizable 'types' of regional sheepdog were to be found all over Europe towards the end of the nineteenth century. The German Shepherd Dog is generally thought to have been the result of crossing two such regional 'types', i.e. the fusion of Thuringian 'blood' with Württemberg 'blood', a crossing of Central German dogs with South German dogs. However, it should be noted that some early German writers on the breed include dogs from the Province of Saxony with those from the Thuringian states, and speak of Swabian rather than Württemberg 'blood'. Parts of the ancient Duchy of Swabia eventually became part of the later Kingdom of Württemberg, which was itself subsumed by what is now the federal state of Baden-Württemberg.

## THE FOUNDING CLUB

The German Shepherd Dog came into being on April 22nd 1899 with the formation of the founding club, the Verein für Deutsche Schäferhunde (SV) eV. Rittmeister (cavalry captain) Max von Stephanitz was elected as the first president – a position which he held until deposed in 1935 – with Arthur Meyer as vice president, secretary and studbook controller. Sadly, Herr Meyer died on December 29th 1900 and von Stephanitz became the driving force of the new club. Other founding members included three master shepherds, two hotel keepers, an architect, a barrister, a town mayor, and – adding an international flavour – one factory owner from Austria and another from Switzerland.

It is sometimes suggested that the crossing of Thuringian and Württemberg animals took place only after the formation of the SV but this is not so. The early studbooks give the results of many such crossing before 1899, the most famous of which was Hektor von Schwaben SZ 13 – winner of the Sieger title in both 1900 and 1901 – who was actually born on July 12th 1898.

## VARIATIONS IN TYPE

Those same studbooks also give some idea of the tremendous variability in the animals originally registered by the SV. They included smooth-coated dogs, long-coated dogs, rough-coated dogs, curly-coated dogs, wire-haired dogs, and even the so-called 'altdeutsche', a shaggy-coated animal very much like the Old English Sheepdog or Bobtail, and usually wholly black, brown, or grey in colour. The vast majority, however, were smooth-coated types from Thuringia and Württemberg, which were basically grey, or yellow-grey, in colour.

## WORKING DOGS

Right from the beginning the German Shepherd Dog was seen by von Stephanitz (and others, of course) as essentially a working dog, and for this reason training qualifications have always been available. Until the early 1920s the following were used by the SV:-

**HGH** = Herdengebrauchshund (dog in use with the flocks)
**KrH** = Kriegshund (War dog)
**SH** = Sanitätshund (Red Cross dog)
**PH** = Polizeihund (Police dog).

Strictly speaking, the HGH qualification was awarded by the various Shepherd societies rather than the SV, though the latter used the test for the herding competitions which they organised. The PH qualification – the forerunner of the modern SchH3 – was conceived as a civilian version of the service dog qualification (PDH =

*Courage and control: The German Shepherd's instincts to guard and to protect have been finely tuned in its role as a police dog.*

*Photo courtesy: New York Police Department.*

Polizeidiensthund). The PH became the most common of the training awards, though relatively few animals were so qualified. The KrH and SH were rather specialised and not widely obtained.

Max von Stephanitz described the dogs from Thuringia as often being small though stocky, generally wiry and coarse, frequently lacking in good tail carriage, but usually having the much-prized erect ears and wolf-grey colouring. It was also said that they were vigorous workers but could become wild and almost uncontrollable if left in kennels! On the other hand, von Stephanitz thought that Württemberg dogs were mostly quite large though fleet of foot, and had good tail carriage. Erect ears were sometimes lacking but Württemberg dogs were usually of a calm and steady temperament.

## ORIGINAL BLOODLINES

Writing in 1914, breed historian Ferdinand Kautsky traced the 'bloodlines' of the leading animals in early breed history to the mixing together of five basic sources. These were as follows:-

*Group 1* Dogs from the kennels of Herr Wachsmuth at Hanau near Frankfurt, especially the Thuringian pair Roland and Courage, whose antecedents are unknown except to the extent that they were from Thuringian tending dogs.

*Group 2* Dogs from the kennels of Herr Sparwasser at Frankfurt which were mainly of Thuringian origin, though he did have some Württemberg 'blood'. Of special importance were Lene (Sparwasser) SZ 156 and her sons, the litter brothers Horand von Grafrath SZ 1 and Luchs (Sparwasser) SZ 155.

*Group 3* Dogs from the kennels of Herr Eiselen, then at Heidenheim on the Brenz in the Swabian Alps of Württemberg. Eiselen (whose kennel name was von der Krone) was a founder member of the SV, whereas neither Wachsmuth nor Sparwasser ever became club members. The Thuringian breeding pair, Max von der Krone SZ 160 and Sali von der Krone (not registered) were to become very influential in the breed.

*Group 4* Thuringian 'Herdengebrauchshunde'. Dogs actually working with the flocks. The Klostermansfeld and Birken kennels provided many examples, being owned by master shepherds Goymann and Arnoldt respectively, both of whom were founder members of the SV.

*Group 5* Württemberg 'Herdengebrauchshunde'. Again, these were animals actually working with the flocks. The most important were the females Fides vom Neckarursprung SZ 19 HGH, Mores Plieningen SZ 159 HGH, Madame von der Krone the Elder HGH (not registered) and the male Carex Plieningen SZ 158 HGH. To this group should be added Audifax von Grafrath SZ 368 HGH who was bred by a shepherd in Augsburg, though von Stephanitz said that he was of Swabian working stock.

## THE BREED'S PROGENITOR

Of all the early dogs the most important was undoubtedly Horand von Grafrath SZ 1, who is usually described as the 'Stammvater' (progenitor) of the breed. He was born of pure Thuringian stock in the Sparwasser kennels on January 1st 1895 and was named Hektor Linksrhein by his first owners. He later came to the Krone kennels of Eiselen,

*A keen sense of smell has proved of value in tracking and search situations.*

*The calm, sensible temperament of a working dog is a key factor in the breed's make-up.*

*Photo: Steph Hobrook.*

who sold him to von Stephanitz (for 222 marks) on January 15th 1898. The first nine numbers in the SV studbook were allocated to the kennel of von Stephanitz, and Horand was duly registered as 'Hektor Linksrhein, known as Horand von Grafrath (SZ) 1'. All early studbooks referred to Horand in that way, but later, when reprinting became necessary, it was decreed that his own original entry should remain as above but that elsewhere he would be shown simply as 'Horand von Grafrath (SZ) 1'.

Von Stephanitz regarded Horand as the very essence of the new breed as he wished it to be, namely a calm and sensible working dog who could, and would, do man's bidding as required. Horand quickly built a reputation for producing the right qualities in his own progeny and for being able to ensure prepotency in such matters in his offspring. As it happened, his status was further enhanced when his name came to be used to underwrite that of his paternal grandsire, Pollux SZ 151, whose name had begun to appear on pedigrees where it had no right to be! To combat this, early writers on breed

matters took to using the term 'Horand-blütig' (Horand strain). In the narrow sense this applied to those animals carrying the 'blood' of either Horand or his litter brother Luchs (Sparwasser) SZ 155. In the wider sense the term applied to those animals which were acknowledged to carry the 'blood' of Pollux. So 'Horand-blütig' in the wider sense included the progeny and descendants of Kastor SZ 153, Fritz von Schwenningen SZ 20, and Lucie von Starkenburg SZ 131.

I suspect that many readers of this book will be pet owners rather than breeders or workers of German Shepherd Dogs. If that is so, then they may well be unaware of the very great emphasis which Max von Stephanitz and others – notably Tobias Ott of the 'vom Blasienberg' kennels and Dr Ferdinand Sachs of the 'vom Hain' kennels – placed upon the working qualities of the breed. Not for nothing was the watchword "Shepherd Dog breeding is working dog breeding"! I have no idea whether or not von Stephanitz was ever aware of the Humphrey and Warner classic, *Working Dogs*, but his work was clearly vindicated in their research.

Breaking down the pedigrees of the annual Sieger Title winners in show, performance, and tending – up to the year 1923 – Humphrey and Warner produced details of those animals which appeared to be above average in producing both show and working champions. They used a version of the arbitrary mathematical system based upon Galton's Law – Galton actually called his system the Ancestral Law of Inheritance – which gives values for pedigree placement. The results of their study showed the very great influence of Horand von Grafrath, mainly through his sons Hektor von Schwaben and Baron von der Krone SZ 162 and his daughter Nelly Eislingen SZ 11. Horand's litter brother Luchs (Sparwasser) led directly to the great working dog Siegfried von Jena-Paradies SZ 1339 KrH, PH, SH, who became the first Leistungssieger (performance sieger) in 1906. The Pollux son Fritz von Schwenningen was noted for his influence on working 'bloodlines'. The Württemberg animals, Carex and Mores Plieningen, together with Fides vom Neckarursprung, were also shown to be leading influences.

BREED INFLUENCES
Pedigree dogs have to conform to a Breed Standard, most of which is concerned with structural matters, coat colour, and the like. So it is inevitable that leading male showdogs will have most influence on breed progress because they will be more widely used at stud than lesser dogs. But in a breed which was

originally conceived as first and foremost a working dog and which rose to be the leading service dog in the world, it is also inevitable that the best male 'performance' dogs will be bred on in the hope that 'like will produce like'. A simple, though arbitrary, method of showing influential animals is by way of tail-male bloodline tables – which means showing the direct male lines of descent– and the appendices included here relate to German Sieger and Siegerinnen, for both show and work, from 1899 to 1913. The show championships started in 1899, the tending championships in 1901, and those for performance in 1906. These tables clearly show the influence of Horand von Grafrath,

*Pedigree dogs must conform to the Breed Standard in order that true type, temperament and construction are maintained.*
*Photo: Jack Oliver.*

mainly through his son Hektor von Schwaben, but they say nothing about his influence through his daughters, nor about inbreeding to him.

Horand sired two Sieger titleholders in Hektor von Schwaben (1900 and 1901) and Peter von Pritschen SZ 148 KrH (1902). The latter was little used at stud but was a great working dog who might well have won the Leistungssieger title had it been available before 1906. Hektor was undoubtedly the best Horand son, producing not only the full-coated Roland vom Park SZ 245 (Sieger 1903) but the unregistered Heinz von Starkenburg and the litter brothers Beowulf SZ 10 and Pilot SZ 111. Heinz has no real claim to fame, except that one of his two registered progeny was the black Roland von Starkenburg SZ 1537, Sieger in 1906 and 1907, who was to exert great influence on the breed in show terms!

The litter brothers Beowulf and Pilot are the dogs upon which the reputation of Hektor von Schwaben is really built. Their dam was a Horand daughter so that they were very closely inbred on the 'Stammvater'. The Pilot line led in direct male descent to the Sieger for 1908, 1910, and 1913, and to another pillar of the breed in Horst von Boll SZ 8306 PH. Beowulf sired Beowulf vom Nahegau SZ 733 (Sieger 1905) but was an exceptional sire of females. Not only did he sire the dam of Roland von Starkenburg, but he produced the Siegerinnen for 1902 to 1906, which included the litter sisters Hella von Memmingen SZ 329 and Vefi von Niedersachsen SZ 339! The sisters were out of Nelly Eislingen SZ 11 – a Horand daughter – so were inbred on Horand!

## BLOOD FUSION

It is important to understand the fact that, in the early years of breed history, breeding took place at two levels. The first (Hochzucht) incorporated the high-bred lines involving Horand von Grafrath and his direct descendants. The second (Gebrauchszucht) was intended to produce working dogs and thus included further injections of the "blood" of animals actually working with the flocks. The antecedents of many such herding dogs were unknown. In later generations, of course, the 'blood' of high-bred and working dogs tended to be fused. This had the effect of reducing inbreeding to lower levels than might otherwise have been the case; to give a bit more quality to purely working dogs; to renew working ability in what otherwise might have degenerated into mere showdogs; and to mould the various types of dog which formed the breed into the basic GSD.

Much has been made of alleged wolf ancestry in the breed, and it is certainly true that the early stud books did show a handful of matings between wolves and dogs. Von Stephanitz himself knew Wölfi vom Wolfsnest (Zuleika-Saar) SZ 65, born in January 1899, whose maternal granddam was shown in the stud book as 'Zamba-Saar (she-wolf)'! But, for the most part, the products of wolf-dog matings had little influence on the breed. The leading showdog, Phylax (von Eulau) the Elder DHSB 8618, who was never registered by the SV and whose name was subsequently changed to Bursche (von Wandsbeck), was reputed to carry wolf blood. He did breed on, to a limited extent, through his daughter Krone vom Park HGH SZ 349, a respected name in working circles. The contention that Phylax carried wolf 'blood' seems to have been first mooted by Richard Strebel in 1905 when he published the authoritative *Die Deutschen Hunde*, though I believe that the grounds for his views on this point are untenable.

But Mores Plieningen SZ 159 HGH did have an enormous influence in the breed – she was, after all, the dam of Hektor von Schwaben – and she is said to have had a male wolf as great-great-grandsire. She

*Am. Can. Ch. Welove Du Chien's R-Man: 1995 Futurity Victor, 1996 Maturity Victor, Twice US Select Champion 1995 and 1996. When exported from its native home, the German Shepherd took North America by storm.*

*Ashbey Photography. Photo courtesy: Jane Jerner.*

appears to have been basically black, but with streaks or stripes as markings. I have always been particularly interested in this bitch because I believe her to be the source of black colouring in the breed, which is the result of a recessive gene – as it is in the wolf – rather than the dominant gene which produces black in most breeds of dog.

## THE SPREAD OF THE GSD

Both Britain and the USA imported breed specimens before the First World War, but they were few in number and not registered as GSDs, being shown as 'miscellaneous' or 'foreign sheepdogs'. It was not until after the war that the GSD became popular in both countries, though the USA had a breed club from 1913, as opposed to the 1919 origin of the first British club. In Europe the GSD quickly spread beyond the German borders and national breed clubs sprang up. Austria and Switzerland had GSD clubs not long after the turn of the century; France followed in 1910, and Belgium and Holland joined the others in 1912. All of these countries originally began with German stock of high-bred lines and most instituted Sieger-style Championships which were usually won by SV-registered animals.

Switzerland tended to go her own way but

the other countries worked closely with the SV. Austria first awarded a Sieger title in 1906, when it was won by Roland von Starkenburg SZ 1537, and thereafter, up to 1914, it was won by a succession of top German dogs including Wotan vom Emstal SZ 6813 PH and Ali von der Sudenburg SZ 11028 PH, both noted producers of excellent character. The title of Siegerin was not introduced in Austria until 1912 when it was won by Hermina Edelweiss SZ 12095, a Beowulf granddaughter out of a Roland von Starkenburg daughter.

Belgium only produced Sieger title holders in 1913, when the Sieger was the well-known Apollo vom Hünenstein SZ 31621 PH, who was also French Sieger in 1914. The Siegerin was Cora Dreiburg SZ 31229 PH, who, in that same year, was also Siegerin in Austria and France. Cora was a Norbert vom Kohlwald SZ 9624 PH daughter whose dam was a daughter of Roland vom Starkenburg. Norbert himself was German Sieger in 1911 and 1912, the first French Sieger (in 1912) and the first Dutch Sieger (also in 1912). Strangely enough, both France and Holland had made up Siegerinnen in 1911, a year before the male title was awarded. The French winner in 1911 was Herta vom Saartal SZ 10320, another Roland daughter, while the winner in 1912 was the famous Hella von der Kriminalpolizei SZ 13748, German and Dutch Siegerin in both 1911 and 1912.

With the outbreak of the First World War – ironically the event which really brought the GSD to the notice of the English-speaking world – shows and titles were placed in abeyance until the conclusion of hostilities. One exception to this general rule appears to have been Holland, which awarded Sieger titles in both 1915 and 1916!

*See Appendix for:*
*1, Tail-male bloodlines of Sieger 1899-1913.*
*2, Tail-male bloodlines of Siegerinnen 1899-1913.*
*3, Tail-male bloodlines of Leistungssieger 1906-1913.*
*4, Tail-male bloodlines of Tending Sieger 1901-1913.*

# 3 THE GERMAN SHEPHERD PUPPY

Making all the correct decisions when buying a puppy is very important because, if you buy the wrong type of breed to suit your needs, you will create a very unhappy situation for both you and the puppy. Remember, a dog that has a normal, healthy life can live for approximately ten to twelve years and, on rare occasions, longer. We assume that in buying this book you have already decided on a German Shepherd Dog.

We suggest that you find out, by buying some of the dog publications, or by inquiring through your national German Shepherd Dog Breed Club, whether there is a breed show – that is a show that is specifically for one breed – in your area. If there is, then go along and have a look at the adult Shepherds, because that is what a puppy will grow up to be like. Ask the owners of the dogs if you can handle their animals, and talk to the owners. Most dog people are only too pleased to answer questions or to give advice on their particular breed. Learn what the GSD is bred for, and what it is capable of, before you actually purchase your puppy.

*Think long and hard before taking on the responsibility of owning a dog.*

*Photo: Steph Holbrook.*

## FINDING A BREEDER

It is very important to find a breeder of high integrity. There are thousands of breeders out there breeding a great variety of dogs; to select one from all these, we advise you to contact the Breed Club Secretary. She will be only too pleased to put you on to the genuine breeders, not dealers, in your area. If, by chance, they have no puppies themselves, they will put you in touch with people a little further afield.

When you have found a breeder who seems to have the litter you are interested in, do not be afraid to ask questions. A genuine breeder is only too pleased to answer all your questions providing they realise you are genuinely interested in the litter – you would be surprised how many timewasters there are. Questions that you should be asking include such matters as whether the parents of the puppies have been hip scored; whether they have been haemophilia tested; whether you can see both parents, if this is possible, but definitely the mother; and when it would be convenient to see the litter.

Do not be upset if the breeder asks you questions: Where do you live? How big is your garden? Are you at work all day? What exactly do you intend for your dog? Breeders are just genuinely concerned about what kind of people are buying their puppies and what kind of life they will offer a puppy.

## MALE OR FEMALE

In our experience, if you want a family companion, both males and females have their advantages and disadvantages. If you want to keep your dog in the house, then a female has the advantage of being smaller – although a German Shepherd Dog often takes up far less room than small breeds that jump up on the furniture and seem to get under your feet more and, on the whole, are not as obedient as a German Shepherd Dog. Once over the puppy stage your dog will have picked his spot and will generally lie

*Both male and female German Shepherds are equally loyal family companions.*
*Photo: Steve Nash.*

there unless disturbed. As for which is the more faithful – well, we find there is little difference between the sexes; both make very loyal family members.

Females have the disadvantage of having a season approximately every six months, which will start any time after they are six months of age – if indeed this is a problem, as it only lasts for an average of 14 to 18 days. This is where your dog run also shows its usefulness because, when your female is in season, instead of leaving bloodstains on your kitchen floor, she will be outside in the run. You must mop up immediately with disinfectant as you will be amazed how the odour will attract your neighbours' dogs, so we also advise that as soon as she shows signs of being in season you put her on a course of veterinary amplex tablets. There are also several spray canisters that will assist in making the season less of a problem. If you use the tablets and sprays you will find them a very effective way of keeping the local dog fraternity at bay.

If you have decided that you want to be involved in showing your GSD then a female is the best choice. A male puppy, if he does not make the show quality to succeed in the show ring, is then only of pet standard, but a female puppy of good breeding with no outstanding faults and good hips, even if she wins little in the ring, can, with the usual amount of luck, be a very good producer of show-winning progeny. Any top breeder will tell you that luck plays a considerable part in breeding excellent winners. You can have the best puppy you have ever bred, anatomically, but, as we have said, it only needs one missing tooth when the dog is of showable age and that relegates it to companion quality, as far as the breeder is concerned.

## COLOUR

The colour of the GSD is very much a matter of individual taste for the pet owner. If you are not sure about colour then go to a show and have a look at the adult dogs there, as the colour alters in the time from puppyhood to, roughly, two years of age. See which colour appeals to you. Then you would have to enquire about the colour of the parents of the litter you have decided on because, by

*The colour of German Shepherds is varied.*

*All-black and all-white German Shepherds are fine as companions, but they are not popular as show dogs. Photos Steve Nash.*

and large, those puppies will, for the most part, finish up approximately the same colour as their parents; but nothing is guaranteed in dog breeding.

Colours are varied in the GSD. There are black/gold, black/pale gold, and bi-colour – that is, predominantly black with gold eyebrows, black all over the head and body and just the bottom of the legs gold. Then there is sable (also called grey); there are variations of colours for the sable, from dark to golden, which is a mixture of black and gold hair on the back running down the top half of the legs. There is also all-black and all-white – all-white dogs are disqualified from the show ring worldwide.

Most genuine breeders avoid the white GSD. We, personally, have never seen a white GSD puppy in all the litters we have looked at in over 32 years in the breed. If anyone tells you they are very rare, so therefore they cost more money, it is because 99 per cent of genuine breeders do not want them and will not breed them. In Germany, towards the end of the 19th century, after years of study over most of Europe's working Sheep and Cattle dogs to produce one uniform type of

GSD, the final touches were being drawn to a conclusion by a small group of intelligent breeders headed by Capt. Max von Stephanitz. Since that time the breed standard of the GSD has changed very little over the years. The current British Breed Standard for GSD states on colour 'Blues, Livers, Albinos, White [i.e. almost pure white dogs with black noses and near whites] highly undesirable'. The American Standard says blues and livers are serious faults, while whites are to be disqualified. The choice is yours.

*Think carefully about the future plans you have for your German Shepherd before making a final decision.*

*Photo: Steph Holbrook.*

## SELECTION

Before you do purchase a puppy it is important that you have decided what you intend to do with him or her. Will you be showing him, or working him, or will he be a companion? Do not go to a breeder and tell him you only want the puppy for a companion – then, when he is of showable age, which is six months, you show him, end up at the back of the class and then blame the breeder for selling you a puppy of inferior quality. So be sure you tell the breeder exactly what you want from your puppy.

When selecting a puppy, never consider the one that runs away and hides from you, or who shows signs of being distressed when handled, or who stands completely rigid, taut in his muscles and shivering, with his tail tucked tightly under his tummy – avoid this one at all costs even if he is the best-looking one offered to you. Always go for the one that runs directly to you and shows no fear when being handled. He should be quite happy with you when you stroke him and play with him. In other words, select one that is full of himself; this is the one that can be trained later and one of which you will be justifiably proud.

## SHOW PUPPIES

If you decide you want a show puppy you must inform the breeder as early as possible so they can select from the best of the litter. If this is your first puppy, you are going to have to rely on the breeder's honesty in selecting one that, in their opinion, is of suitable show quality. That means the puppy is of good conformation, of good colour and coat, and sturdy and healthy in appearance with a happy character. When we are selling puppies that have this show potential we never guarantee anything, except that the puppy is displaying the promise to make the show ring. For every puppy that has the potential for showing, out of 20 or 30

*This nine-week-old Steffen-Haus puppy, bred by Jane Steffenhassen in the USA, has the makings of a Champion.*
*Photo courtesy: Steffen-Haus kennel.*

puppies probably one or two will actually make the show ring.

Decide what colour Shepherd you prefer. Always remember that if you want your adult Shepherd to have a nice black saddle, then you must choose a puppy at eight weeks with plenty of black colouring on the face (especially the muzzle) and all over the body to the top of the legs. When first born this puppy would, to the inexperienced eye, appear to be almost completely black but, on closer inspection, the eyebrows would be gold and, possibly, the feet. Therefore, you can see that by the time that the puppy is 12 months of age he should have developed a nice black saddle, and a black muzzle and mask – a light-coloured muzzle detracts from the true Shepherd expression – with the rest being gold marking and finish, which is the true, typical, Shepherd colour when adult. Although colouring is of secondary importance, especially in companion dogs, we have never heard either an exhibitor or a novice owner say they dislike a rich black and gold adult Shepherd.

We have already spoken about visiting shows to observe how full-grown Shepherds behave and what they look like. Now, after choosing a show puppy, you must see what is expected of him, because Shepherds are shown and judged quite differently from

*A promising male puppy aged eight weeks.*
*Photo courtesy: Terry and Lilly Hannan.*

*At seven months of age, this female youngster is showing excellent potential.*
*Photo courtesy: Terry and Lilly Hannan.*

*The mature show dog: Ch. Jonimay Shannan aged five years.*

*Photo courtesy: Terry and Lilly Hannan.*

The puppies should be lively and inquisitive.
Photo: Alan Jones.

The litter should be reasonably evenly matched in size and weight.
Photo: Alan Jones.

most other breeds. You might think it is quite simple to get your puppy to run around a show ring out in front of you, but not pulling too hard to make judging him impossible. When you visit your local GSD breed training club you will find it is not as simple as it seems. Some young animals love running around the ring; but some do not, and it takes a lot of patience, time and correct training to achieve this.

## COMPANION PUPPIES
To the complete novice's eye the puppies selected as companion quality will appear to be almost identical to the ones which the breeder has graded show quality. We are assuming you have gone to a breeder who only breeds from good-quality bitches and

who, over the years, has established a very dominant bitch line. Consequently that breeder will have used a dog to complement the bitch, a dog who, more than likely, will have established himself in the breed show ring. So do not think that because you are buying a puppy only as a companion, that he or she will not make a very fine specimen on reaching maturity. The companion puppy will leave the litter and go out into the wide world much more quickly than will most show puppies.

Indeed the puppy that finds himself taken home to be a member of a loving family will probably have a much more rewarding life then some of the puppies that are retained or sold for the show ring. Puppies that are sold as companions will be taken out for regular

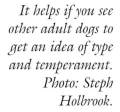

*It helps if you see other adult dogs to get an idea of type and temperament. Photo: Steph Holbrook.*

walks with the family in the park, woodlands or countryside, and will be played with, which is what they like doing most – being out with their owners to whom they are devoted. The show puppy, when he is taken out, is usually taken to the training club and then to dog shows when he is old enough.

BASIC EQUIPMENT
It is important that you have the basic equipment for the puppy's well-being – the correct lead, a stainless-steel bowl, a comb, a glove and a sleeping bed. Always buy a lead of good-quality leather, approximately six foot long and three-quarters of an inch wide, with a strong clip to secure it to the choker. However, your puppy will not need a choker until he is about six months old. Your first collar should be of leather, or a good-quality canvas or a nylon material. The collar must be fully adjustable so that, as your puppy grows, you can adjust it to suit the puppy's neck. When he has outgrown this he is ready for a choke chain. You will need one approximately 22-24 ins for a female and 24-26 ins for a male. Do not buy a fine-linked or a round-linked choker as this, over a period of time, will wear away the hair on one side of the neck, leaving a gap in the coat. Always use a long-linked choke chain.

Buy a stainless steel bowl, it will last for years. If your puppy starts to chew the bowl then remove it from him as soon as he has finished eating – the reason being that his jaws will soon be strong enough to tear the

*The choice is made!*
*Photo: Alan Jones.*

bowl and this could result in serious damage to his mouth. A stainless-steel bowl can be washed easily. Depending on what you feed your puppy, some of the complete foods, once dried on, can take some removing from the bowl if it is plastic; also, washing the bowl immediately keeps flies away when the weather is hot.

Your puppy will want something to sleep in. There are plenty of beds of all sizes and prices on the market, but a very large, strong, plastic, oblong bed is probably the best buy. It is easy to clean and disinfect. Buy two pieces of bedding so that you have one spare while the other is being washed. If your puppy is sleeping in the house, put his bed out of the way so that he has some privacy and you are not always moving it to get to a cupboard.

INDOOR CRATES
If you want to put him somewhere while you are doing your housework and you do not

want him under your feet, you can build, for want of a better word, a play pen. This only need be 2ft 6ins. high and 5ft. square. Make it so that the corners hook together then, when you do not require it, just fold it away. It can be used indoors and it will also stand on your patio or any paved area, but this idea is only temporary, as the puppy will soon be big enough to jump out of it if he has a mind to. Put a few toys in with the puppy so that he will not get bored too quickly. So, whether you use this method or the permanent run as mentioned below (which is the one we recommend), it is important not to leave the puppy in there too long. Do not let him start barking and then take him out; take him out before he starts being a nuisance to you and your neighbours.

Once your puppy is out of the puppy stage (12 months) you should be able to leave him for short periods without putting him in his run, but do not forget – this is a very intelligent breed and he will soon get bored just lying in the crate. That is when he may still get up to mischief and the outside run comes into its own. The puppy cannot get up to mischief in there – that is his place and he can do what he wants in there, except bark.

## OUTSIDE RUNS

We always advise pet owners to have a dog-run out in the garden – somewhere that is the puppy's own space, somewhere you can put him when you want to do housework, or where he can wait if he has come back from a walk and is in need of cleaning before he goes into the house. Also, if you are a keen gardener, a nine to ten week-old puppy will wreak havoc in a garden until he is old enough to be trained to behave himself.

Your puppy will appreciate somewhere he can be put where he can do whatever he wants without being told off, or scolded for chewing something he should not have done. If you make it a nice experience for your puppy, for example putting him in this private place with a large knuckle-bone so that he can chew away on it and not get anything stuck in his throat, he will be happy to go in there when he gets older and not think he is being punished and consequently, as soon as you are out of sight, start barking.

Do not leave him in there for too long for the first few weeks; as with everything else, increase it slowly. The run needs to be large enough for your puppy to walk around in, but it is not there for him to exercise himself in. It needs to be approximately 9ft by 6ft by 6ft high, with smooth paving stones for the floor, and with a wooden bed for him to lie on, approximately 3ft square. If you want to use it while you go out for a few hours, you

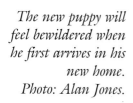

*The new puppy will feel bewildered when he first arrives in his new home.*
*Photo: Alan Jones.*

*Give your puppy a chance to explore his new surroundings.*
*Photo: Alan Jones.*

should cover it with corrugated plastic sheets set at a slight angle, so the rain can run off, keeping your puppy nice and dry. If you use new timbers 3 ins by 2ins, make them into frames; use 2 ins square mesh fastened to the wooden frame with strong staples; stain the wood frames, place one or two garden tubs and hanging baskets around the run, put some bedding plants in and you will find the whole thing does not look the eyesore that some of them do.

## OUTSIDE KENNELLING
If your puppy is going to sleep outside he will need a kennel. You have, basically, two choices of kennel, wood or building blocks. For the average companion owner, wood is far more practical than a permanent block construction. Some people among the show fraternity prefer the building-block type, because some dogs chew. We have found, in our experience, that if you do have a block-built kennel and the dogs chew, it is the doors that most of them chew whether they are constructed of wood or block. We have been using wood kennels for over thirty years and never had any problems, apart from usual wear and tear.

If you want light and heating in the kennel you will have to have it wired up and the cable boxed in so the dogs cannot get to it to chew. But, providing the kennel is dry and draught-proof, with some clean bedding inside, your dog will survive moderately cold weather. There are several good sheepskin-imitation blankets on the market – vetbed being one of them; and, when they are dirty, just pop them in the washing machine, they come up like new.

## COLLECTING YOUR PUPPY
When the day finally arrives to collect your puppy you should receive from the breeder a pedigree, confirmation of the dog's registration and a diet sheet. If the registration is with the breeder at the time of purchase, make sure the breeder signs the back of the registration form. You must also sign your section of the form and return it with the appropriate fee to the national Kennel Club. It will then be returned to you stating that you are the owner.

We like our puppies to be eight weeks old before the new owners collect them, especially if this is the first dog they have had. You will need to know, prior to bringing the puppy home, what the breeder has been feeding him on so that you can have the same diet awaiting his arrival; then the sudden loss of his brothers and sisters is not accompanied by introducing him to strange food, all in the same few hours of leaving his first home.

## ARRIVING HOME

When you do finally arrive home with the puppy of your choice, remember that your puppy is just a baby; although he may look strong and healthy and want to run about, you must build up the exercise very slowly. Do not throw objects 20 or 30 yards away and then let your puppy gallop after them until he can hardly stand. Just roll a ball a few yards and let him bring it back to you, always making a fuss of him after every throw.

## SETTLING IN

If your puppy is sleeping in the house, usually the kitchen, put his bed in a draught-proof area. If you want to feed the puppy inside for the first few nights, feed him in the same area. Choose a position in the room where you will not have to keep disturbing him once he has settled down; it is no use putting the puppy in a corner where you are forever opening cupboard doors to get kitchen utensils out. So it is important to select the correct spot.

## HOUSE-TRAINING

When you first begin house-training your puppy, do not expect results immediately. We all want our pups to be house-trained as soon as possible for obvious reasons but, with perseverance, you should soon have your puppy fairly reliable. We have always tried to explain to people that, if you relate young puppies to babies and toddlers, you will not go far wrong. It takes babies a long time before they are completely potty-trained, so you will have to have patience with your puppy. The most usual times when a puppy will want to relieve himself is on first waking up and after meals.

If the weather is fine, as soon as your puppy has finished his meal, take him outside. It is very important to stay with your puppy until he has finished his ablutions, firstly so you know he has relieved himself and secondly to make a fuss of him and tell him what a good pup he is. Always take him to the same spot in the garden; if you make this a routine your puppy will soon realise this is what he must do. If the weather is too bad to let a small puppy out, put newspaper down in the doorway and, as soon as he has finished his meal watch him very closely. Once a puppy has decided it is time for toilet he will squat very quickly, so try to get the puppy on the same spot on the newspaper every time. Never punish a puppy for relieving himself in the wrong place unless you actually catch him in the act. Tell him "No" very firmly and take him outside. Never punish the puppy if he has been left in the house for too long; that is your fault and you will only confuse him.

## FEEDING

If you do want to change your puppy's diet for any reason, do so over several days, providing that your puppy is eating what you initially fed him. We have always brought our puppies up on the same simple formula- feeding four times per day. We give porridge oats for breakfast with a little milk and honey and we have never had any problems adding an egg two or three times per week. Lunch consists of a complete puppy food; there are many on the market. If the breeder has told you what he has been feeding then, if the puppy is looking good on this, do not change it. Tea-time is a repeat of lunch, and supper is a repeat of breakfast.

On this feeding routine your puppy should have healthy stools and little of them. Also this diet builds muscle and not too much fat. Never allow your puppy to become too fat; you do not need to have seen or owned lots of puppies in order to know if yours is too fat or too thin. So long as their bones are strong and they are well covered without seeing their ribs too easily, you will not go far wrong. Always make sure the puppy has clean water available after eating, especially after lunch and tea-time feed. Do not worry too unduly if your puppy does not eat too much for the first 36 hours. It is a big step for the puppy, leaving the safety and companionship of his litter mates and the protection of his mother, but with a steady temperament, he will soon get over this and be back to his normal eating habits.

If you have taken our advice in an earlier paragraph and built yourself a dog run, always feed him in there. Put him in there after exercise so he can sleep without being disturbed. Also put things in there for him to play with; we are not big believers in giving a puppy personal things such as old slippers and shoes, because a puppy cannot distinguish between old and new. The first time you leave a pair of good shoes out and your puppy is in the house, he will probably think they have been left out for him – and who could blame him? We usually put an empty soft-drinks bottle (plastic) in the run with the puppy, after removing the screw-top; they will chew on that for days. When it starts to break up, throw it away and replace it with a new one. There are some fascinatingly shaped, and remarkably strong, rubber toys to play with and pass the time away.

MEALTIME TRAINING
You can train your puppy to do quite a lot by incorporating training into meal times. Before you give your puppy his meal, make him sit; as soon as he has done so, give him his bowl of food while praising him. If you want your puppy to return to you – the exercise known as the recall – do it with food. Get one of the family to hold him in the sit position a few yards away. You hold his bowl in the same position as for the sit exercise, call your puppy's name and give the command "Come". When he arrives in front of you give him the command "Sit".

*To begin with, the puppy may miss the rivalry of eating with his littermates.
Photo: Steve Nash.*

Remember, you must at all times have much patience when training your puppy.

Once your puppy has the basic idea and will come when you call him, replace the bowl of food with a small tidbit. Once you have the basic control of your puppy, do not go too far with a training programme of your own, because if you discover that Obedience and Working Trials are going to be the side of dog sports which you enjoy most, you might train bad habits into your puppy which would take a lot of correcting.

## SOCIALISATION

When your puppy first arrives home, he probably will not have heard any of the noises he is going to come across in your kitchen – the washing-machine, the vacuum cleaner, the television, people in and out all day. So let him investigate them at his own speed. If he approaches an unusual object such as a mop-bucket in the middle of the kitchen floor, encourage him, once he has got there and sniffed at it a few times; tell him what a good pup he is and fuss him.

His time as a puppy is probably the most important of his life as far as training is concerned, so socialisation is paramount in this breed. Let him explore everything and encourage him to do so. The time to really build up the puppy socialisation programme is after his inoculations at approximately 14 weeks of age. You should, by now, have got him lead trained in your own garden. When you first take your puppy outside your own boundaries, let him sit by your gate, especially if you live on a busy road with heavy traffic. Take him out when the traffic is at its lightest, talk to your puppy, all the time encouraging him. If you have a school nearby, it is ideal to stand outside when the children are coming out; not many children can resist the charms of a young puppy.

Take your puppy in the local park where you will meet other dogs. There will certainly be plenty of people and children there, and people and children love stroking puppies. Town is also an excellent place to walk around with your puppy; there is everything there that your puppy will come across in the course of his life, noise, people, buildings, traffic; it is ideal. If your puppy wants to approach people, let him – but always on the lead. Encourage this unless it is obvious that the people do not want the attention of a young puppy. Remember, dogs are not everyone's cup of tea, so you must appreciate other people's views.

## PLAY

Along with the socialising comes play. Most puppies love playing tug-o'-war with a piece of old rag, but be careful not to drag the cloth out of the pup's mouth as he will be

*Puppyhood is a time for learning, and socialisation is an essential part of the education you provide.*

*Puppies can learn a lot during play sessions – but make sure that young children are always supervised.*
*Photo: Alan Jones.*

teething up to the age of six months and his gums will be tender. Let your puppy get a firm grip on the cloth, then you just hold it and let the puppy do the tugging. Throw a rubber ring for him, just a few yards while he is still young; encourage him to fetch and return it to you and make a fuss of him but, like all other aspects of training, do not overdo it; stop while he is enjoying it.

## CAR TRAVEL
Most people with a dog like nothing better than to drive out into the country with their family and pet and have a nice leisurely walk in the fresh air, so it is essential that part of your puppy's training covers car travel.

If you have an estate car it makes things more bearable for puppy and family. Most puppies, after the first few initial journeys, have very few problems with travelling, but it must be said that if you have bought a puppy who is a poor traveller it can make things awkward, to say the least. There are several things you can try to make travelling less of a bad experience for the puppy. The most distressing situation may be not the puppy that is sick after the first few miles, but the one that drools and salivates from the first

minute of getting into the car to arriving at your destination, as such a puppy can dehydrate quite a lot. If you are travelling any sort of distance you must make water available as soon as you reach your destination.

So, what to do about it? Once the puppy has settled in with you (about two or three days), when your car is parked in the drive, sit your puppy in the back of it for a few minutes while you are within his sight, making his focus of attention you, not the car. But only keep him in there for a few minutes to start with; build up the length of time slowly over the next few days. Try sitting in the back of the car with the puppy and play with him for a few seconds before you leave him in the car on his own. Try giving him one of his meals in there so he associates being in the car with pleasure or fun things. Give him a large bone to chew on, always making sure not to leave him for too long at any one time. When you decide it is time to take him on his first journey, just drive up the road and back, do not swing the car about, do not set off very quickly and do stop gently. Make your first few journeys very short, no longer than a few minutes. Leave the windows open so that there is always plenty of fresh air flowing to the back of the car. Never feed your puppy just before the journey. If you are going out for the day take his meals with you and feed him when you arrive at your destination.

## VETERINARY CARE
When you buy your puppy from a reputable breeder, he will have told you that your puppy has been wormed at least twice and also when to worm him again. We always buy our worming tablets from the vet. When you take your puppy along to the vet for his first inoculation at ten weeks, ask your vet about worming. He will weigh the puppy and give you the proper dosage. After six

months of age your puppy will then need worming twice yearly for the rest of his life.

Do not allow puppies or adult dogs to lick humans, especially around the mouth and particularly with children. Do not let them eat off plates, bowls, pans etc. that are used by humans. Always make sure your children, especially, wash their hands after handling your puppy. Your puppy will require inoculations at approximately ten weeks of age, as mentioned previously. He will receive one inoculation on his first visit; your vet will then give you another appointment for two weeks later for the second inoculation in this course.

Your vet will also give your puppy a thorough examination for his general well-being and will hopefully tell you that you have a healthy, robust puppy. After he has completed his course of inoculations he will require a booster every 12 months. It is vitally important not to take your puppy off your property until one week after his last inoculation.

GROOMING

You should have a few simple pieces of grooming equipment. A metal comb (not too fine) and a wire brush, or a glove which incorporates wire brush on one side and polishing cloth on the other. Just a few minutes grooming every day will keep your dog clean and leave a shine on his coat. A German Shepherd's coat is a double coat. Its undercoat is of a very woolly texture and approximately twice a year your adult Shepherd will lose his coat. At this stage your dog will need more attention to grooming, as the undercoat will loosen and need to be groomed out. The top coat will look rather dull and dry and the puppy may lose a few pounds in weight. Do not worry: this is quite normal and, as soon as they have finished casting, they return to their normal weight and the coat recovers its usual lustre.

If your dog does get into a muddy mess after long walks in the countryside, providing it is not too bad, let the coat dry completely and then comb and brush it out; but, if it is in such a mess as to make this impossible, fill a bucket with warm water and, using a clean cloth, wash your dog down all over, starting with the back and work your way to the muddier parts – legs, belly, tail. Do the same again with clean water, then dry thoroughly with the dog's own towel kept especially for such occasions. You do not have to soak your dog to the skin; just the top coat will require washing. Of course, always do this operation outside unless you have the facilities inside.

Once you have finished, put plenty of newspaper down and let your dog lie on it just to soak up any excess moisture from his underparts. Once your dog is dry, give the coat a quick brush and it will look as good as it did before the walk. Observe these simple grooming operations and your GSD will always look well turned out – a dog to be proud of.

LEAD TRAINING

The most common thing the novice owner asks is: "At what age should I start training my puppy?" There are lots of answers to that. Mostly it depends on what you, yourself, want from your puppy. Lead training is your first job; we advise you to do this in your garden on the lawn, well away from garden walls, furniture etc., because some puppies react like a horse being broken in for the first time and throw themselves about all over the place. If you were introducing him to the lead for the first time near any of the aforementioned objects and he banged into them with his legs or hocks, or, worse still, banged his head against them, it could cause serious injury; so always use an area of grass where the puppy can throw himself around for a few minutes without causing himself any injury.

## ELEMENTARY OBEDIENCE

All dogs, whether show, working or companion, benefit from training in elementary obedience work – and if your Shepherd shows particular aptitude for work, the achievements are probably more rewarding for both dog and owner than in the show ring. There are very good dog training clubs throughout the world. Some train all breeds, some specialise in one particular breed.

Once you experience the pleasure of getting your puppy to sit when you tell him to, and to retrieve an object thrown across your kitchen floor, you may very well get the bug and want to start more intensive training. So we suggest you start training your puppy from approximately four months of age. Never try to do too much at one session; just start with a three or four minute exercise. Never do too much so that your puppy becomes bored, and always finish while he or she is enjoying it; and play with him so he associates working with pleasurable fun.

When you first start to train him in simple obedience – Sits, Stays and Heel Work – always do it on a lead. It is not very difficult to teach your puppy to sit. Just hold a tidbit in your hand and let him smell it, but do not let him taste it. Hold it in front of and above his head, pushing him gently backwards with the other hand on his chest. Once he has sat down, give him the reward and make a fuss of him. Repeat this exercise several times and you will be surprised how quickly he catches on to what is expected of him.

When you teach your puppy the Sit/Stay, sit your puppy in front of you, and keep telling him to Stay while you move backwards a few inches at a time. If he looks like moving, stop and tell him to Stay, then return slowly back towards him. Keep practising this until you can move backwards the full length of the lead and then return to the puppy, to the position where he will be sitting at your left leg.

With this exercise do not keep him in the Stay position for too long; just a few seconds is enough until you have confidence that he

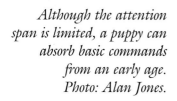

*Although the attention span is limited, a puppy can absorb basic commands from an early age. Photo: Alan Jones.*

*As your puppy gets older, he will benefit from attending a training club.*
*Photo: Steve Nash*

will not move. From this you can move on to the Recall to handler from the Sit position. With your pup sitting in front of you, approximately six feet away, quietly call him to you so that he walks to you, while you are pulling your lead in, like landing a fish. Make

him sit directly in front of you. Keep him there for a few seconds, then, with the command Heel, place your lead around the back of you and guide him around to the Heel position at the side of your left leg, finishing up in the Sit position.

Heel work should be started once your puppy has relaxed while he is on the lead. Take the lead in your right hand so the lead is across your body and, with your left hand, have a tidbit to start with. If he goes out in front, just give a gentle tug on the lead with the command Heel, and pat the side of your left leg at the same time. As with all exercises, do practise just a little at a time, so that it does not become a chore for the puppy.

Along with the heel work you will now have a very basic idea of what is needed of your dog from a working point of view, and you will have decided whether you want just a well-adjusted companion or if you want to advance both your puppy and yourself into the world of working dogs.

First of all you must find your local dog training club; most do a first-class job but some are really just for companion dogs. If you want a club that trains for competition and you cannot find one yourself, get in touch with the breed club and ask for your nearest competitive GSD training club.

*Ondine and Ondra v Steffen-Haus: Despite their young age, these youngsters already show a calm, settled approach to life.*

*Photo courtesy: Steffen-Haus kennel.*

# 4 DIET AND NUTRITION

Nutrition has never been the sole domain of the medical practitioner or of the veterinary surgeon. It is relatively recently that the medical profession has developed clinical nutrition to the point where there are professors in the subject, and that veterinary surgeons in companion animal practice have realised that they have an expertise to offer in this area of pet health care. This is curious, because even the earliest medical and veterinary texts refer to the importance of correct diet, and for many years veterinary surgeons working with production animals such as cattle, pigs and sheep have been deluged with information about the most appropriate nutrition for those species.

Traditionally, of course, the breeder, neighbours, friends, relatives, the pet shop owner and even the local supermarket have been a main source of advice on feeding for many pet owners. Over the past fifteen years there has been a great increase in public awareness about the relationship between diet and disease, thanks mainly to media interest in the subject (which has at times bordered on hysteria), but also to marketing tactics by major manufacturing companies. Few people will not have heard about the alleged health benefits of 'high fibre', 'low fat', 'low cholesterol', 'high polyunsaturates', 'low

*A balanced diet is essential in order to produce good bone and substance.*

*Photo: Alan Jones.*

saturates' and 'oat bran' diets. While there are usually some data to support the use of these types of diets in certain situations, frequently the benefits are overstated, if they exist at all.

Breeders have always actively debated the 'best way' to feed dogs. Most German Shepherd owners are aware of the importance of good bone development and of the role of nutrition in achieving optimal skeletal characteristics. However, as a veterinary surgeon in practice, I was constantly amazed and bewildered at the menus given to new puppy owners by breeders. These all too frequently consisted of complex home-made recipes, usually based on large amounts of fresh meat, goat's milk, and a vast array of mineral supplements. These diets were often very imbalanced and could easily result in skeletal and other growth abnormalities.

Domesticated dogs usually have little opportunity to select their own diet, so it is important to realise that they are solely dependent upon their owners to provide all the nourishment that they need. In this chapter, I aim to explain what those needs are, and in the process dispel a few myths and hopefully give some guidance as to how to select the most appropriate diet for your dog.

## ESSENTIAL NUTRITION

Dogs have a common ancestry with, and are still often classified as, carnivores, although from a nutritional point of view they are actually omnivores. This means that dogs can obtain all the essential nutrients that they need from dietary sources consisting of either animal or plant material. As far as we know, dogs can survive on food derived solely from plants – that is, they can be fed a 'vegetarian diet'. The same is not true for domesticated cats, which are still obligate carnivores, whose nutritional needs cannot be met by an exclusively vegetarian diet.

## ENERGY-GIVING FOOD

All living cells require energy, and the more active they are the more energy they burn up.

*Diet must be quantified according to a dog's energy requirements.*
*Photo: Alan Jones.*

Individual dogs have their own energy needs, which can vary, even between dogs of the same breed, age, sex and activity level. Breeders will recognise the scenario in which some litter-mates develop differently, one tending towards obesity, another on the lean side, even when they are fed exactly the same amount of food. For adult maintenance a German Shepherd will need an energy intake of approximately 30 kcal/lb body weight (or 65 kcal/kg body weight). If you know the energy density of the food that you are giving, you can work out how much your dog needs; but you must remember that this is only an approximation, and you will need to adjust the amount you feed to suit each individual dog. This is best achieved by regular weighing of your dog and then maintaining an 'optimum' body weight.

If you are feeding a commercially prepared food, you should be aware that the feeding guide recommended by the manufacturer is also based on average energy needs, and therefore you may need to increase or decrease the amount you give to meet your own individual dog's requirements. In some countries (such as those within the European Community) legislation may not allow the energy content to appear on the label of a prepared pet food; however, reputable manufacturing companies can and will provide this information upon request.

When considering different foods it is important to compare the "metabolisable energy", which is the amount of energy in the food that is available to a dog. Some companies will provide you with figures for the "gross energy", which is not as useful because some of that energy (sometimes a substantial amount) will not be digested, absorbed and utilised.

There are many circumstances in which your dog's energy requirement may change from its basic adult maintenance energy requirement (MER):

| Work | |
|---|---|
| Light | 1.1 - 1.5 x MER |
| Heavy | 2 - 4 x MER |
| Inactivity | 0.8 x MER |

| Pregnancy | |
|---|---|
| First 6 weeks | 1 x MER |
| Last 3 weeks | 1.1 - 1.3 x MER |
| Peak lactation | 2 - 4 x MER |
| Growth | 1.2 - 2 x MER |

| Environment | |
|---|---|
| Cold | 1.25 - 1.75 x MER |
| Heat | Up to 2.5 x MER |

Light to moderate activity (work) barely increases energy needs, and it is only when dogs are doing heavy work, such as pulling sleds, that energy requirements are significantly increased. Note that there is no increased energy requirement during pregnancy, except in the last three weeks, and the main need for high energy intake is during the lactation period. If a bitch is getting sufficient energy, she should not lose weight or condition during pregnancy and lactation. Because the energy requirement is so great during lactation (up to four times MER), it can sometimes be impossible to meet this need by feeding conventional adult maintenance diets, because the bitch cannot physically eat enough food. As a result she will lose weight and condition. Switching to a high-energy diet is usually necessary to avoid this.

As dogs get older their energy needs usually decrease. This is due in large part to being less active caused by getting less exercise, e.g. if their owner is elderly, or there are locomotor problems such as arthritis, but there are also changes in the metabolism of older animals that reduce the amount of energy that they need. The aim should be to maintain body weight throughout old age, and regular exercise can play an important

*A working police dog must cope with high levels of stress as well as coping with a heavy workload.*

*Photo: Kind permission of the Metropolitan Police.*

part in this. If there is any tendency to decrease or increase weight this should be countered by increasing or decreasing energy intake accordingly. If the body weight changes by more than ten per cent from usual, veterinary attention should be sought, in case there is a medical problem causing the weight change.

Changes in environmental conditions and all forms of stress (including showing), which particularly affects dogs with a nervous temperament, can increase energy needs. Some dogs, when kennelled for long periods, lose weight due to a stress-related increase in energy requirements which cannot easily be met by a maintenance diet. A high-energy food containing at least 1900 kcal of metabolisable energy per pound of dry matter (4.2 kcal/gram) may be needed in order to maintain body weight under these circumstances. Excessive energy intake, on the other hand, results in obesity, which can have very serious effects on health.

Orthopaedic problems, such as rupture of the cruciate ligaments, are more likely to occur in overweight dogs. This condition, which often requires surgical intervention, can occur in the older German Shepherd and may present as a sudden-onset complete lameness or a gradually worsening hind leg lameness. Dogs frequently develop heart disease in old age, and obesity puts significant extra demands on the cardiovascular system, with potentially serious consequences. Obesity is also a predisposing cause of non-insulin dependent diabetes mellitus, and has many other detrimental effects on health, including reducing resistance to infection and increasing anaesthetic and surgical risks. Once obesity is present, activity tends to decrease and it becomes even more necessary to decrease energy intake; otherwise more body weight is gained and the situation is made worse.

It is important to prevent the development of obesity in juvenile German Shepherd puppies. This is often made difficult by the public image of the roly-poly puppy encouraged by the media. These overweight puppies are more prone to the development of skeletal problems such as hip dysplasia and osteochondritis. They also then have a lifelong predisposition to adult obesity with the multitude risks this brings. Dogs, especially bitches, are also more likely to develop diabetes mellitus if they are overweight. Prevention of obesity in all breeds of dog is essential to avoid such conditions as described above.

Energy is only available from the fat, carbohydrate and protein in a dog's diet. A gram of fat provides two-and-a-half times as much energy as a gram of carbohydrate or protein, so high energy requirements are best met by feeding a relatively high-fat diet. Dogs rarely develop the cardiovascular conditions, such as atherosclerosis and coronary artery disease, that have been associated with high fat intake in humans.

Owners may think that protein is the source of energy needed for exercise and performance, but this is not true. Protein is a relatively poor source of energy because a large amount of the energy theoretically available from it is lost in 'meal-induced heat'. Meal-induced heat is the metabolic heat 'wasted' in the digestion, absorption and utilisation of the protein. Fat and carbohydrates are better sources of energy for performance.

For obese, or obese-prone dogs, a low energy intake is indicated, and there are now specially prepared diets that have a very low energy density; those which are most effective have a high fibre content. Your veterinary surgeon will advise you about the most appropriate type of diet if you have such a problem dog. Incidentally, if you do have an overweight dog it is important to seek veterinary advice in case it is associated with some other medical condition.

## CHOOSING A DIET

The first important consideration to make when selecting a maintenance diet is that it should meet the energy requirements of your dog. In some situations, specially formulated high-energy or low-energy diets will be needed to achieve this. Other nutrients that must be provided in the diet include essential amino acids (from dietary protein), essential fatty acids (from dietary fat), minerals and vitamins. Carbohydrates are not an essential dietary component for dogs, because they can synthesise sufficient glucose from other sources.

Do not fall into the trap of thinking that if a diet is good for a human it must be good for a dog. We only have to look at a dog raiding the dustbin or eating faeces to see that what tastes good to a dog would not be so appealing for the owner. There are many differences between a human's nutritional needs and those of the dog. For example, humans need a supply of vitamin C in the diet, but under normal circumstances a dog can synthesise its own vitamin C, and so a dietary source is not essential. The amount of nutrients that a dog needs will vary according to its stage of life, environment and activity level.

## FEEDING FOR GROWTH

Growing animals have tissues that are actively developing and growing in size, and so it is not surprising that they have a relatively higher requirement for energy, protein, vitamins and minerals than their adult counterparts (based on the daily intake of these nutrients per kg body weight).

Birth weight usually doubles in seven to ten days and puppies should gain 1-2 grams/day/lb (2-4 grams/day/kg) of anticipated adult weight. An important key to the successful rearing of neonates is to reduce the puppies' energy loss by maintaining their environmental temperature, as well as by ensuring sufficient energy intake. Bitch's milk is of particular importance to the puppy during the first few hours of life, as this early milk (called colostrum) provides some passive immunity to the puppy because of the maternal antibodies it contains. These will help to protect the puppy until it can produce its own immune response to challenge from infectious agents.

Survival rate is greatly decreased in puppies that do not get colostrum from their mother. Orphaned puppies are best fed a proprietary milk replacer, according to the manufacturer's recommendations, unless a foster mother can be found. Your veterinary surgeon will be

### GROWTH AND DEVELOPMENT

*A puppy achieves half its adult weight by four months of age.*
*Photo: Steph Holbrook.*

able to help if you find yourself in such a situation.

Obesity must be avoided during puppyhood, as so-called 'juvenile obesity' will increase the number of fat cells in the body, and so predispose the animal to obesity for the rest of its life. Overeating is most likely to occur when puppies are fed free choice (ad lib) throughout the day, particularly if there is competition between litter-mates. A better method is to feed a puppy a daily ration, based on its body weight, divided into two to four meals per day – the number decreasing as it gets older. Any food remaining after twenty minutes should be removed.

In 1987 growth studies were carried out using two groups of puppies, one group fed free-choice and the other group fed twice daily for 30 minutes. This showed that the time-restricted group consumed less food but still achieved similar adult size to the group fed ad-lib. By consuming less food the puppies were less likely to develop diseases of overnutrition.

Limiting food intake in growing German Shepherd puppies has also been associated with fewer signs of hip dysplasia. This is of extreme importance in this breed due to the high incidence of hip problems. More German Shepherds have been hip scored than any other breed, showing how seriously the breed is taking the problem. Weight control is in the hands of the puppy owner and it cannot be stressed too strongly that preventing overweight puppies can reduce problems with hip dysplasia later in life.

Proper growth and development is dependent upon a sufficient intake of essential nutrients, and, if you consider how rapidly a puppy grows, usually achieving half its adult weight by four months of age, it is not surprising that nutritional deficiencies, excesses or imbalances can have disastrous results, especially in the larger breeds of dog. Deficiency diseases are rarely seen in

veterinary practice nowadays, mainly because proprietary pet foods contain more than sufficient amounts of the essential nutrients. When a deficiency disease is diagnosed it is usually associated with an unbalanced home-made diet. A classical example of this is dogs fed on an all-meat diet. Meat is very low in calcium but high in phosphorus, and demineralisation of bones occurs on this type of diet. This leads to very thin bones that fracture easily, frequently resulting in folding fractures caused simply by weight-bearing.

Development of a good skeleton results from an interaction of genetic, environmental, and nutritional influences. The genetic component can be influenced by the breeder in a desire to improve the breed. Environmental influences, including housing and activity level, can be controlled by the new puppy owner with good advice from the breeder. However, nutrition is one of the most important factors influencing correct development of the puppy's bones and muscles.

In growing puppies it is particularly important to provide minerals, but in the correct proportions to each other. The calcium:phosphorus ratio should ideally be 1.2-1.4:1, and certainly within the wider range of 1-2:1. If there is more phosphorus than calcium in the diet (i.e. an inverse calcium:phosphorus ratio), normal bone development may be affected. Care also has to be taken to avoid feeding too much mineral. A diet for growing puppies should not contain more than two per cent calcium. Excessive calcium intake actually causes stunting of growth, and an intake of 3.3 per cent calcium has been shown to result in serious skeletal deformities, including deformities of the carpus, osteochondritis dissecans (OCD), wobbler syndrome and hip dysplasia. These are common diseases, and while other factors such as genetic inheritance may also be involved, excessive mineral intake should be considered a risk factor in all cases.

If a diet already contains sufficient calcium, it is dangerously easy to increase the calcium content to well over three per cent if you give mineral supplements as well. Some commercially available treats and snacks are very high in salt, protein and calories. They can significantly upset a carefully balanced diet, and it is advisable to ask your veterinary surgeon's opinion of the various treats available and to use them only very occasionally.

A growing puppy is best fed a proprietary pet food that has been specifically formulated to meet its nutritional needs. Those that are available as both tinned and dry are especially suitable to rear even the youngest of puppies. Homemade diets may theoretically be adequate, but it is difficult to ensure that all the nutrients are provided in an available form. The only way to be sure about the adequacy of a diet is to have it analysed for its nutritional content and to put it through controlled feeding trials.

Supplements should only be used with rations that are known to be deficient, in order to provide whatever is missing from the diet. With a complete balanced diet nothing should be missing. If you use supplements with an already balanced diet, you could create an imbalance and/or provide excessive amounts of nutrients, particularly minerals.

Nutritional management alone is not sufficient to prevent developmental bone disease. However, we can prevent some skeletal disease by feeding appropriate amounts of a good-quality balanced diet. Dietary deficiencies are of minimal concern with the ever-increasing range of commercial diets specifically prepared for young growing dogs. The potential for harm is in overnutrition from excess consumption and supplementation.

## FEEDING FOR PREGNANCY AND LACTATION

There is no need to increase the amount of food being fed to a bitch during early and mid-pregnancy, but there will be an increased demand for energy (i.e. carbohydrates and fats collectively), protein, minerals and vitamins during the last three weeks. A bitch's nutritional requirements will be maximum during lactation, particularly if she has a large litter to feed. Avoid giving calcium supplementation during pregnancy, as a high intake can frustrate calcium availability during milk production, and can increase the chances of eclampsia (also called milk fever or puerperal tetany) occurring.

During pregnancy a bitch should maintain her body weight and condition. If she loses weight her energy intake needs to be increased. A specifically formulated growth-type diet is recommended to meet her nutritional needs at this time. If a bitch is on a diet formulated for this stage of her life,

*The bitch needs top-quality food when she is feeding her puppies. Photo: Alan Jones.*

and she develops eclampsia or has had previous episodes of the disease, your veterinary surgeon may advise calcium supplementation. If given during pregnancy, this is only advisable during the very last few days of pregnancy when milk let-down is occurring, and preferably is given only during lactation (i.e. after whelping).

## FEEDING FOR MAINTENANCE AND OLD AGE

The objective of good nutrition is to provide all the energy and essential nutrients that a dog needs in sufficient amounts to avoid deficiency, and at the same time to limit their supply so as not to cause over-nutrition or toxicity. Some nutrients are known to play a role in disease processes, and it is prudent to avoid unnecessarily high intakes of these whenever possible. The veterinary surgeons at Hill's Science and Technology Centre in Topeka, Kansas, are specialists in canine clinical nutrition and they are particularly concerned about the potential health risks associated with too high an intake of the following nutrients during a dog's adult life: protein, sodium (salt) and phosphorus.

These nutrients are thought to have an important and serious impact once disease is present, particularly in heart and kidney diseases. Kidney failure and heart failure are very common in older dogs and it is believed to be important to avoid feeding diets high in these nutrients to such an 'at risk' group of dogs. Furthermore, these nutrients may be detrimental to dogs even before there

*Nutritional needs will change as a dog gets older. Photo: Steve Nash.*

is any evidence of disease. It is known that salt, for example, can be retained in dogs with subclinical heart disease, before there is any outward evidence of illness. Salt retention is an important contributing factor in the development of fluid retention (congestion), swelling of the limbs (oedema) and dropsy (ascites).

A leading veterinary cardiologist in the USA has claimed that 40 per cent of dogs over five years of age, and 80 per cent of dogs over ten years have some change in the heart – either endocardiosis and myocardial fibrosis (or both). Both of these lesions may reduce heart function. Phosphorus retention is an important consequence of advancing kidney disease which encourages mineral deposition in the soft tissues of the body, including the kidneys themselves, a condition

known as nephrocalcinosis. Such deposits damage the kidneys even more, and hasten the onset of kidney failure.

As a dog ages there are two major factors that determine its nutritional needs:
1. The dog's changing nutritional requirements due to the effects of age on organ function and metabolism;
2. The increased likelihood of the presence of subclinical diseases, many of which have a protracted course during which nutrient intake may influence progression of the condition.

Many German Shepherd owners are aware of a condition called gastric dilatation and torsion, commonly known as 'bloat'. This potentially life-threatening condition was previously thought to be due to the ingestion of a high fat or carbohydrate meal. Current thinking is that bloat is due to aerophagia (the intake of large amounts of air with a meal), common in greedy individuals, and the predisposing factors may be:

- Genetic make-up

- Competitive feeding

- Strenuous exercise around meal times

- Excitement at feeding time.

The last three factors encourage rapid eating. Special highly digestible diets are available from veterinary surgeons to feed to at-risk individuals.

Energy requirements usually decrease with increasing age, and food intake should be adjusted accordingly. Also the dietary intake of some nutrients needs to be minimised – in particular, protein, phosphorus, sodium and total energy intake. Dietary intake of other nutrients may need to be increased to meet the needs of some older dogs, notably essential fatty acids, some vitamins, some specific amino acids and zinc. Unlike humans, calcium and phosphorus do not need to be supplemented in ageing dogs – indeed to do so may prove detrimental.

## THE UNDERWEIGHT GERMAN SHEPHERD

German Shepherd Dogs are often presented to their veterinary surgeons because of weight loss or failure to maintain adequate body condition. This is especially true in the case of older dogs and in those with a nervous disposition.

The German Shepherd Dog has an increased incidence of a pancreatic disease called exocrine pancreatic insufficiency. This condition leads to an inability to digest fat from the diet. Affected dogs lose weight, are voraciously hungry and produce very bulky, pale, foul-smelling soft faeces. The coat condition often deteriorates too. The condition requires a blood test to confirm the diagnosis, although the clinical signs are usually highly suggestive of the condition. Once the diagnosis is certain, treatment involves a special highly-digestible, fat-restricted diet together with supplemental pancreatic enzymes in the form of a powder added to the food. Response is usually very favourable but the treatment can be expensive.

Exocrine pancreatic insufficiency can also be complicated by an overgrowth of bacteria in the small intestine. This further decreases food digestion and absorption. Affected dogs require the addition of oral antibiotics as well as the pancreatic enzymes.

Many German Shepherds will benefit from a more highly digestible diet, especially if they have a tendency to lose weight when stressed. Very nervous individuals can also be affected with a condition called anal furunculosis. This is a painful condition causing ulceration and infection under the tail and around the anal area. It is more common in dogs that hold their tails very close to their bodies, hence the link with nervous and stressed individuals. Treatment is often aggressive and involves antibiotics, a highly digestible diet to prevent diarrhoea and tail-soiling, and it may even necessitate surgery.

## INTERPRETATION OF LABELLING ON PET FOODS

Labelling laws differ from one country to the next. For example, pet foods sold in the USA must carry a Guaranteed Analysis, which states a maximum or a minimum amount for the various nutrients in the food. Pet foods sold in Europe must carry a Typical (as fed) Analysis, which is a declaration of the average amount of nutrients found from analysis of the product.

## COMPLETE VERSUS COMPLEMENTARY

In the UK a pet food must declare whether it is Complete or Complementary. A Complete pet food must provide all the nutrients required to satisfy the needs of the group of pet animals for which it is recommended. At the time of writing there is no obligation for a manufacturer to submit such a diet to feeding trials to ensure that it is adequate.

In the USA some manufacturers submit their pet foods to the feeding trials approved by the Association of American Feed Control Officials (AAFCO) to ensure that they meet the nutritional requirements of the National Research Council (e.g. the Hill's Pet Nutrition range of Science Plan products). A Complementary pet food needs to be fed with some other foodstuff in order to meet the needs of the animal. Anyone feeding a complementary food as a substantial part of a dog's ration is obliged to find out what it should be fed with, in order to balance the ration. Failure to do so could result in serious deficiency or imbalance of nutrients.

## DRY MATTER

The water content of pet foods varies greatly, particularly in canned products. In the USA there is a legal maximum limit (78 per cent) which cannot be exceeded, but no such limit is in force in Europe and some European canned petfoods contain as much as 86 per cent water. Legislation now makes it compulsory for the water content to be declared on the label and this is important, because to compare one pet food with another, one should consider the percentage of a nutrient in the dry matter of food.

For example, two pet foods may declare the protein content to be 10 per cent in the Typical Analysis printed on the label. If one product contains 75 per cent water it has 25 per cent dry matter, so the protein content is actually $10/25 \times 100 = 40$ per cent. If the other product contains 85 per cent water, the protein content is $10/15 \times 100 = 66.6$ per cent. This type of calculation (called Dry Weight Analysis) becomes even more important when comparing canned with dry products, as the water-content of dry food is usually only 7.5-12 per cent.

You can only effectively compare pet foods if you know:
1. The food's energy density
2. The dry weight analysis of the individual nutrients.

## COST

The only valid way to compare the cost of one food against another is to compare the daily feeding costs to meet all the needs of your dog. A high-energy, nutritionally concentrated type of diet might cost more to buy per kilogram of food, but it could be cheaper to feed on a cost per day basis. Conversely, a poor-quality, poorly digestible diet may be cheaper per kilogram to buy, but actually cost more per day to feed, because you need to feed much more food to meet the dog's requirements. The only valid reason for feeding a food is that it meets the nutritional requirements of your dog. To do that, you need to read between the marketing strategies of the manufacturers and select a diet that you know provides your dog with what it needs.

## HOME-MADE DIETS

What about home-made recipes? Well, theoretically it is possible to make a home-made diet that will meet all the nutritional requirements of a dog, and all foodstuffs have some nutritional value, but not all published recipes may actually achieve what they claim. The reason is that there is no strict quality control of ingredients, and the bio-availability of nutrients may vary from one ingredient source to another. If you feed a correctly balanced home-made diet, they are often time-consuming to prepare, usually need the addition of a vitamin/mineral supplement, and if prepared accurately can be expensive. Variations in raw ingredients will cause fluctuations in nutritional value.

The only way to be sure that a home-made diet has the nutritional profile that you want is to mix all the food ingredients plus supplements, treats, snacks, scraps etc. in a large pot, homogenise them and have a sample analysed chemically (this costs well over £100 (US$160) for a partial analysis). Compare this analytical content with the published levels for nutrient requirements.

You may feel that feeding an existing homemade recipe passed on to you, or developed over a number of years, is adequate. But how do you know? What is the phosphorus level of the diet that you are feeding? An undesirably high level of intake may take a long time before it results in obvious problems.

Sometimes the condition of your dog(s) will give you an idea that all is not well with the diet you are feeding. One of the most common questions asked by breeders at dog shows is "Can you recommend a diet that will keep weight on my dogs?" Unless there is a medical problem (and in such cases you should always seek veterinary attention first), the only reason why dogs usually have difficulty maintaining their weight is, simply, that they have an inadequate energy intake.

This does not mean that they are not eating well – they could be eating like a horse, but if the food is relatively low in energy content, and if it is poorly digestible, your dog may be unable to eat sufficient food to meet its energy needs. Large, bulky faeces are an indicator of low digestibility. A poor-looking, dull, dry or scurfy coat, poor skin and other external signs of unthriftiness may also be an indicator of poor nutrition. How many "poor-doers" and dogs with recurrent infections are on a diet with a marginal nutritional level of adequacy?

## SUMMARY

The importance of nutrition has been known for many years and yet, sadly, it is still surrounded by too many old wives' tales, myths and unsubstantiated claims. The emergence of clinical nutrition as a subject in its own right has set the stage for the future. Hopefully, in the future we shall hear about the benefits and dangers of different feeding practices from scientists who can base their statements on fact, not merely opinion. Already we know that a dog that is ill has different nutritional requirements to a healthy dog. In some cases, dietary management can even offer an alternative way to manage clinical cases. For example, we currently have the ability to dissolve struvite stones in the urinary bladder simply by manipulating dietary intake instead of having to resort to surgery.

But please note, dietary management is not "alternative medicine". Proper nutrition is the key to everything that a living animal has to do, be it work or repairing tissues after an injury. It is not an option; it is a crucial part of looking after an animal properly. If you own a dog then you should at least ensure that the food you give supplies all his/her needs, and avoids the excessive intake of energy or nutrients that may play a role in diseases which your pet could develop.

# 5 *TRAINING THE GERMAN SHEPHERD*

The training of dogs is a very deep and complex subject, with many varied views on the rights and wrongs of objectives and methods. Whole books have, over the years, been written about it. However, having spent over forty years being deeply involved with the training of dogs, I will endeavour to add my contribution and to help the German Shepherd enthusiast in this essential part of their care for their dog.

## PRINCIPLES OF TRAINING

Dogs are pack animals and thrive best with good leadership. If the dog does not experience true leadership the system suffers and this, in the domestic dog, results in disobedience and lack of control. If we accept this as fact, then we need to understand what true leadership within the pack really means. Leadership does not mean bullying or abuse of the dog but, because the dog is also a submissive animal, results can be achieved by bullying and abusing. However, this is not nature's way. A true pack leader is one who is greatly admired by the dog, yet the dog must respect, and be impressed by, that leader's ability to assert dominance in a fair and understanding manner.

The strength of the dog's character has to be studied to assess what it would take to impress that particular dog, as over-correction to the nervous or insecure dog would be damaging to the future relationship, just as a soft spoken word and a wag of the finger would be totally pointless to the confident, high-drive dog.

*Tegg Sch111 and her daughter Nixie CDex UDex, WD open: The character of a dog must be assessed and training methods adapted accordingly.*
*Photo: Keith Allison.*

In dog training we are simply trying to create desirable habits in the dog for our benefit. In obedience training we are creating desirable habits, not only for ourselves, but for the benefit of the dog and its role as our companion in society. Owning a dog is a commitment which we take on for the lifetime of the dog, and I just cannot understand what pleasure is derived from owning a dog which is not trained in at least the basic rudiments of obedience. The teaching of right from wrong, or to put it into dog training terms, the acceptable and the unacceptable, should start as soon as the young puppy has settled into its new environment, with the emphasis being on the word 'teach'.

## BASIC OBEDIENCE

Basic Obedience is a term used for general control of the dog and a term which, in my opinion, is quite often undervalued. So often, in my professional capacity, I am told by caring and well-meaning owners that, apart from this problem or that problem, their dog is really very obedient and under control – that is, until they are asked to remove the dog lead and control the dog, or put the dog in a down position and walk away for a short distance, or walk the dog on lead through a group of people without it pulling, avoiding or jumping up. Not until people see a demonstration of good obedience do they realise what can be achieved and what, in fact, is missing from their dog-and-master relationship.

## COMPULSION VERSUS INCENTIVE

When I first started on the road to a lifetime of dog training in the early 1950s, I was lucky enough to be associated with a very talented and gifted man who, for his era, had an uncanny understanding of dogs. Although little known or remembered outside our own village, here was a man with a talent for getting the best out of a dog without the abuse or pressure that I was to witness being used by others. Although the terms compulsion and incentive were not even in this man's vocabulary, he unwittingly gave me an insight into the balance needed for successful dog training.

In those days most results in dog training, particularly in the world of competition, were often achieved by over-compulsion and pressure, with frustration and temper being evident. Although this is, sadly, still the case in some training systems, like most sports and pastimes progress has been made simply because more and more people have become involved. Study has been given to the subject of the training of dogs and, over the last few decades, several sports have joined the ones already in existence, thus giving more ideas and thought to the subject. Hence dog training classes have grown, and continue to grow, at a tremendous rate and several can be found in most towns and cities. Unfortunately, this has brought with it a surge of so-called qualified trainers and canine behaviour people who, although they may have attended this or that course, or spent time with so-and-so, are not always doing the dog training world a service. In some circles, rejected and condemned out of hand is this piece of equipment or the use of that sort of method, and substituted is a pocketful of liver or other treats which are fed to the dog at every opportunity. Also, we now have several new ideas in equipment which does not train the dog but merely restricts his movement for the duration of the training lesson.

Let us compare the two alternatives using the basic and simple exercise 'sit'. If we give the command Sit and press the dog's bottom to the ground, we will get a result. The result may not be long-lasting but a result, nevertheless, is achieved. If we repeat this action, and make refusing or moving immediately a little unpleasant, then we get a better result. By repetition the result becomes more effective. Now, let us compare that with the passing of a food incentive over the dog's head slowly and giving the word 'sit'. It could be that the dog, because of the body posture, takes up the sit position by accident, but is still praised and given the tidbit. If this is repeated and always preceded by the word 'sit', then the dog picks up the idea and begins to respond on hearing the word, but only in anticipation of the food reward. The reader will have noticed that, in the first example, Sit was classed as a command, and in the later one 'sit' was a word. In other words, in the former the dog was given a command by its leader who was showing the dog by compulsion what was required and in the latter a word-association method was being used.

So which method do we approve of and which will give the best results?
Example One: Through the use of the dog's submissive instinct, the dog was being compelled to respond. The dog received no praise or reward but became obedient to the command. Therefore this method lacked incentive.
Example Two: On his own terms, and if he was in the mood for food reward, the dog responds on hearing the word 'sit'. If he is distracted, or not in the mood, he will refuse. This method lacked any form of compulsion. Conclusion: Common sense and a combination of both methods.

## BASIC OBEDIENCE EXERCISES

We can take the five elementary exercises for basic obedience to be walking the dog to heel properly, both on and off leash, to sit and to lie down, to stay in either of these positions and to come when called. In other words teach the dog to understand and respond to the commands Heel, Sit, Down, Stay? and Come. Please take note of the question mark after the word stay, which will be explained later.

You will need the following equipment: a strong well-made dog leash (I prefer one inch flat leather of approx. four feet in length [1.2 metres] giving comfort in the hands), collar or slip collar (several types are available depending on the strength and drive of the dog), a ten-metre length of cord, a five-metre length of cord, a two-metre length and finally a short length (boot laces are ideal for the final piece).

### HEELING ON LEASH
This should be one of the easiest things to teach a dog yet it appears that the average

*Timing of correction and praise is all-important in heelwork.*
*Photo: Keith Allison.*

dog owner has more problems with heelwork and the recall than with any other exercise. If collar and lead training had been done at the puppy stage with praise and relationship balanced with encouragement to walk correctly, then correction with the adult dog would have been avoided. However, this is very rarely the case. Therefore this chapter is for the owner who has a walking problem with the adult dog. The choice of collar will have been made before training begins, as I refuse to advocate which piece of equipment to use because, as stated earlier, every dog is different. Because dogs are required to work on the left-hand side of the handler through almost all dog sports and competitions – police dogs, service dogs and guide dogs etc. – for the purpose of this chapter we will do the same.

### About-turn correction

Hold the leash (a little more than one metre in length) in the right hand, let it hang loose across your body to the dog's collar and take a few paces forward. If the dog walks close to your side and shows good interest in you, then consider yourself very lucky at this point and apply the following only when distractions are present. As the dog walks ahead with a view to taking the strain of the leash, take the leash in the left hand also, give the command Heel and turn about smartly, giving a jerking action with the leash, and begin walking in the opposite direction, praising the dog at this point and releasing the left hand immediately from the leash. The dog will be surprised and will now be behind. He will have to overtake before he can take strain again. As he begins to get ahead, the exercise is repeated. If the timing of correction and the praise are cleverly balanced, the dog should be impressed and show respect.

Repeat this several times more using command only, i.e. no correction by the leash. In other words, the dog will respond to command, thereby avoiding the correction. However, if the dog still requires a correction, so be it. Again, if the timing is correct, progress will be very quick and rewarding. This we will call the about-turn correction method which, in my opinion, is the most effective method for the strong and severely pulling dog. We then have to consider how to maintain the heel position without the about-turn.

### The side-step correction

Taking the leash again in the right hand and starting as before, take a few paces forward. Whether or not the dog surges forward with a view to pulling (and he should not do this if the about-turn method was done correctly), give the command Heel and, placing the left hand on the leash, take a smart step to the right and give a correction backwards with the leash, once again praising and releasing the left hand. Repeat this several times until the side step without the correction has been achieved.

### The left-turn correction

The chances are that if the two previous lessons have gone well over a period of time, the dog will now be walking reasonably well with about-turns, right turns (being only half of an about-turn), and side steps being quite competent. The distance in a given straight line can be increased. However, more difficult is the turning to the left. Once again, start with the leash in the right hand, take several paces forward with your dog now walking reasonably close to the left leg, take the leash loosely in the left hand, give the command Heel, jerk the leash in a backwards direction and turn smartly to the left, releasing the left hand from the leash and praising the dog. Repeat this several times until the left turn can be effected without the correction.

*The first stage of heeling off-leash using a training line.*

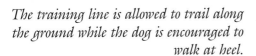

*The training line is allowed to trail along the ground while the dog is encouraged to walk at heel.*

*A short line keeps the dog in position.*

*Heeling with the lead and the training line detached.*

## HEELING OFF LEASH

Teaching the heeling of the dog on leash can take as little as ten minutes in total, or many separate sessions over a period of time, depending on the skill and timing of the trainer or handler. Now it is time to remove the leash and in its place attach the ten-metre training line. Passing the line behind your back into your right hand, let the remainder of the line fall to the ground. Now begin to walk forward, giving the command Heel; after several paces it should be possible to drop the line altogether and continue forward, praising and flattering the dog as you go.

Should the dog stop due to the weight of the line, simply replace the line with a shorter one and repeat. Practise all the turns and side steps as before and enjoy the rapid progress. Should the dog refuse at any time, pick up the line quickly, give a command and a correction and start again. Remove the long line and replace with a shorter one and repeat until all that is left is the very short line attached to the dog. Leave the short line attached for the next few training lessons, going back to a longer line if failure is experienced.

The final stage is to pass the short line through the collar, this time holding both ends in the left hand, give the command Heel and walk forward. After several paces release one end of the line and draw it away from the collar, encouraging and praising the dog throughout. Now your dog is walking to heel without leash. We have cleverly removed the leash by a gradual process. Fortunately for us the dog cannot measure the length of a piece of cord and conforms to the requirement of the trainer or handler. For the potential competition dog, other incentives can now be used to create attitude and drive, such as a food or toy reward.

## SIT

Most dogs living in a domestic situation will be familiar with the word 'sit' from puppyhood. They may not always respond to the word but, nevertheless, the chances are that an attempt has been made to achieve the sit on command. This is usually attempted with the dog in front of the owner. The dog now thinks that the command to sit means not only to put his rump to the floor but that he must be in front of his handler, as praise or food reward has consolidated this.

In dog training, and certainly for the competition dog, there are two positional sits to teach: the sit in the Present Position, which is in front of the handler, and the sit in the Basic Position by the left leg of the handler facing forward. It may be necessary, therefore, to practise the sit at the basic position more than in the present position. If the dog sits in front on the command, simply move yourself to the basic position and, if necessary, reward him from this position. After several practices of this, you will have to insist a little more strongly to achieve a compulsive sit.

If the Sit has not yet been attempted, the basic position is the one to start with. With the dog on leash by your left leg, give the command Sit and press the dog's bottom to the floor with the left hand, holding him in this position with reassuring praise. Repeat several times before insisting with a little more compulsion, remembering throughout to keep the dog happy with praise and reassurance. Next you can begin to incorporate the Sit in the basic position with walking to heel. Take several paces forward and give the command Sit as you slow down to make the sit position. It is advisable to give the command just before stopping, rather than putting the brakes on suddenly and expecting the dog to anticipate. After several practices of this, you should find the dog taking up the sit position on command

## THE DOWN
*Photos: Keith Allison.*

*Do not apply undue pressure when teaching the Down.*

without any physical help and, eventually, taking up the sit position simply because you are slowing to a halt. That is an attentive dog beginning to pick up body signals.

For the sit in front, simply sit the dog at heel, move to the front of the dog and with praise or food reward make it pleasant to be in this position. Take a few paces backwards, calling the dog to Come and Sit. Repeat several times each lesson and both sits will be achieved.

## DOWN
In theory the teaching of the Down position should be relatively easy, in that we now have a dog under control sitting in the basic position. From this basic position – i.e. both handler and dog facing forward and with the dog on leash which again is held in the right hand – place the left hand behind the withers of the dog (just behind the shoulder blades) give the command Down and press in a downwards and slightly sideways direction. You will find that the dog may take up the down position for comfort. However, if the dog struggles and shows objection, do not show annoyance or use undue pressure but simply repeat the performance in a calm soothing voice, although being physically

*Maintaining the Down position despite distractions.*

assertive with the left hand.

It may be necessary with dogs of a more timid nature to bend your knees and go downwards with the dog, using a reassuring tone of voice, while still insisting with the left-hand pressure. As soon as the dog takes the down position, hold him still with the left hand, which will now change from pressure to heavy stroking, and give reassuring praise. After several seconds, praise gently and release the dog by walking forward with the dog at heel for several paces. Repeat this exercise several times until you feel that progress is being made; that is the time to stop the lesson. When you take up the teaching of the 'down' on the next lesson things should be a little easier and, after several lessons, the dog should go into the down position on hearing the command and feeling the left hand, now gently, touching the wither area.

Now it is time to try the down position without going through the sit. Walk the dog to heel on leash for a few paces at a casual pace, stop, give the command Down and apply a left-hand touch to the wither; if your earlier lessons have been successful, the dog should take up the position, if not then a few more lessons through the sit are required. When the down on command has been achieved, we can start the down at a distance – one of the most important and useful exercises to teach the dog.

## DOWN AT A DISTANCE
So far with the down we have spoken in terms of giving the command and then applying the explanation, in this case using the fingers of the left hand to put pressure onto the wither. For downing a dog at a distance the principle is the same. With the dog on a training line and free of the handler, a distance of approximately three metres is purposely created by the handler by stepping away from the dog. The command Down is

given and the handler immediately and quickly advances to the dog and effects the down by the left-hand pressure as before. This action is repeated until the dog anticipates and goes into the down position to avoid the pressure. Reassuring praise is given throughout.

Next the distance between handler and dog is increased gradually, remembering to advance towards the dog immediately the command to down has been given. If timing is correct and the dog is responding, he will begin to down on command without the handler having to advance towards him, thus giving a down on command from a distance.

## STAY
This is where I probably differ from most other trainers when it comes to basic obedience training. Many trainers put so much emphasis on this exercise and bring in different words for different stays. When I started my dog training many years ago 'stay' meant just that. Then, in the early seventies, a new concept came into Obedience competition. In some dog training circles 'stay' means 'I will be returning', but if the word 'wait' is used that means 'I will be calling you to come to me'. I have never been able to come to terms with this sort of thinking and to me a stay is a stay; if I want to call my dog to me I will do so; if not, he should, in theory, remain where he is until further notice.

However, over the years, I have found it unnecessary to use the word stay at all. In other words, if I give the command Sit and walk away from the dog, then he should sit until further notice, and if the command is Down then he should down until further notice. What the handler is doing, or where the handler goes for the duration of the stay exercise, is of no concern to the dog. This becomes evident in the advanced positions in Obedience competition, or the sit and down

*The Stay exercise is built up gradually.*

out of motion in the Schutzhund sport, where one command only is allowed. I would therefore advocate the training of the stay in the following manner.

Having taught the dog to sit at the basic position, repeat the word 'sit' in a reassuring tone and step half a pace to the right, stepping back immediately. If successful, repeat this, now going one pace to the right, pause a moment and return to the dog. If successful one pace to the right, pause for several moments and return. Then two paces to the right, then three and so on. Sooner or later the dog will want to move, probably in the direction of the handler. Here the commands No and Sit are given very abruptly, and with a correction back to the exact place and position that the dog was left in.

Now start the whole exercise again, this time moving a little quicker, and after a pace to the right try walking a few paces forward and returning to the dog immediately. From this stage it is just a matter of increasing time and distance away from the dog by gradual, successful progression, remembering that movement without permission should be corrected firmly and speedily, making the act of moving not very pleasant.

## THE DOWN STAY

If you think about it, the work for this exercise has already been covered. We have already taught the dog to down on command from a distance in an earlier section. If the dog will down on command and we can walk to the dog to the basic position, there should be no problem in repeating the command Down and walking away from the dog again. However, it would pay to spend a little time, as in the teaching of the sit stay, by giving the Down command from the basic position and moving to the right, making progress as in the sit stay training.

*If the dog attempts to move, correct with a verbal command – "No" or "Sit".*

RECALL

This is definitely the most important exercise to teach the dog and probably one of the most misunderstood. The teaching of the recall should be started in the puppy training stages, where the dog's name is called, along with the command to come, and lavish praise given to the puppy with the use of the occasional food reward. Coming to you should be very pleasurable from the early stages and the teaching of the formal recall later will be very easy. However, let us look at what happens to the dog that has not been puppy trained correctly.

The vaccinations are all complete and now the young dog is taken to the park or some other recreation area. The dog is let off the leash to have a good romp and play until it is time to curtail this pleasurable experience and take him home. OK so far, the puppy may well come on the first occasion. You may be lucky and have success on the next occasion, but now the trouble starts. You are actually recalling the dog to deprive him of something that was giving him a great deal of pleasure. Put yourself in the dog's position for a moment. Recalling means the end of pleasure, refusing to recall means a little more freedom; now the handler gets very irate and begins to show annoyance, worse still punishment may be given when the dog is finally caught. Next day the dog hears the recall and remembers the previous discomfort and decides not only not to recall but to avoid being caught. More punishment follows etc. etc. – now the dog is not trusted to be off the leash and the dog owner blames the dog. Crazy!

Here is how to avoid this happening, or even to correct it once it has happened. From the early stages of letting the dog off the leash, attach a long thin line (about ten metres in length) and let the dog drag this around with him. Pick up the end of the line, call the dog by name with the command

Come and jerk the line quickly towards you. Praise the dog as he comes in, using the line again should he stop on the way. Praise, and hands on for relationship, are very important at this stage, as recalling must always be a pleasurable experience. A food reward may be given to the dog at this time, or a toy or ball produced as a reward. Having made a fuss of the dog, release him to continue his recreation. Repeat this several times during his free recreation until the dog begins to come willingly, avoiding the tug of the line, and enjoying the pleasure you show when he comes. In other words, there are many times when the dog is recalled without him connecting this with it being an end to his freedom. When it is time to put on the leash or to put him back in the car, spend time with a little playing and praising before doing so.

Now the dog is recalling when the long line is attached and he is coming willingly. As he probably connects the wearing of the line with the understanding that you have control over him, remove the long line and try the shorter line, then a shorter line still and so on. The final line need only be the length and weight of a boot lace but psychologically the dog still connects it with your control. If timing and the skill of showing pleasure and relationship has been correct, then remove the final piece of line and enjoy.

THE 'NO' COMMAND

Apart from creating desirable habits in the dog via basic obedience training, we have to deter undesirable habits. In theory this ought to be easier as we only have the one word of command to work with. When the dog does anything which we do not approve, we give the command No and the dog should cease what he is doing. It is that easy – or is it?

Let us take some examples. First of all indoors: the dog who jumps on table, kitchen units or furniture.

As we must be careful not to get into the habit of going for the dog's collar to give a correction, I find that a very good aid indoors is, once again, to have the dog on a short piece of line – not so long as to get wrapped around any furniture but enough to take hold of from a short distance to give a tug correction. When the dog is in the act of jumping on the furniture give the command No and immediately give a sharp tug downwards using the attached line. Release the line immediately and do not relate any further. I firmly believe that further scolding does no good whatsoever and that corrections should always be short and sharp and given impressively but without aggression. Once again we ask how severe do we have to be with the correction and the answer is always the same: severe enough to get a result and impress the dog. If the dog is not impressed you are wasting your time, and if the correction is too severe then you are bordering on bullying rather than correcting.

JUMPING UP

This habit has usually been created by unthinking owners when the puppy is small and when jumping up is no big deal. In fact, when the owner is dressed in casual clothing, jumping up to be played with is even encouraged. Then, as the dog gets bigger and the jumping up gets to become a nuisance, or the owner is dressed in clothes which mean that jumping up from the dog is a problem, something has to be done. This is rarely the dog's fault and avoidance from puppyhood would have been the answer. However, in the adult dog it is a problem which we have to correct.

First of all let us ask: Why is the dog jumping up? The answer is for hands and voice. The dog gets relationship from our hands in caressing, and from the voice in praising, so let us not punish him for that. Rather, let us make the act of jumping up

unpleasant, having regard for his reasons. As the dog jumps up, give the command No and raise the knee in order to make contact with your dog's chest area, followed by squatting down to the dog to give hands and voice to the dog in reassurance. The reason for the reassurance is in order that the dog does not blame you for the discomfort but takes the blame and connects it with the action of jumping up. With the more confident dog the command Sit can be given after the knee correction, and there can be a pause before squatting to give reassurance.

Now, if the dog does show respect about jumping up to you but continues to jump up at other people, the correction is different. With the dog on leash, set up an opportunity with a friend or a member of the family. Have your assistant walk towards you and, as the dog goes into jumping up mode, give the command No followed immediately by a sharp and effective correction downwards. Repeat the exercise several times until on the command No the dog does not attempt to jump up. If this training has been successful, set up the situation again, this time giving the command Sit as the assistant approaches. Effect the sit position physically, if necessary, and repeat this until the dog goes into the sit position automatically as someone approaches him.

**ADVANCED TRAINING**

In a single chapter there is not sufficient space to go in depth into all aspects of training and the methods used. Here, however, are some of the exercises used in advanced training.

THE RETRIEVE

For the pet dog retrieving can be fun and a means of giving the dog exercise. In the competition dog it becomes more precise and formal. Whatever the reason for teaching the retrieve, certain things have to be taken on

*The dog must stay at the handler's side when the retrieve article is thrown.*

*On command, the dog goes out to retrieve the dumb-bell.*

board. First of all the dog must be taught not only to run out for the thrown article, but to want to give it up to the handler. Many a dog will run and pick up the thrown object, but with a view to possessing it. It is a very big mistake to chase the dog to try to take away the object. He will begin to enjoy the game of chase, and returning the object to handler will be the last thing on his mind.

The object thrown can, of course, be anything the owner wants it to be – a stick, a ball etc. However, in competition the article is usually of a wooden or plastic dumb-bell shape and is, in fact, called a 'dumb-bell'.

## THE NATURAL RETRIEVE

I find the best method for the dog with a good drive and interest in articles is for the dog to be, once again, attached to a long training line. The dog is offered the dumb-bell, with a command suitable for the exercise such as 'fetch' or 'bring' or 'carry' etc. For the purpose of this chapter let us use 'fetch'. On taking it, he is praised and flattered. Do not be in a hurry to take the dumb-bell from the dog at this stage, particularly if he has a firm grip. After a while, certainly before the novelty of carrying it wears off, take the dumb-bell using a command such as 'leave', 'give', 'drop' or 'out' etc. For the purpose of the chapter we will use 'leave'. Praise the dog once more. Carrying the dumb-bell for you will become very pleasurable for the dog.

After several lessons place the dumb-bell on the ground in front of the dog, give the command Fetch and advance towards the dumb-bell with the dog still on line. If you are lucky and the dog picks up the dumb-bell from the ground, praise him immediately and run backwards, giving the command Come while tugging slightly on the line. After several paces backwards, squat down and welcome the dog into you with rewarding flattery; let the dog hold the dumb-bell for several seconds before taking it. A skilful trainer could, at this point, begin to play tug with the dumb-bell to obtain a firmer grip until given the release command. This will create a good attitude from the dog to the retrieve exercise, but take care that things are on your terms. Sit before being allowed to chase, and sitting in the present position when he returns, can be brought in later and are effected as in Basic Obedience, the only difference being that the dog now has something in his mouth.

## THE NOT SO NATURAL RETRIEVE

This is for the dog with less interest in the dumb-bell. Again with the dog on line, throw the dumb-bell around and try to create a desire in the dog to chase it. If the dog picks up the dumb-bell for a while, then go into the squat position to praise and continue as in the previous section. For the dog with even less interest, the dumb-bell may have to be attached to a very thin cord and dragged along the floor to create the desired interest from the dog. If the dog has no desire to retrieve at all then a forced retrieve might be considered. However, I think this is totally unnecessary for the pet dog and a job for a professional trainer in the competition dog.

With the pet dog it may not be necessary to have the dog stay before the object is thrown, but with the competition dog the stay while the article is being thrown, and the sending of the dog on command, will have to be taught. Then there is the procedural taking of the article and the finish to the basic position for point scoring.

Once the retrieve has been taught, the pet owner can change to a ball or other object. If you are using a ball I would strongly recommend the type that has a rope passed through it, to avoid the chance of the ball becoming lodged in the dog's throat. These are now available at most pet suppliers. The potential competition dog must now be encouraged to retrieve other objects which will lead on to future scent discrimination work for Obedience Competition or for the tracking and searching exercises in the sport of Working Trials etc.

## SCENT DISCRIMINATION

This is a term given to an exercise in the sport of Obedience where the dog has to distinguish between an article or cloth bearing the scent of his owner, or later the scent of the judge, from other scented articles and decoy articles. I would recommend that, once your dog is retrieving different articles, you have a colleague lay out, in line, several heavier objects of similar size to the one you are working with. These objects must not bear your scent. Now let the dog see the required article being placed among them. As the dog knows the command Fetch, I would use this to take the dog over the articles, praising him when he nears the correct one.

I appreciate that there will be experienced handlers who would rather bring in a new word at this point to help the dog know that this is a new exercise being taught. This is a personal choice and I myself do not see the need to do this as the dog will, through experience, pick up the signals and set-up of the situation and know that the command Fetch simply means to go and bring the one he has been taught to bring.

Once the dog is getting the idea of retrieving from a group of other articles, turn the dog away from seeing where the correct one is being placed. Now he will have to find the correct article by the use of his nose, as he did not see the position in which his article was being placed. Similar articles can be used so that the dog has a choice and a decision to make. Now begin to 'give the dog scent', either by placing your hand over the dog's nose in order that he takes the required scent, or by placing a cloth over the dog's nose to give him the scent of the article to be retrieved, bearing in mind that, in the more advanced classes, the article required will not bear your scent but that of the judge.

## SEARCHING

This is an exercise appertaining to the sport of Working Trials in which the dog has to go into a marked area containing several small articles, not visible to the dog and, by using his powers of scent, retrieve to its owner any article bearing human scent. The dog needs to be a very good retrieve dog and very keen to work diligently in the task of searching. To

start teaching this, hold the dog on leash and have a colleague pace out the given area which, in competition, would be a square measuring 15 paces by 15 paces for the first stage of qualification and 25 paces by 25 paces for all other more advanced stages. However, it would be advisable to train the dog on smaller areas until he gets the idea of what is required.

The area is marked by pushing a pole in each corner of the 'square', as it is known in the sport. Your helper then walks the whole area to disturb the vegetation by foot pressure and then, in view of the dog, throws several objects within a few paces of the centre. The helper should then walk out of the area and stand behind the handler. The handler then walks to the area, taking care not to get too close or step inside the area and gives the dog the command Fetch. If the dog has very strong retrieve drive, he will go to investigate what was thrown by the assistant and, with praise and encouragement, will simply retrieve his first find to the handler.

Getting him to repeat the action for the other articles is the tricky part as he has never been asked to do two retrieves in a row. If the dog gets confused, give a fake throw in the direction of the centre of the area and then the command Fetch. If this fails, leave the dog sitting outside the area and, walking towards the centre of the area, pretend to place something. Return to the dog and repeat the fetch exercise. With practice the dog will get more proficient and should soon be retrieving several articles from the area.

The next stage is not to let him see the articles being placed inside the square but to bring him along after the square has been prepared. Now he will be required to do his first real 'search for articles'. Three will eventually be the requirement for the Companion Dog stake and four in the succeeding stakes of Working Trials. This is

*Encouraged by the handler, the dog finds his favourite toy. This is the first stage in tracking.*

*The dog is then introduced to the line and the tracking harness.*

## TRACKING
*Photos: Keith Allison.*

only one brief training method for a very complex test, and there are many variations, but, for the purpose of this chapter, it is one method to consider.

## TRACKING

Tracking is the practice of a dog following the exact route taken by a person who has previously walked that route and, in doing so, has disturbed the vegetation or ground simply by the pressure of the footprints. Tracking is very useful to the training of the police dog in order to follow the route of a suspect or in the finding of a lost person. Tracking for competition features in the sports of Working Trials and Schutzhund, in which training is very intensive. It is a very fascinating subject which could fill a book all to itself but I will give food for thought in a condensed version. I will endeavour to give several alternative methods of teaching tracking.

Having been involved in tracking for over thirty years, I have witnessed many changes in the training of this fascinating discipline. Originally the method I was using, like most handlers in the sport of Working Trials, was to have the dog held by an assistant and let the dog watch as the handler walked in a straight line away from the dog, calling his name and letting him see his favourite toy being taken away from him. The toy or article would then be placed on the ground and, on the handler's return, the dog, attached to a leash, would be allowed to tear up the line of

*A demonstration of deep-nose tracking.*

track in order to find the article, where a great deal of praise would be lavished on the dog and the whole exercise repeated.

After a few repetitions of this, the dog would be introduced to a harness and line, which is the mandatory equipment used for Working Trials Sport. After several similar lessons and when the dog has reached the stage where he does not see the laying of the track, the time lapse is increased, as is the distance of the track, bringing with it turns and curves. Different articles would be used and the dog praised on the finding of each. Although this now sounds a ham-fisted way of teaching tracking, many a handler has had great success with this method over the years and I took several dogs to the high level of Tracker Dog Excellent by using variations of this method. In fact it is still the favourite at

a lot of police dog training schools, as it creates a fast tracker dog and, for those who think speed is of the essence in order to catch a criminal, the method is still popular. However, for the competition dog things have become more exacting, and precise work is now a necessity in order to obtain high scores.

Food is now used by many handlers in teaching their dog to track. A small piece of food is placed by a starting pole and then placed at very regular intervals along the track. The dog or puppy is then brought, on leash or line, to the start of the track and, with encouragement, begins to discover that, when it follows the scent of disturbed vegetation, it repeatedly finds food reward. Articles are introduced in later lessons when the dog is very proficient at following the

*In some situations, the dog will free-track, without a leash or a harness.*

## THE CLEAR
### Photos: Keith Allison.

track. The dragging of food is another method used with the reluctant dog.

Of late I have become very enthused by a method to which I have given a lot of thought and planning. Having competed with several dogs in the Schutzhund sport over the last six or seven years with Working Trials trained dogs, I am now training a puppy for the first time purely for the sport of Schutzhund, where absolute accuracy is required and deep-nose tracking is essential.

Start with the puppy as young as possible. Tread an area of about two metres square and place within it many small pieces of food, preferably cooked beef or similar. Carry the puppy to the area and place him inside it. At first there will be no result but he will inevitably sniff the ground as there are many tempting rewards there for him. Finding the food reward becomes connected with the scent of disturbed earth or grass, as each time the dog leaves the area there is never a food reward to be found and only by returning to the area will he be successful.

I find that praise and a command to track can be introduced at this stage, as progress is being made and the puppy begins to get excited at being carried to the scented area. Now the shape of the area is changed to four metres long by one metre wide, the puppy being introduced to the scented area at one end and will now progress along, finding his food en route to the other end. Turning around to check behind, or returning back along the disturbed area to check for missed food, I do not think is a problem. With progress the disturbed area now becomes the width of two shuffled footprints by maybe twenty-five metres long and the result is fascinating. As the released puppy makes his way along the 'track' successfully finding his food reward, commands and encouragement can now be introduced. With this method the puppy teaches himself to track and never connects it with anything to do with the

*The dog must wait for the command before he jumps.*

*The handler must retain control until rejoining the dog on the other side of the jump.*

handler. I prefer the puppy to be free-tracking on this style for several months before attaching a line to his collar, thereby avoiding the risk of any compulsion or pressure. Later, articles are introduced, a line is attached and a more formal attitude can be taken, by which time the puppy, or by now the young dog, is quite competent in the art of tracking. These are condensed versions of tracking styles but should be a help to the would-be enthusiast.

## AGILITY

In the early seventies successful working trials competitors were asked to provide entertainment, at game fairs and the like, by taking along their jumping equipment and evolving different obstacles for the dogs to negotiate. Other inventive tests were included which brought with them a great following and support. In those early days I was involved as a competitor but, in the late seventies, after several time-consuming dog-training contracts overseas, I was amazed to find that the interest had grown so much that the sport of Agility had taken off at a tremendous pace. With it came mini horse jumps, the tyre in a frame, the see-saw – and the rest is history. The sport now has a very large following in the world of dog training. Although it is very exciting and entertaining, I would not consider that it should be the first choice, or the only sport, for the German Shepherd dog. But having expressed that opinion, jumping your dog can be great fun, whether it is for competition or just for convenience. However, care must be taken

### THE SCALE
### Photos: Keith Allison.

*With correct training, the athletic German Shepherd should have no difficulty clearing this obstacle.*

*The scale is upright and 6ft in height.*

not to start jumping your dog too young, and the dog must be in top physical condition. In the sport of working trials there are three pieces of jumping equipment in the Agility section.

### 1. The Clear

In this exercise the dog is required to clear a hurdle 3 ft in height and to be under control at the other side until the handler is told to join the dog. The teaching of the clear jump starts with getting the dog to jump over a very simple height, and then to increase it by lifting the bar of the clear jump gradually until the required 3ft is achieved.

## 2. The Long

For this a 9ft spread is created using five equally spaced boards, varying slightly in width, and individually supported on a slight angle, to give the impression, from the dog's eye-view, of it being one continuous spread. The dog is required to jump over the boards and to be controlled at the other side until the handler is told to join the dog. To teach the long jump, have the dog jump over one board to start with. Then, one by one, add another board until all five boards are being traversed. The boards are then opened up gradually until the dog is capable of clearing the required 9ft distance.

## 3. The Scale

The scale jump is a vertical wall of wooden boards slotted into grooved uprights. The dog is required to scale over the apparatus and be controlled on the opposite side until the handler recalls the dog back over the wall. The training for this is a controversial subject as I do not go along with slotting the boards in, one after another, until this progression reaches the required height. This method does teach the dog to clear the equipment – but the time comes when he realises that it is getting a little too high, and then problems arise. The dog has been taught that he must jump high if he is going to get over. He now realises that to be successful he must try to put his feet on top of the wall. He will then throw himself off the top in order to land on the other side.

A better method of teaching the scale is to have the training apparatus made in such a way that the two boards, each 6 ft in height, are hinged at the top, and they can make an A-frame of varying heights. The dog starts by walking along a 12 ft spread. Then the hinged apex is gradually lifted to make a steeper and steeper A-frame until the two sides come together to make the required 6ft. With this method, the dog is taught not only how to run up the boards, but also how to use the boards in descent, thus reducing the risk of injury.

In Schutzhund sport we find only two obstacles to negotiate.

## 1. The Brush jump

With the dog at the basic position a dumb-bell is thrown over a solid brush-topped jump one metre in height. The dog is then sent to jump over, pick up the dumb-bell and return to the handler, presenting the dumb-bell. The training for this is the same as for the training for the clear jump – doing it through natural progression.

## 2. The A-frame

In Schutzhund the scale jump has been replaced by an A-frame, as this was thought to be a safer way of showing the dog's agility prowess without the physical stress caused by continuous scale-jumping and would, supposedly, give a longer competitive working life to the dog. My own experience tells me that if the dog is taught to scale correctly, the working life of the dog is about the same in both sports. However, this has been a topic for discussion and debate for many years and I am sure will continue to be so.

The design of the A-frame has been described when we were discussing the scale jump. Two boards, each 1.9 metres long and 1.5 metres wide are hinged together in order to make the shape of the letter A. The size, when opened, is 1.8 metres vertical. The dog has to sit in the basic position; the handler then throws a dumb-bell over the frame and, after a three-second pause, sends the dog to retrieve. A command to jump and a command to retrieve is allowed; any other command or assistance is penalised. The dog is expected to run up one side of the jump and down the other, pick up the dumb-bell and return by the same route. The teaching of this is the same as is described earlier in the teaching of the scale.

## THE A-FRAME
### Photos: Keith Allison.

*After the dumb-bell is thrown the dog must wait in the Sit position for three seconds before going out to retrieve.*

*The command to jump and the command to retrieve are allowed. Any other assistance is penalised.*

*A swift return to the handler with no deviation.*

PROTECTION WORK

The necessity of teaching a dog to protect is a controversial subject and I do not intend to go too deeply into the arguments for or against this activity. However, I will state to those who are sure their dogs will protect them should the need arise, without the necessity of training them, that they are only kidding themselves and are being totally unfair to their dog. If a dog is capable and, indeed, expected to protect, then is it not reasonable to teach him how and when to do this, in order to control any such incident? A dog reacting on his own initiative could surely be a liability to its owners, not an asset. In the two sports where protection work is a requirement, Working Trials and Schutzhund, there are several exercises to prepare for.

In Working Trials we have:
1. Quartering the area for hidden persons.
2. Test of courage.
3. Search and escorting of the prisoner.
4. Recall from a running criminal.
5. Chase and detaining an escaping criminal.

In the Schutzhund sport we have:
1. Searching for the hidden helper.
2. Stopping an escaping helper, including defending himself under attack from the helper.
3. Transporting the helper, including defending his handler.
4. Defence against further attack, and courage test.

The reader will notice the use of the term 'helper' in the sport of Schutzhund and the term 'criminal' or 'prisoner' in Working Trials. These are traditionally the terms used and mean, simply, the person involved in the trial who will test the standard of the dog's ability to perform the required tasks. For the purpose of this section I will use the term 'helper'. The reader will also have guessed,

**PROTECTION WORK**
*Photos: Keith Allison.*

*The correct bite for protection work.*

having seen the list of requirements, that a very high standard of control is essential. Lack of control in both these sports will, or should, result in disqualification from the test.

Although the two sports have their differences in technique and in judging, they both require the dog to detain by gripping the protected arm. In Schutzhund this will be an obvious bulky arm-guard but, in Working Trials, the protection may be concealed under clothing to simulate a more realistic situation.

Training starts with the dog being encouraged to pull on a rag or sack until the desire is strong and the prey drive is created. The protection sleeve is then substituted and stronger work develops. The drives in the dog have to be carefully monitored and the balance of prey drive and defence drive kept in the correct proportion in order to maintain the necessary control.

The main difference between these two sports is the situations in which they take place. The protection work in Schutzhund takes place in an arena such as a football field or stadium and is therefore very stereotyped, with the test being performed in the same order at all events. Working Trials protection work can take place wherever is convenient for the event, taking into account that the scenario simulates a practical police-type situation.

### 1. Searching for the Helper

In Schutzhund the dog must first check five obvious hiding places before reaching the helper who will be concealed in hide number six. In Working Trials the helper could be anywhere which is practical for a hiding place, e.g. up a tree, in a gully, behind bales of hay etc. However, the dog is required in both sports to indicate by barking. In

*The courage of the dog is tested by stick threats.*

Schutzhund the dog is required to contain the helper by pressing towards him with a very strong attitude, whereas in Working Trials the dog is only required to indicate to the handler that he has found someone.

## 2. Test of Courage

The Working Trials dog can be tested in almost any fashion compatible with safety and quite often the judge, who has full jurisdiction, will come up with ingenious ideas to test the courage of the dog. In Schutzhund the courage test is, again, stereotyped in that the dog will always be tested for courage by stick threats. Having competed with several dogs in both sports over many years I think it fair to say that, because of the nature of the tests, the Schutzhund dog tends to show a stronger attitude to the courage test. However, that is a personal opinion and will no doubt be a topic for discussion among enthusiasts.

## 3. Stopping the Escape

In Schutzhund the helper will try to escape from a distance of several metres from the dog, who will be watching and waiting anxiously. As soon as the helper makes his move, the dog will very quickly come into action and stop the escape by firmly gripping the protection sleeve. After being commanded to leave he will then have to protect himself from the attacking helper by gripping the sleeve once more. In Working Trials the escaping person can be a hundred metres away from the dog and handler. The handler will ask him to stop and, on refusal, will send his dog to stop him by gripping the protected arm.

## 4. Escorting

In both sports escorting the helper back to the judge is very similar. With the dog in the heel free position, the handler will command the helper to walk ahead with the handler and dog following a few paces behind, the dog being vigilant and ready for the inevitable attack on his handler.

*Waiting for the escape.*

### 5. The Recall from a Running Person

This very difficult test appears only in the Working Trial sport. The dog is released in the same way as in the stopping of the escaping runner, but, when the dog is in full flight and anticipating a catch, the handler is required to call the dog back again. I will leave it to the reader's imagination as to what standard of control is needed to perfect this test.

*The escape is stopped by gripping the protection sleeve.*

# 6 *THE WORKING GSD*

The working ability of the German Shepherd Dog is one of its most respected characteristics. This, combined with the breed's intelligence and its knack of being able to work things out for itself, makes it the ideal choice for a variety of tasks. Those breeders who have followed the original concept, that the German Shepherd should be "a good guardian of home and flock", have been well rewarded by the loyalty and devotion shown to their dogs by those who work with the breed.

## GUIDE DOGS

The role of a dog leading a blind person is not a new one. The Metropolitan Museum in New York possesses a Chinese scroll, dating from the 13th century, showing a blind man being led by a dog. Similar scenes have been depicted in wood cuts, paintings and engravings from the 16th century. Gainsborough (1727-1788) in his painting *Blind Man on a Bridge* shows a dog leading its master. It was not until the 1920s that formal techniques were used to train what we now refer to as a guide dog for the blind.

The guide dog movement started in Germany. The German Red Cross Ambulance Dogs Association trained dogs to help find the wounded on the battlefields. Seeing the potential of these dogs, the Association started training some of them to lead veterans who were blinded during the First World War. By 1919 over 500 war-blinded men had been provided with a guide dog and many of these were German Shepherds.

By the mid-1920s the popularity of the German Shepherd had spread enormously. The German Red Cross were having difficulty acquiring enough suitable dogs, so the German Ministry of Labour gave the task of providing guide dogs to the German Shepherd Dog Association. A large new training school at Potsdam was opened in 1923. Rapid progress was made and by the early 1930s they had trained over 4,000 German Shepherds as guide dogs.

The controller of this school identified three key factors which are essential to producing successful guide dogs – fundamental principles that have not changed. They are:

1) Selecting good-quality dogs which are physically sound and of good temperament.
2) Matching the dog's ability to the owner's ability and requirements.
3) Continuing to give support once the dog and owner have returned home after training.

## SPREADING THE GUIDE DOG MOVEMENT

The reputation of the work being carried out at the school in Potsdam spread worldwide.

In 1927 one visitor to the school was an American lady, living in Switzerland, called Dorothy Eustis. She went on to be largely responsible for initiating the guide dog movement in America and Great Britain. At her kennels, known as Fortunate Fields, she was breeding and training German Shepherds for the army, police and customs services. The principal purpose of Fortunate Fields was to develop a selective breeding programme that would produce dogs suitable for a wide range of work. Later on this included careful selection of stock suitable for guide dog work.

In 1928 Dorothy trained her first two German Shepherd guide dogs. An enthusiastic young American, Morris Frank persuaded Mrs Eustis to provide him with one of these dogs. He acquired Buddy, and the two of them then returned to the United States. Shortly afterwards Dorothy Eustis also returned to her native country and, in partnership with Morris Frank, set about the daunting task of launching 'The Seeing Eye'.

By 1931 Dorothy Eustis was in a position to send William Debetaz, an instructor from The Seeing Eye school in America, to train the first four British guide dogs and their owners. They were all German Shepherds, or Alsatians as they were then known in the UK. The training time of one of the dogs was interrupted while she produced a litter of puppies. Once she had recovered she went on with her training to become one of the first four guide dogs. The routine neutering of guide dogs was not introduced until the 1960s. In the 1930s, when The Guide Dogs for the Blind Association relied on adult dogs donated by the public, German Shepherds and Border Collies were the most common breeds offered.

## THE PUPPY REARING SCHEME
Due to the popularity of the German Shepherd in the 1920s, many people were prepared to pay high prices for the breed and, inevitably, this encouraged a great deal of indiscriminate breeding, resulting in many shy, nervous specimens. With the onset of the Second World War pedigree dog breeding declined, resulting in fewer good-quality German Shepherds being offered to the Association. Attention was turned to other breeds. A variety were tried – Border Collies, Dalmatians, Airedales and all types of Retriever. Only the Border Collie, at that time, was judged to have the qualities needed, but after the war the German Shepherd reappeared in greater numbers as guide dogs. It was some time before the quality of the Labrador improved enough for it to be considered suitable for regular use as a guide dog, which seems surprising as the breed now dominates the guide dog population the world over.

With the variety of types being offered at the time, the wastage rate was high. Finding healthy dogs with a confident attitude was difficult. For over thirty years the Association obtained dogs from various sources including farmers, dealers and breeders. These dogs were neither bred nor reared for this highly specialised and demanding work. The need for puppies to be reared specially as prospective guide dogs was recognised. A puppy rearing scheme was introduced in the mid-1950s, followed by a small breeding programme. By the end of 1961 the Association owned two German Shepherd and five Labrador brood bitches.

## THE GSD'S SPECIAL NEEDS
The Labrador's qualities proved to be a more suitable match for the increasing diversity of applicants requiring guide dogs. The breeding programme had to develop and to produce a wide range of dogs, both in size and temperament. Tall men need a large dog, and the elderly, or physically less capable, require a sensitive temperament that is easy

## THE TRAINING PROCESS
*Photos: Alan Jones, courtesy of the Guide Dogs for the Blind Association.*

*The early stages of training. The new recruit is wearing a bodypiece rather than a full harness. The trainer is working on artificial obstacle avoidance where the dog must learn to negotiate obstacles allowing sufficient room for the handler.*

*Working in full harness, this dog is being taught straight line work. By working in a kind of grid system, the dog will learn to go back on course after negotiating obstacles.*

*Kerb work: The dog must learn to stop at kerbs. In most cases, the dog is taught to sit, although some special needs may require a dog to stand.*

Obstacle avoidance off-kerb. The dog finds the kerb, and after the appropriate stop, he goes into the road to negotiate the obstacle. The dog must then return to the safety of the pavement at the earliest opportunity and then re-establish the origional straight line.

*This training begins under controlled conditions with a vehicle being driven by another instructor. The dog is taught to stop if a vehicle approaches.*

*The dog must learn to stop if he steps off the kerb and then a vehicle appears. Ultimately, it remains the decision of the handler when to cross the road.*

*Regular training sessions at the railway station will include steps, lifts, getting on and off a train and safely negotiating a busy, noisy platform.*

*Platform edge awareness is being taught at a railway station.*

*The dog must stop and stand at the start of a flight of steps. This applies going up and down steps.*

*Find the door: The dog is trained to find the door of a building.*

*The door must then be negotiated safely.*

*Road junctions and pedestrian crossings are safe places to cross the road.*

*The dog must cross in a straight line without wandering or deviating.*

*Left turn: The dog takes the handler to the kerb and then turns in the direction indicated by the handler.*

*Find the van: The end of a training session.*

*It is important that all the dogs enjoy their training sessions, and they are rewarded with plenty of praise.*

to handle. In the UK during 1996 less than five per cent of the dogs that qualified as guide dogs with new owners were German Shepherds.

There are many reasons for the decline in numbers used. The more sensitive types are suited to guide dog work, but these dogs find the time spent in the kennel environment during the lengthy training programme an additional burden. The breed is generally slow to mature; add sensitivity to this equation and they are then inclined to take longer to adapt to change, which all adds to their training time. Not all blind people want a German Shepherd; or perhaps someone in the immediate family is reluctant to have one living with them; also, not all working environments will accept a German Shepherd on the premises on a daily basis.

The German Shepherd Guide dog needs an owner who can keep pace with their long stride – a sympathetic handler who is agile, quick-thinking and able to provide the German Shepherd with the level of work that the breed requires.

## THE IDEAL QUALITIES
The ideal guide dog must be:
Stable and of a pleasing disposition.
Not neurotic, shy or frightened.
Reasonably energetic but not hyperactive.
Non-aggressive.
Of low chasing instinct.
Possessing an ability to concentrate for long periods.
Not easily distracted.
Willing and responsive to the human voice.
Confident with and tolerant of children.
Confident with and tolerant of other animals.
Not sound-shy.
Able to show a level of initiative.
Not too dominant or self-interested.
Adaptable to change.
Possessing an acceptable level of hearing, and of mental and body sensitivity.
As free as possible from hereditary defects.

## TRAINING A GUIDE DOG
The puppy walking scheme for prospective guide dogs has proved to be a major factor in the success rate currently enjoyed by the Guide Dogs for the Blind Association. The

Association was the pioneer of early socialisation, which is widely recognised as being of fundamental importance in ensuring the development of acceptable temperamental characteristics.

Puppies are placed in homes from the age of six weeks. The aim is to rear a puppy in a family environment and for it to be socialised in a variety of situations. The puppy must get used to all the sights and sounds of a busy town life. It has to learn to walk slightly ahead of the handler and should ignore distractions. It is also house-trained, taught good social behaviour and basic obedience responses. This period of early training lasts on average for one year, during which the puppies are visited and assessed on a monthly basis, while at walk, by a member of GDBA staff.

German Shepherds normally come in for training at 14 months of age. They are taken to one of the regional training centres for assessment and further training. Initially they are taught the straight line procedure, kerb stops, turns (left, right and back) and speed control. Once these skills have been developed they are then taught obstacle avoidance – at first these obstacles are solid stationary objects, such as lamp-posts and letter-boxes, then there are moving objects, namely people.

The sheer size of the German Shepherd can tend to clear the pavement, but speed control in busy areas is an important aspect of their training. They are inclined to rush their work and enthusiastically anticipate commands, if allowed to do so. The correct approach from the handler is essential in order to develop a calm, relaxed, steady attitude from the dog. On average it takes nine months to train a guide dog.

In the later stages of training the dog is matched to a suitable blind owner. The needs and circumstances of the client are assessed, as well as their lifestyle, fitness and temperament. It is important to match the capabilities of the client with the ability of the dog. Training the dog with the client can take up to four weeks. The flexibility of the residential course allows for the variety of client ability. The rate of progress will depend on the aptitude of the owner and the dog's acceptance of the change of handler and circumstances. This stage can be very taxing for the German Shepherd.

The new blind owner will be taught how to handle the dog in all the different situations and environments that the dog experienced during training. The owners are also taught basic dog psychology, feeding, grooming and general care procedures. When the guide dog owner returns home with their new dog, their instructor will visit them to practise the routes they do regularly, for example going to work, to school and to the shops, to ensure the safety and confidence of the dog and owner in their new role together. All guide dog owners are visited on an annual basis throughout the dog's working life. More frequent visits will be made if required. Most Guide dog owners who have lived and worked with a German Shepherd request another one when the time comes for a replacement.

## LEWIS AND BARCLAY
*Working with a German Shepherd guide dog has been a joy for Lewis Price, 46. He says: "Once you have had a GSD you want another one. They have a bit of extra something."*

Although the characters of his two German Shepherds have been quite different – Berry was a dominant bitch while Barclay, aged five, is a gentle giant – Lewis has found both to be fun to work with, and very responsive, calm and "nosy".

"Whereas my Labrador was a slave in harness and did everything you asked to the letter, sticking rigidly to her regular routes, I

*Barclay: A dog to trust.*

find the GSDs do the same routes well but, because it is familiar, they have a look in all the driveways and notice everything that is going on around them.

"What they really like is to go into town where it is more difficult, with more obstacles to guide me through. Then they rise to the occasion and start to concentrate."

Thinking ahead has also been another common trait of his GSDs, Lewis says. "Again, my Lab would follow our regular routes religiously with every corner a perfect right angle, whereas Berry and now Barclay seem to be more aware of their wider surroundings, and if they think they recognise a quicker way to get somewhere they will take you diagonally to achieve it. If Barclay recognises that we can get more

speedily to the pick-up point where we meet my wife each evening he will want to take control – never mind that it is two hours early!

"But seriously, I can trust him totally because he is so switched on. If I got a bit lost and he knew the general direction, I could just let him take me there. He is very perceptive."

As a social person who likes to get out and about Lewis also finds that, whatever image people may have of German Shepherd Dogs generally, when they are in harness people lose their fears.

"With my Labrador, wherever we went I always had someone coming up wanting to fuss the dog and talk about her, which is fine because guide dogs are not that common and it is good that people take an interest. When I got Berry I thought at least with a GSD I won't get so much attention. But it was quite the opposite. They are such big, beautiful dogs that they are a magnet. I get more attention now than ever."

Working with Barclay six, sometimes seven, days a week, Lewis says that not only have his guide dogs given him dignity by allowing him to be more independent, they have become an important part of the family. And again the GSDs score highly as great characters.

"We have had our disagreements, such as the time we went out just after Christmas leaving Berry, the cat and a cooked pheasant wrapped high up on a shelf, only to find when we got back that Berry had got it down and eaten the lot. So the dog had pheasant

for lunch and I seem to recall we had Cornish Pasty.

"But overall, when they are not there, because we have gone somewhere and they have stayed with someone overnight, I absolutely miss them."

## COLLEAGUE AND FRIEND
*Lorna Smith of Lanarkshire, Scotland, needs her guide dog to be able to cope with travel and people, and is delighted with Andrea's adaptability.*

Lorna says: "My first GSD was wonderful and I was very sad when she developed health problems that meant she could not work any more. Happily she went to stay with a friend of mine and lived for another four years. I have worked with all breeds of

*Lorna and Andrea.*

guide dog but after Fudge I always said that I would prefer another GSD. They are just so in-tune with you.

"People talk about dogs having a sixth sense, but with Fudge, and now with Andrea, I agree that there is something there. If I am feeling worried or happy it seems to transmit to Andrea and she feels it too. We were getting ready to go somewhere one day and I must have been feeling a bit uptight about it and she came out in sympathy with an attack of the runs!"

Unlike the majority of guide dogs, Andrea was actually bred outside the Association, but her pedigree was so good that the Guide Dogs for the Blind breeding manager bought four puppies from the litter. Andrea showed her quality by finishing puppy training and advanced training at 22 months, when she and Lorna were first introduced.

After an intensive four weeks of training together at one of the Guide Dog centres under the expert eye of an instructor, dog and owner go home for the first time.

Lorna says "It must be quite hard on the dog when it first starts to train with you, changing allegiance for the third time in its short life, and for the instructors who have to let go and let you take over. But Andrea adapted quickly and seemed to accept that this was the way it was going to be, so she would go along with it, which is typical of her.

"But it is when you get home for the first time that the work really starts. The first year is the hardest with a new dog. You are all the time learning about each other and developing a trust. But if you answer the regular questionnaires absolutely honestly about any problems you are having, then everything can usually be ironed out as you go along."

Lorna has found her German Shepherd Dogs easy to build a rapport with. "Andrea is a marvellous wee girl. In harness she takes her job very seriously and her only aim is to please. I have no sight at all so she is doing 110 per cent of the work when we go out and she is extremely aware of our surroundings and cautious about obstacle avoidance. If she does occasionally get things wrong, like going into the wrong shop, she would get very upset if I scolded her so I have to reassure her and move her on.

"Off duty she is a darling and full of fun, always hiding things and wanting me to play with her squeaky toys. Her favourite pleasure is the park. I have to keep her in check when there are people around because she can get a bit boisterous. But generally people seem to love her."

Guide Dogs are not only matched to their owner for character, they have to be able to fit in with the owner's lifestyle and work. In Lorna's case that means liking people and travel.

"My work as a regional charity fund-raiser means that I do lots of travelling and meeting people and my Andrea is wonderful at both. On aeroplanes we sit in the very back seats where the engine noise is quietest and she squeezes herself into the seat next to me without any fuss. On one occasion a stewardess had put blankets across two seats in order to give her more room, with me sitting across the aisle, but I had to say no, because she would not like not being right next to me.

"She also loves children and when I take her into schools she is very well behaved, enjoying the fuss. She fits in brilliantly with me and is a friend as much as anything."

## GUIDE DOGS FOR THE BLIND USA

In the UK a single programme, the Guide Dogs for the Blind Association (GDBA) provides all the guide dogs for blind Britons. Regional centres are found in various locations, but training standards are uniform and national. Close to 5,000 dog-person

*German Shepherds
are used exclusively as
guide dogs by some
training programmes
in the US.*

teams are working currently. In the US, the
picture is different in a number of ways, with
more competition being the main one. Less
than ten years after the 1929 establishment of
The Seeing Eye, Inc., a second programme
started up in Michigan, called Leader Dogs
for the Blind. After World War II, additional
schools were founded, and by 1997 there
were at least 14 such training institutions.
There were over 7,500 teams working in
1997 and about 1,300 graduating each year.

The first years in the movement featured
the German Shepherd Dog almost exclusively,
but in later years the percentage has dropped
precipitously until now about 70 per cent of
guide dogs are Labrador Retrievers, 10 per
cent Golden Retrievers, and 10 per cent
GSDs. A variety of breeds make up the
remainder, including Doberman Pinschers,
Boxers, Australian Shepherds, Poodles, and
Lab-Golden Retriever crosses. This last
phenomenon originated in the UK, where it
is said that such a crossbreed is the most
common dog trained for work with the
blind.

Two or three programmes in America still
exclusively train GSDs for the blind. One is

Fidelco Guide Dog Foundation, which had
begun as a GSD breeding kennel and became
a full-fledged training institution in 1981.
Until then, they had supplied pre-selected
dogs to existing schools. Fidelco trains in the
blind person's home, compared to all others
requiring the blind person to come to the
schools. Eye Dog Foundation, where Erich
Renner used to work, still specializes in
GSDs. The Seeing Eye, Inc., beginning in
the early 1990s, is implementing a policy to
increase the proportion of GSDs and hopes
to reach the goal of 60 per cent in each of its
graduating classes.

Guide Dogs USA, Inc. is Erich Renner's
school and has operated in Arizona, Nevada,
and California. Erich uses only German
Shepherd Dogs, and almost only females at
that. Erich, besides being a fervent lover and
exhibitor of the breed, prefers the GSD for
practical reasons as well. In many minds, the
dog's coat with its adaptability to any
climate, and the temperament, self-
confidence, and eagerness to work found in
the German Shepherd Dog are unparalleled.
Erich states that the alert, prick-eared, intense
impression that the Shepherd gives is one of

the reasons that blind people with GSDs are almost never attacked or molested by criminals, citing as an example his contention that the few blind women who have been accosted on the streets of Los Angeles, all used Retrievers. He feels that these "birddogs", as he calls the Retrievers, "seem to think that service for the blind is a game", whereas to the GSD it is their very reason for living.

That may seem somewhat anthropomorphic, but Erich has had deep insight into the psyche of the GSD for over half a century. There is no doubt that the psychological advantage of the GSD's expression and reputation has deterred many a would-be perpetrator of crime in other venues. The properly bred and selected, healthy GSD tends to solve problems faster and with more confidence, and this breed's walking speed and stride is purportedly better adapted to that of most humans. Erich also exclusively uses females, as males tend to be too large for the owner to hold on to the harness comfortably, and are more aggressive and self-willed, even if castrated. Spaying does not noticeably change the females and as a matter of fact has some health advantages.

## POLICE DOGS IN THE UK

Many attempts have been made to use dogs as assistants in police work. There are records of rural police constables in the 19th century using their own pet dogs to catch poachers. These dogs were usually trained by their owners with the assistance of the local gamekeeper and were used on the patrol of large estates. In 1888 the use of Bloodhounds to track down 'Jack the Ripper' was unsuccessful. In 1909 London and North Eastern Railway Transport Police successfully trained and used dogs to assist the transport police to locate and remove vagrants from their rolling stock. Although

the extensive use of the German Shepherds by the armed forces in Germany during the First World War as messengers, guards and sentries attracted attention from Britain and the United States, little progress was made in developing their use.

One incident did, however, shoot the breed to stardom and established the breed's popularity worldwide. At the end of the Second World War a German Shepherd puppy, abandoned by the retreating Germans, was rescued and taken back to America by an army sergeant. The dog received extensive training and went on to appear in many films as the Hollywood star Rin-Tin-Tin.

Successful use of police dogs on the Continent during the 1920s stimulated interest at the Home Office. A study was carried out to examine the type of training required, how long the training took and which breeds would be best suited for police work. An experimental police dog training school was established but still only limited progress was made. At the outbreak of the Second World War any dogs that had been trained were recruited into the armed services. These where few in comparison to the number the Germans deployed.

Attitudes and financial constraints blocked any proposals for developing any extensive use of the dog. Then, in 1951, sergeants from the Metropolitan and the Birmingham Police and the Surrey and Lancashire Constabularies were sent to Germany to study the dog training methods of the German police. It was after this visit that formalised training on an organised scale was introduced. On their return these men trained a small number of dogs each and, following this early initiative, regional dog sections were established.

## UK TRAINING

Dogs are acquired either by the police force's own breeding scheme or as a gift or a purchase from the public. The German Shepherd is one of the many different breeds that they use. Ideally the dog should be about twelve months old and have a confident, self-assured nature. The initial training course lasts thirteen weeks. During this period the dog is taught the basic skills of heel work, on and off lead, the retrieve, agility, then tracking on soft and hard surfaces and to search for persons or property out in the open or inside buildings. Criminal work is taught in the later stages of the training programme. The success of a good police dog is down to team-work. Both handler and dog rely on each other totally. The selection of suitable handlers is vitally important. The police dog is only as good as the handler demands. As a team, they are only as effective as circumstances at the scene of crime allow; the handler is dependent on the co-operation of his fellow officers. As little disturbance as possible at the scene of crime will give the dog and handler the best chance of success.

TRACKING

The dogs are taught to follow the scent of ground disturbance e.g. crushed grass, disturbed earth. Only a minute proportion of personal scents contribute to the track as a whole. Therefore the type of ground the dog is tracking over is often an essential factor leading to success or failure. In an experiment it was proved that a dog can successfully track in woodland for up to 24 hours after the event, on pastureland up to 18 hours later. Hard surfaces such as roads and pavements reduce the tracking time to about half an hour in the daytime and an hour at night.

SEARCH

(this includes people, property, bodies, drugs, firearms and explosives)

---

**The following list illustrates the complexities of scent discrimination.**

**Personal scent:** Sex, Race, Parts of the body.
**Additional but not totally personal:** Clothing, Occupation, Footwear, Shoe polish.
**Ground:** Earth, Gases, Insects, Microbes, Vegetation, Decay.

---

### Searching for a person

Unlike the track scent, which can be disturbed or even destroyed by movement or the prevailing weather conditions, the scent of a hidden human can be detected as a wind-borne scent in open ground from a considerable distance. Within a building a dog can track the scent from the point of entry, or indicate a source of human scent to the handler.

### Searching for property

When searching for property the dog will retrieve any article bearing human scent or it will indicate, by barking, for example, at an irretrievable article.

### Searching for bodies

There are two main factors that affect how a body is detected – the length of time the body has been dead and the depth of burial. There are dogs specifically trained to detect bodies that have been deeply buried for some time. In instances where bodies have been buried in a shallow grave, or even left in the open in a clothed state, depending on the weather, and whether it is an exposed or a sheltered site, the dog can locate the scent from an item of clothing for some time after death.

### Searching for drugs

German Shepherds are more than capable of being trained to search for drugs but experience has shown that the Labrador, Spaniel, Pointers and Border Collies are more socially acceptable in the types of environment where they are expected to undertake this work. These breeds are also smaller, so the dogs find getting into confined spaces easier. All drugs have quite a definite scent, which dogs are taught to identify. I have been asked to stress the point that the dogs are not addicted to the drugs; they are simply taught to associate the indication of the scent with play. 'Active' drugs dogs will indicate a find by barking, scratching or digging. 'Passive' dogs are taught to indicate a find by sitting immediately.

### Searching for firearms and explosives

All explosives give off a strong odour. Even a new firearm has a scent. It will have been contaminated during proof-firing by the black powder explosive contained in the cartridge case. The dogs trained to detect explosives are taught to recognise the scent and to indicate the substance found by barking or sitting; they are not taught to retrieve, for obvious reasons!

### Criminal work

The dog is taught two types of criminal work. Firstly to circle and bark at a criminal who submits and remains still. Secondly to attack, on command, a criminal who is running to escape, whether armed or otherwise. This type of arrest is usually used as a last resort. If a dog is used to effect an arrest, all other officers must be instructed accordingly and should do nothing in any way to distract the dog from its task.

*Agility jumps test the dog's fitness, strength and obedience.*

### THE TRAINING PROGRESS
*Photos: Alan Jones, courtesy of the Greater Manchester Police Dog Section.*

*In the initial stages of training the dog is taught basic Obedience skills.*

The dog is fitted with a tracking harness so that he knows that he is working. The handler attaches a tracking line to maintain contact with the dog. This is particularly important when the dog is working in undergrowth or at night.

Items may be placed along the route and the dog must find them.

The end of the search and the 'suspect' is found. The trainee police dog is immediately rewarded with his favourite toy.

*The police dog must learn to apprehend a suspect. The handler shouts a challenge to the suspect before releasing the dog.*

*The dog detains the suspect by gripping the arm protector. The suspect attempts to shake the dog off, testing his determination and courage.*

*The dog is rewarded with his toy.*

*The dog must also learn to work at close quarters.*

*In training, life-like situations are created to give the dog an understanding of what is required.*
*Here, the suspect is attempting to intimidate the dog.*

*The suspect turns and runs away.*

*The dog is released to take up the chase.*

*The dog finds the suspect and goes in to hold.*

*The dog holds the suspect until the handler arrives at the scene.*

*The dog is joined by his handler and recalled.*

*Police dogs must also learn to work inside. Disused buildings make an excellent training environment.*

*The hander is encouraging the dog to search for the suspect.*

*The dog is given sight of the suspect. This encourages him to continue the search.*

*The suspect is located and the dog barks to alert his handler.*

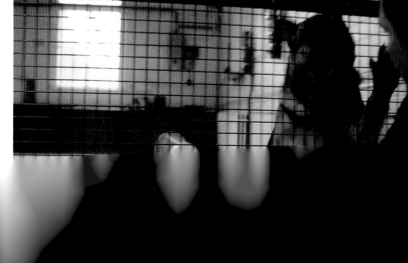

## PC MARK ROBSON AND BOSKO

"What exactly makes the German Shepherd so outstanding at police work is hard to answer, but in my opinion it is because the breed as a whole is so intelligent. Throughout the training, it is not a case of teaching the dog to do something, but simply showing the dog what needs to be done. The Shepherds are so adaptable and seem to enjoy the work so much, they are always eager to learn. It is as if they accept and understand that they are a working breed."

It is impossible not to be inspired by PC Mark Robson's enthusiasm and love of the breed, which comes across with every word. More than an interest, the Shepherd is his work and his life. As the only police dog handler who has bred, trained and works his own dog, he is unique in the British police force and justifiably proud of two-and-a-half year old Brezburg Bosko, who qualified as a fully-fledged police dog six months ago.

"Bosko was bred from a German bitch that was originally brought here for showing purposes, mated with a Dutch import dog with a working background," Mark explains. Having applied to join the dog section of Cleveland Police himself, he had always had ambitions for Bosko within the force. "I started doing a little with him when he was very young, introducing him as early as possible to nose work and getting him used to as many situations as I could. Even at the stage when I was still having to carry him around, we went in the car to shopping precincts, the train and bus station and the town centre. All the noises around the home that can potentially be a shock to a dog – the vacuum, the washing machine, noise from a garage – I started to get him accustomed to them. I also joined the local Schutzhund Club, so that we could make a start in learning the protection side of training, chasing and tracking, all using the correct equipment."

The youngster's thorough preparation stood him in good stead, as both Bosko and his trainer were taken on. The pair's solid performance throughout the initial 13-week training course enabled them to finish with flying colours. So impressive was the dog's ability, that Bosko's son Danni has been purchased by the Force in the hope that he will show the same aptitude for police work. If all goes well and Danni eventually joins the Cleveland operation, the father-son duo will be another first.

## RECRUITING POLICE DOGS

The care that Mark put into Bosko's breeding and early education loaded the odds in the dog's favour in a canine profession where the strictest of entry criteria apply. Only 1 in 25

*PC Mark Robson with police dog Brezburg Bosko, and son Brezburg Danni, aged 12 weeks.*

young dogs who begin training turn out to be suitable for the work and eventually reach the required standard. No risks can be taken where lives, safety and precious public resources are at stake.

The high failure rate is also partly a result of a 'recruiting' method that is very much a business of trial and error. Although several forces are now experimenting with breeding programmes, most prospective police dogs are offered as gifts.

"The most frequent situation is that a pup has been purchased by someone at eight weeks old, kept for a year or slightly longer, and then that owner, for whatever reason, finds they can't handle it," says Mark. "It could be a family problem, or that the dog doesn't like young children or, more often than not, simply that the dog is too much of a handful and the owner hasn't realised the demands of keeping a dog from a working breed.

"We will take the dog on trial and assess it. If we believe it could have potential, it is allocated a trainer. If it is clearly not going to be suitable for police work, it can either be returned to the owner or we will find an alternative home with someone who is not going to come across the problems that arose previously."

## INITIAL TRAINING

Dogs must be no older than 18 months, the age at which the majority start their training. "Some do begin earlier, if they are showing the right mental attitude," Mark explains. "With those we take on younger, we have the opportunity to do a little preparatory work with them, hopefully bringing out the better aspects of the dog's behaviour as we go, so that when they start the training they are a good prospect. The advantage of a breeding programme is that by the time they are old enough to train you have a good idea

*PC Mark Robson and Bosko in action leaving the Cleveland Police Force helicopter.*

whether they are going to be suitable or not, so it is worthwhile in cutting down the failure rate.”

The initial police dog training course lasts for 13 weeks, though allowances are made for slower learners that still show promise. Nose work and tracking skills provide the grounding on which the job will be based and are the priority:

“We will track almost every day for the first fortnight to see if the dog has the ability he needs in that direction. It is more or less a case of brainwashing the dog into using its nose. Then there is a certain amount of obedience and some agility work. We will then start the dogs on a hessian rag, then a bite-bar, then progress to a protective sleeve.

“In the early days we also need to assess the dogs in a building and on all kinds of surfaces. Some dogs, for example, dislike a linoleum floor. If a dog won’t accept a slippery floor we generally have to say goodbye to it, because the majority of work in towns involves buildings with corridors, like schools and factories, and if they are uncomfortable on lino that is no good.

“The amount of tracking done generally decreases as the training continues, if the dogs are happy. What increases as time goes on is working at a distance, away from a handler. The dog has to come to realise there are jobs to be done away from ‘dad’ and to work independently. He must realise that dad will not always be there to back him up. When he finds a criminal 600 or 700 metres away in a wood, he has to sit and hold and bark until the handler arrives. So we build up the distance between the handler and dog gradually until the end of the course, by which time the dog has to be a good standard – not an excellent standard, but at a point where he has a good grounding and is efficient enough to go out on the streets.”

ON THE BEAT
Training then continues, interspersed with working shifts, with the onus on the dog’s handler to help him progress to the more advanced stages and trial work. Those who fail to complete the course have proved unsuitable for one of a number of reasons.

“Often they have no aggression when it is needed, have poor hips or other health problems. Some dogs we take are great at everything but don’t seem to have a nose on their heads, be it for food or for toys. Most commonly, though, they lack enough self-confidence.”

Confidence, Mark believes, is the key personality trait when it comes to selecting a young dog that could have the potential to make it in the police force.

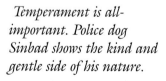

*Temperament is all-important. Police dog Sinbad shows the kind and gentle side of his nature.*

"When you are judging a pup, you are looking for a bold, playful dog that is solid in construction and has a lot of drive. We throw all kinds of things for them, to see if they are the sort of dog with a strong prey instinct who wants to chase, including, for example, bunches of keys or a spanner, because many dogs will turn their noses up at metallic objects. There must be a real urge to retrieve – to go away and bring things back to you, and to use their nose.

"A gift dog coming from outside the Force has to have been well socialised, be good with traffic and be able to travel well by any mode of transport, be it a fast-moving car, van or helicopter. Dogs that are continually travel sick are no use to the police."

## CONSTRUCTION

Soundness is important, as a dog that cannot stand up to work cannot be an efficient member of the Force. The Breed Standard is used to assess a new recruit, though not as a hard and fast rule. An experienced eye will tell the trainer whether a youngster shapes up.

"The dog must be put together properly. We like it to look the part, though it must not be too big or it will only impede itself when it has to work in a small or cramped area. Sound hips, of course, and dentition are other important areas. In the early days of training, in particular, there is a lot of bite work done on protective sleeves. If the dog's teeth are going to be dropping out we will be liable for continual vet's bills. We do have older dogs that have been in the Force a number of years which have actually had lost teeth replaced by chrome, metallic ones – quite a sight for a criminal when those are bared!"

## TEMPERAMENT

Although construction is considered to a certain extent, temperament is the crucial factor in whether a dog will make the grade. "Police work requires a strong, bold character, but you do not want an aggressive dog as such. When it comes to situations such as dealing with people that are vulnerable, like the elderly or young children, then the animal must not frighten them or be likely to bite. The dog must be trustworthy. The aggressive side needs to be there, but it must be controlled. More or less like flicking a switch, the handler has to be able to turn the aggression on and off."

## THE COMPLETE ALL-ROUNDER

In Mark's opinion, the German Shepherd's strength, instincts and sensitivity combine to make it the ultimate police dog.

"I have worked with other breeds such as gun dogs, and we do use others at work for the drugs and explosives side, for example Springer Spaniels, mainly because they fit into smaller places and are quicker. However, the Shepherd is so versatile.

"Although the dogs do have their own personalities, as a rule the ones we take are quite a similar type. They are all well-motivated all-rounders. For safety, and to be efficient, a police dog has to be an all-rounder, with ability in tracking, searching, and chasing work, and reliable enough for public relations. We would much rather have a dog that is second best at everything than brilliant at only one thing.

## THE HANDLER

It is the handler's job to channel the dog's instincts and control the on-off switch that gives the police dog the ability to be a school-child's friend one minute and criminal's worst nightmare the next.

"The handler is the key. It is a huge responsibility. Yet the trained German Shepherd is so sensitive that more often than not he reads the situation himself from the tone of his handler's voice and the body language. It is the challenge the handler gives that will trigger the latent aggression in a dog.

"On the other side, if I am down for whatever reason, or have had a bad day, and I get him out, I find he is feeling just the same as me. It will knock his drive and his enthusiasm. He knows, because it is transmitted in the tone of my voice, and he can feel if I am tense. The bond between the handler and his dog is vital. You keep each other happy."

That bond, on which the effectiveness of this crime-busting team pivots, grows throughout the young dog's early education. At first it is generally circumstance that throws man and dog together. Later, the two become a partnership based on mutual respect and not a little affection.

"In the first instance it is often a case of a man being allocated whatever dog comes along," Mark explains, "though if it is anticipated that a youngster might be particularly hard, it will go to an experienced handler. Those that are perhaps more sensitive, or slower to learn, could go to a novice handler so that the two can bring each other on. Some dogs are so strong in their character that they try to rule the roost. Those, obviously, need to go to an established handler who knows the score and knows when correction is due. A novice could easily spoil a dog like that – one that might have been a good prospect.

"The handler works together with the dog all the way through the course. One man will only have one general-purpose GSD, although he may have an additional specialist dog of another breed. If it completes the training, the dog then becomes that handler's permanently, living with him at his home.

"The relationship between the handler and dog brings everything else together and makes it work – it is the most important element of all. By the end of the training, the bond between the two must be really strong, and getting stronger. At the end of the day, the dog must back up the man in every situation. If a dog does not particularly like his handler, then he is not going to stick up for him. Dogs go downhill rapidly if you go overboard with training or if they are not happy. If there is a good bond, the dog will give 100 per cent to please you, whatever you ask."

Bosko's 'beat' tests the strength and quality of that relationship daily. As part of an urban force, one day's challenge might be to help in dispersing a violent crowd, the next to track a stolen vehicle across waste ground. Then, that afternoon, he could be leaping through a burning hoop at an obedience demonstration, or posing for a photograph with smiling schoolchildren. So what are the most satisfying moments, for PC Robson and Police Dog Brezburg Bosko?

"Our job involves a lot of searching, either of buildings or for missing people. Ninety-nine out of 100 times, a criminal has actually gone. Occasionally they are still in there, hiding somewhere behind a closed door. The dog loves it! When Bosko starts barking, it's such a thrill. Unbelievable."

POLICE DOGS IN THE USA
In 1958 five officers from the St Louis Metropolitan Police Department were selected from a group of volunteers to go to England to attend an extensive 14-week training programme at Keston Police Dog Training School. On their return to the USA they trained their own dogs and began patrolling the streets of St Louis. The Board of Police Commissioners were quick to approve the employment of dogs to assist the department in its fight against crime and the St Louis Police Canine Department began. It has gained a national reputation as a training centre for the development of police canine teams. Officers from all over the United

States of America and the Royal Canadian Mounted Police have been to St Louis for canine training.

They only use German Shepherd males. These are dogs that have been donated to the department by the public. They prefer the physical and mental attitude the GSD can offer and its willingness to learn. It has excellent tracking and search skills and finally, when up against a criminal on the run, it looks the part. In St Louis, Canine Officers are eligible for a special award presented by the department to man and dog teams for work well done.

## OFFICER MICHAEL ROBERTSON AND K-9 DUKE
*Extract from a newspaper report of an incident*
On Wednesday, September 12th 1997, at 11:00am, Officer Robertson responded to a foot pursuit of a suspect who was wanted for violation of the Missouri Controlled Substance Law. The pursuing officers lost the wanted suspect but they thought that he may have run into a vacant building. The suspect was wanted for selling "crack" cocaine and was known to carry a hand-gun. The pursuing officers advised Officer Robertson that the side door to the residence at 3455 Nebraska had been forced open and they thought their suspect could be inside.

Officer Robertson made the proper announcements and when there was no response, he released his K-9 Duke with the command to "find him". Duke indicated, by barking, that the suspect was hiding in a dark corner of the basement. As Duke got closer to the suspect, he began kicking at Duke in an attempt to escape. K-9 Duke apprehended the suspect by the left leg and held on. The suspect quit resisting, K-9 Duke was ordered to release, and the suspect arrested without further incident.
*The suspect was subsequently charged with a variety of offences.*

## OFFICER KEVIN MELCHIOR AND CANINE CHAMP
*An extract from a police report*
On July 2nd 1994 at 10:15am district patrol officers received a radio assignment for 'burglars in the building'. Upon the district officers' arrival at the building they were met by the supervisor of the business who stated that he had responded to an alarm and he observed a suspect inside the building. The district officer requested additional cars to surround the business. As the officers entered they observed a suspect attempting to escape through a door. The officers pursued the suspect and apprehended him.

The district offices requested Canine to respond. Officer Melchior and Canine Champ responded. The business is a very large tube-fabricator warehouse approximately 400,000 square feet. The warehouse was full of boxes and barrels, some full of parts and others empty. There were hundreds of places for a person to hide, where they would never be found by an officer. Officer Melchior and Canine Champ entered the warehouse with one of the district officers as a backup.

Prior to releasing Canine Champ, Officer Melchior made the proper announcements and, after waiting a reasonable amount of time and not getting any response, Officer Melchior released Champ with the command to "Find him".

Canine Champ worked the west section of the warehouse and did not give any indication of the presence of a suspect. After working about 30 minutes continually, Officer Melchior gave Champ a break and watered him down. The temperature outside was 90 degrees and it was even hotter inside. Officer Melchior and Champ were the only canine team working, so the search had to be completed by them.

Officer Melchior gave another announcement and there was no response to

*Officer John Undersinger with Blix, officer Joseph Dobbs with Caesar, and officer Michael Robertson with Duke.*

it, and he again released Champ with the command to "Find him". Champ searched another 15 minutes and the search team got to the section of the warehouse that had the lunch room with the soda and candy machines. Both of these machines had been broken open by using a cutting torch that the company owned. The money in the machines had been removed.

As Champ was searching the area of the machines, he became very excited and Officer Melchior knew that someone was in the general area. At about this time Officer

Melchior was advised by radio that the suspect already arrested had stated that there was another suspect in the warehouse and that he was a former employee of the company and that he was possibly armed with a pistol.

Canine Champ started to run east through the warehouse toward a stack of boxes and steel tubing, which was stacked up about 20 feet high. As Champ was running toward these boxes he was barking and growling and Officer Melchior advised the backup officer that Champ was indicating that the suspect

*The handler and police dog build up a relationship of trust, knowing they can work together in critical situations.*
*Photo courtesy: New York Police Dept.*

was in that area. Champ began to run around the stack of boxes and tubing, barking continually. Officer Melchior and the backup officer took a position to cover Canine Champ. The officers could not see the suspect or where he could be hiding. Officer

Melchior ordered the suspect to surrender but there was no response.

Canine Champ started to climb up the boxes and, upon reaching the top, he jumped down out of sight and at that time the officers heard the suspect start to yell to get

*Officer Julia Priest with K9 Bolo. Bolo has dropped on command, but is ready in case the suspect tries to escape.*

*Officer Ed Meyer with K9 Conran, a working police and search dog, trained to detect explosives.*

the dog off him. The suspect appeared at the top of the stack of boxes and was attempting to escape, but Champ had a hold of the suspect's leg and was holding on.

The suspect continued to fight and try to escape from Canine Champ. As the struggle continued, the suspect and Champ fell into a box of tubing on the floor. During the fall and after Canine Champ never let go of the suspect. The suspect hit the tubing first and Canine Champ was on top of him. The suspect continued to fight but Champ held on to the suspect's leg and had him pinned down with his body. The suspect was ordered to lie still and stop fighting the police dog. The suspect complied and Canine Champ was called to the heel position. Officer Melchior ordered the suspect to lie still and he was handcuffed by the backup officer.

The suspect was searched and in his pockets was the money from the machines but no weapon was found. The suspect was escorted out of the building by the backup

officer as Canine Champ and Officer Melchior took another break. After watering down Canine Champ and taking a break, a search was made in the general area where the suspect was apprehended by Canine Champ to find the weapon but none was ever found. The entire warehouse was searched and no other suspects were found. The search took approximately three hours to complete.

Without Champ the second suspect would probably not have been found and, further, the suspect could have harmed an officer because the suspect was probably armed even though a weapon was not found.
*Both suspects were charged with burglary.*

## UK SERVICE DOGS
The Animal Defence Centre at Melton Mowbray supplies trained dogs for all the departments of the British Armed services. The number of dogs required to meet the demand is met by a team of officers

constantly viewing and assessing the many breeds of dog offered to them by the public. Most of these dogs are donated. The breed most frequently used as a patrol dog is the German Shepherd. All dogs entering the centre undergo a basic training course at which they either pass or fail. If successful, they are then matched to a handler from one of the many government services; for some of these this may be their first time attempt at dog handling. Handlers and dogs are then trained together – six weeks for a patrol dog, but a search dog can take up to six months to develop its skills.

*A Sergeant at the Services' Defence Animal Centre in Melton Mowbray, Leicestershire, explains why GSDs are so fit for active life.* Working as a search or patrol dog for the British army or airforce is a highly specialised job that calls for confidence and adaptability – both traits that GSDs usually have in abundance, says our RAF spokesman from the Centre's procurement cell.

For search work, involving seeking out explosives and firearms or drugs, the services use a number of gundog breeds including Pointers and Labrador Retrievers. But for patrol work, involving more time outdoors, security patrolling and guarding military establishments, it is to the German Shepherd Dog that he turns first.

The Sergeant explains: "In our view GSDs are spot-on for patrol work for a number of reasons. Firstly, their size and build commands respect from would-be intruders, so psychologically we are on the right track from the beginning. They are adaptable, cope well with the training, have a coat that can withstand extremes of temperature, which is useful for some foreign postings, and they have a good nose. Finally, there is a more ready supply of GSDs from private homes and rescue centres, which are our main sources."

Dogs that show confident, positive behaviour are taken in by the Services aged between one and three years old. Once they have passed initial suitability and health tests at the Animal Defence Centre, training builds up gradually, with the dogs often "unlearning" things that they may have been taught from puppyhood.

The Sergeant says: "We have to teach the dogs that they will be praised, not scolded, for biting. They might start off in twos and threes barking and biting at a hessian sausage or rag, then progress gradually until they will chase and bite a man in a full body-suit and so on, and will attack under gunfire and will track from scent.

"At first they are often reluctant to bite and stay at all, and it takes time for them to come round to our way of thinking. The main thing is that they have drive and determination, and you can't teach that – they have either got it or they haven't. But if it's there we know how to channel it and, if necessary, temper it for our needs.

"Again, the GSDs cope well through training, showing a real aptitude for work. Roughly speaking we view 1,000 dogs a year overall, take in about half that number, with around half of those passing the training. The pass rate for GSDs is probably about 70 per cent, which is much higher than for the other breeds."

But no amount of training will mean success for the Services unless the dogs work well with their human partners. And though some dogs may spend three or four years with one handler, others working in the Falklands, for example, may have to swap allegiance to a new face every four or five months. So German Shepherd Dogs' adaptability is a prized characteristic.

"We try to minimise the upheaval for the dogs as much as possible by always treating them as individuals," explains the Sergeant. "Each one has its own Service Number, and

Record of Service Book which contains every scrap of information about it, from injections and experience right down to whether it prefers to eat alone. So any new handler can read the book before even meeting the dog and know just about everything about it.

"Once they meet the dog it is a matter of building up trust with exercises, and bonding through grooming, feeding, playing, etc."

There is no doubting the loyalty of German Shepherd Dogs to their handlers and their dedication to their job when the Sergeant recalls this story of Jason, his first dog who worked with him on tour abroad.

"A group of us were doing a demonstration of our work with a line of jumps and sacking tunnels and other equipment. The pace was fast and suddenly I collided heavily with another handler, knocking both of us flat and leaving us slightly concussed. By the time we came to and staggered to our feet Jason and the other GSD had finished their line of jumps in perfect style and were sitting stock still at the end of the course waiting for us. They were both so reliable that they had carried on and finished the job without us."

Even the travelling to postings as far away as the Falklands (8,300 miles) does not seem to bother the dogs who, by all accounts, cope well. That GSDs enjoy their active service, the Sergeant is sure.

"Dogs don't lie and you only have to look at their other end, with tails wagging while they are working, to know that they enjoy it. The work stimulates them mentally and physically and they react by giving it all they've got. They are a perfect breed for our needs."

The Animal Defence Centre supplies dogs for the British Army and Royal Air Force and currently has around 2,500 operational dogs.

## SERVICE DOGS IN THE USA
*Retired Police Dog Handler Roger Haywood visited the huge Davis Monthan United States Air Force Base and met the Air Force Police dogs and handlers.*

The Davis Monthan AFB stands on 640 acres of land originally purchased from the Arizona State Land Department in 1924 for $19.50 and was named by the citizens of Tucson in honour of two local Air Corps Officers killed in military flying accidents, Lts. Samuel Davis and Oscar Monthan.

It is difficult to describe this massive base and give a true impression of the responsibilities of the 355th Security Police Squadron, who patrol its vast area with a military working dog section regarded as one of the finest in the US Air Force. It is an operational airfield for over 100 fighter and special operations aircraft and is also a pilot training centre. However, it is as a storage area for over 5,000 aircraft, withdrawn from service with the US Air Force, Army, Navy and Marine Corps, that the base is famous, and called affectionately 'the Boneyard'. Aircraft are flown to the base, serviced, and then cocooned and stored until needed or sold. There are currently over 1,200 F4 Phantoms, as well as hundreds of B52s there – which are being disposed of under the SALT Treaty. It is estimated that the value of the aircraft stored on the base is in the region of $35 billion (£20 billion).

These details give some idea of the responsibilities that the Air Force police dogs and handlers have in patrolling the base and its storage areas. The dogs used are either Malinois or German Shepherds and, as well as being fully trained patrol dogs, all of the dogs are dual-trained in either drug or explosive detection.

The youngest dog at the base is three years old and the oldest is ten year old Marco who, as well as achieving considerable success as a patrol dog, has carried out operations with the Federal Drug Enforcement Agency and US Customs, detecting drugs which have led to property seizures amounting to $11.5 million (£7 million). Dogs are obtained and trained at the USAF base in Lackland, Texas and then allocated out to bases across the United States.

Handlers are selected from personnel joining the USAF Security Police, also undergoing training at Lackland, Texas. They usually have no previous dog handling experience, but first have to complete their full military training. After training as dog handlers, they are posted to bases for a maximum of three years, when they move on to other Stations; the dogs stay at the original base. There is continual in-house training, which includes gunfire training with the dogs.

## SERVICE DOGS IN SCANDINAVIA

The Swedish Dog Training Centre at Solleftea is responsible for training dogs for the Military, for Customs and for Guide Dogs for the Blind. It was established in 1936 as a dog training school for the Swedish Army. It is now the largest dog training school in Scandinavia. They train only GSDs and Labradors. After 20 years of research and careful breeding they have eliminated the problems of hip dysplasia and arthritis of the elbow from the dogs they use. They are now able to breed healthy dogs that are mentally and physically suitable for all purposes.

The training centre resembles a miniature town; this enables the majority of training to be carried out on site. Both breeds are used as Guide Dogs. It takes six months to train the dog and another month to train the blind person how to work and care for the dog effectively.

This school is also the main supplier of patrol, search and sniffer dogs to all government departments. The guard dog section is the largest; this includes training dogs for the police force. These dogs undertake exactly the same sort of duties as most police dogs the world over – everything from attack on command to attending a crime safety awareness talk at a school. The level of control required for this type of dog is high and a lot is expected of the police dog handler; maintaining the standard of training is very demanding.

A patrol dog for the Army, Air Force or Security Services requires intelligence, endurance and courage. The guarding level expected, and achieved by these dogs does not allow them to be anything other than a one-man dog. They could not be expected to live as a pet dog. At Solleftea they consider the German Shepherd is the only breed suitable for this type of work.

They also train dogs at this school for a role that is essential, particularly to the Scandinavian countries where timber is used extensively. Rot and mould are a major problem. Dogs are used to detect these ever-present invaders of wood, in homes and buildings as well as in electric and telegraph poles. Will we ever exhaust the use a dog's nose can be put to?

For anyone who has ever worked a dog in whatever discipline, even if they have handled other breeds, the extent of German Shepherd's qualities in such a variety of roles would place it as surely one of the most versatile of the working breeds. A breed apart from the rest – perhaps they could be referred to as the Rolls Royce of the working dog world?

# 7 THE BREED STANDARDS

Much has been written of the history of the German Shepherd Dog and how it evolved, therefore it is not my intention to reiterate here what has been so adequately dealt with elsewhere. It is sufficient to begin with the founding of the ruling breed club in the country of the GSD's origin, still the beacon to which other breeds look – the Verein Für Deutsche Schaüferhunde, known throughout the world as the SV.

## THE ORIGINAL BREED CLUB

The SV was founded in 1899 (which was also the year in which the first Breed Standard was produced), with Cavalry Officer Captain Max von Stephanitz as the President. At that time it had 31 members, but it grew at an astounding rate; after 10 years there were approximately 10,000 members and another 10 years on some 40-50,000 members. Today the membership has passed the 100,000 mark, many of them being overseas.

Until his death in 1936 von Stephanitz had been the breed's guru and guiding light. Undeniably authoritarian in his approach, he was responsible for the very existence of the GSD. The title posterity has given to him, 'the father of the breed', is a fitting crown for a man who devoted his life to achieving a vision of canine excellence.

The SV operates entirely and exclusively for the GSD without constraints of any Kennel Club or other overriding body. It organises shows purely for this breed, with its own prerequisites and conditions, the highlight of each year being the SV Bundessiegerzuchtschau – universally known as the Sieger Show – a dog show to which "shepherdites" from all over the world, some 30,000 or more, gather to view the top animals. Entries are currently approaching 2,500, with every adult dog and bitch having attained the mandatory working qualifications before entry. Each year, from this enormous entry of quality animals, a male and a female is selected for the title of Sieger and Siegerin respectively. The SV system does not award the title of Champion to a number of dogs each year, as is the system in the UK and USA.

The first dog to be registered with the SV was Horand von Grafrath, owned by von Stephanitz but bred by Herr Sparwasser. The dog was originally named Hector Linksrhein and registered with the Phylax Society, an early group that did not survive. When von Stephanitz bought the dog he changed its name to Horand von Grafrath (the latter part being the affix of his own kennel) and enthusiastically described the dog as "the fulfilment of our fondest dreams". Here, then, was the beginning.

## THE FIRST BREED STANDARD

In evolutionary terms the GSD is a fairly young breed; unlike some natural breeds it does not have centuries behind it. I have referred to the inception of the Breed Standard and the vision of its authors. The first Breed Standard, produced in 1899, has been adopted by all the countries into which the breed has been introduced. Considering that it was conceived almost a century ago and has needed so little change, it is a quite remarkable testimony to the creator's vision. True, there have been minor variations in some countries, but such anomalies are attributed to errors in the translating of it into their own languages.

Notwithstanding this, I think it is true to say that, from the original Standard through to the present-day version, no changes of significance have been made. Think of superb modern dogs like Odin von Tannenmeise, Fanto vom Hirschel etc.; is it not remarkable that the same Standard fits them also? This is not to say that the authors of the Breed Standard envisaged dogs like these; had they done so they could not have written in such glowing terms of the dogs of their times.

## BREED CHANGES

This leads to another interesting idea. Think again of the outstanding present-day dogs, dogs that we, the judges, consider epitomise the Breed Standard. Then think forward: can you visualise the breed in 50 or 100 years' time? And in what way could the breed improve and yet still retain the present Breed Standard? It is easy to say that we will get a greater proportion of good ones over the years. That is true, but canine history illustrates the fact that breeds do alter, or get better, however you see it. Can we improve upon the ideal dog of today?

I have been involved with the breed for some fifty-five years and I have seen many changes, some good and others not. Fashions have come and gone. I recall the "tall leggy" types, followed by the "long and low to ground" types, and, incidentally, that description was high praise in those days. In some quarters in Britain, what are known as the "UK clubs" members still breed, show and make up Champions fitting this description. They are known as "English type".

On the other hand, the pendulum has, at times, swung right over the other way, with people considering their dogs to be "Germanic type", when, in fact, they are tall, short-bodied dogs with no depth of quarters and shallow rib cages and are far removed from real German type. Dogs in Germany are quite substantial and slightly long, as described in all the Breed Standards; so too are the best British and American dogs.

## GSD TYPE

"Type" is a word that is commonly used when discussing show dogs and is often considered to be a matter of opinion. In some breeds where the Standard is concerned more with aesthetic points, such as coats, this may be so. However, I do not believe this to be true of the GSD Standard for the simple reason that it is principally concerned with the anatomy of the dog. *Proportions determine the type*, and the ideal proportions are laid down in detail, leaving no room for argument or differences of opinion about what is or is not correct. Furthermore, the proportions and statistics first laid down in 1899 were considered to depict the ideal working dog – von Stephanitz's words "to breed Shepherds is to breed working dogs" being the inspiration.

Anatomically, the Standard describes the ideal trotting dog. There are other breeds with their Standards written to describe the ideal construction for a different gait, but do remember that the GSD is a *trotting* dog. The ideal gait for the Shepherd dog in

*In the German Shepherd, it is proportions that determine type.*

Germany was to trot easily and untiringly and so guard the flock in mostly unfenced terrain. Although its role in society has expanded, our requirement remains the same, which is the ideal working dog, balanced and free from exaggeration, steady of nerve, loyal, courageous and tractable.

## THE BREED'S CUSTODIANS

Preserving the Standard has to be the aim (unless, of course, we find, at some time in the future, that it, or some part of it, proves detrimental to the dogs). This brings me to ruling bodies and their role in this. I believe that their role must be as guardians of the breed type, ensuring that breeders and judges adhere to the Standard, and not allowing fads and fashions to creep in and so change the breed. We must never forget what von Stephanitz and his colleagues had in mind: "a dog of medium size, neither too large and clumsy for speed, nor too small to be a good guardian of the home and flock. With the

trotting build of a sheepdog, a noble head and of obvious intelligence, in all, a peer among the canine races." With this in mind, let us not forget that we are merely the custodians of the breed and our aim has to be that we leave it better than we found it.

The judging of dogs is subjective. It will never be an exact science, but if breeders, judges and exhibitors were really familiar with the Breed Standard and stuck to it, fashions would not arise. Let me reiterate, I consider it to be the duty of breed clubs and other ruling bodies to preserve breed type. This is paramount and, of course, the reason why Standards are written. I will discuss later in this chapter the merits of the Standards recognised by the SV, the American Kennel Club (AKC) (US) and the British Kennel Club (KC) (UK) – also with occasional references to a more explicit Standard produced by the British Breed clubs (BBC) from which the KC Standard was formulated.

## EARLY INFLUENTIAL DOGS

The early dogs seemed to show little progress from the original Horand, but in 1920 a real breakthrough came in Erich von Grafenwerth, the Sieger of that year. He was far superior to any dog before him and became a pillar of the breed. He had a slightly wavy coat and unfortunately, it was said, not the best of temperaments, which led to his being sold to a breeder in the United States of America. Nevertheless, he sired many good dogs, the most important, undoubtedly, being the great Klodo von Boxberg, the Sieger of 1925. Klodo, a smaller, grey dog, was chosen by von Stephanitz because he saw that the breed was becoming too tall and square, and lacked the balance of the ideal working type. Klodo set his stamp on the breed and so began a new era. I consider him to be the forerunner of the German Shepherd Dog as we know it today.

Klodo sired many quality animals, the greatest of them being Utz von Haus Schutting and Curt von Herzog-Hedan, each of them founding a dynasty of his own. Utz and Curt became outstanding progenitors. My long-held opinion is that Curt was the more useful of the two. His son, Odin von Stolzenfels, sired good producing offspring, the best of which must be Sigbert Heidergrund, Baldur von Befreiungsplatz and the "Q" litter Durmersheim, especially Quido, though all of them contributed immensely to the evolution of the breed. I consider this line to have been the most correct breed type in terms of construction and harmonious outlines. Utz, though equally successful in his day, led to the Ingo Piastendamm-Lex Preussenblut line which, in my opinion, was too heavy and stodgy, undoubtedly the result of over-compensating in the choice of breeding partners for bitches of light frame.

By 1925 dedicated breeders worldwide were becoming ambitious and many fine dogs were exported from Germany. The Americans were particularly keen; in fact Horand, Klodo and Utz went to the USA and should have laid the foundations of bloodlines to challenge Germany but, sadly, in the ensuing years they seemed to lose their way.

Von Stephanitz did a good job in keeping a tight rein on the breed but, despite this, many faults cropped up in the main bloodlines, faults from which the breed still suffers today. Perhaps with this in mind, in 1930 he chose Herold aus der Niederlausitz as the Sieger. This was a return to the old square type, which was perhaps needed after the faults brought in by Utz, but his choice was flawed and proved to be unpopular with the breeders, who did not follow his lead. Herold was reputed to be 27ins tall, of moderate construction, with glaring yellow eyes! He was eventually sold to Japan. This left the way clear for the trend towards low-stationed, heavily built types first exemplified by Utz and subsequently accepted as the German prototype.

1932 saw, as Sieger, the heavily built Hussan von Haus Schutting, a son of Utz and like him in type, but he did not have a measurable impact on the breed. Very different was the 1933 Sieger, Odin von Stolzenfels, a son of Curt von Herzog-Hedan and a dog of real influence. In 1937 the practice of awarding a Sieger title was discontinued until 1955. In 1936 Captain von Stephanitz died, having lived to see his dream come to fruition, a dream sparked by a chance sighting of a handsome shepherd dog some thirty-seven years earlier. A breed which he had planned had blossomed into one of the world's most noble canines and certainly the most versatile in all areas of dog's usefulness to man.

## UK BEGINNINGS

The breed came to Britain after the First World War, where our soldiers had seen and admired them in Continental Europe. To begin with they were French-bred and not of the same quality as the dogs in Germany. Nevertheless, they were handsome and of obvious intelligence. Because of a strong anti-German feeling at that time, the breed was registered with the Kennel Club as Alsatian Wolf Dog, giving the impression that it was of French origin. In 1924, Wolf Dog was dropped from the name and in 1936 German Shepherd Dog was added in its place. This continued until 1974 when the name was changed to the current title of German Shepherd Dog (Alsatian). The appendix was at the request of the KC.

The first breed club in Great Britain was the Alsatian Wolf-Dog Club; in 1924 the club teamed up with a second organisation, the Alsatian League, and formed the Alsatian League and Club of Great Britain. This was the premier breed Club and still is today, under the title of the German Shepherd Dog League of Great Britain. Other clubs of that time which are thriving today are the Associated Sheep, Police and Army Dog Society (ASPADS) and the British Association of German Shepherd Dogs, the latter having the larger membership, made up mainly of Obedience members from branches spread around the country.

Today there are 48 breed clubs, 36 of them presently members of the Kennel Club Breed Council, whose role is to represent the breed, particularly within the KC, but as yet the Council does not have the influence to impose its wishes for the breed on the KC.

ASPADS was established essentially to promote working trials and so retain and further the working ability of the breed. Such trials became very popular and remain so today. Promotion of the dog in this way helped to rekindle public enthusiasm at a time of indifference and even hostility to the GSD. One must not forget the practical working dogs, either, described in Chapter

*Working ability has always been of paramount importance, and this goes hand in hand with the correct conformation.*

Six. A wonderful union between man and dog evolves within their work, resulting in their rendering one of the greatest of services to humanity.

The Royal Air Force, Army and Police dogs all play their part in furthering the breed, as do the specialist sniffer dogs that are trained to search for drugs, weapons, explosives and much more. All these services continue to the present day and have indisputably helped the breed to survive and grow during those lean years, as have the legendary rescue and messenger dogs used during the war, producing many stories of valiant deeds and lives lost for the love of man.

Two such German Shepherd Dog heroes deserving special mention were Jet of Iada and Crumstone Irma, who were each awarded the Dicken Medal (DM) for bravery – the DM is the equivalent of the Victoria Cross for humans. Both these dogs were owned and worked by the late Mrs Griffin. It was reported that during the wartime blitz on London, Irma and her half-sister between them discovered 233 human casualties. Jet was also a notable worker and, besides his war work, once had to spend three days underground searching for the victims of a terrible coal mine disaster. The use of messenger dogs was adopted in case of a failure of normal means of communication. They require not only special training but also great courage and devotion to duty. These examples illustrate clearly the unique versatility of the German Shepherd Dog. It is ironic that at times it has been the victim of its own usefulness, most notably when used in the role of guard dog.

The special qualities of the German Shepherd Dog make it one of the most consistently popular dogs in this country, both for working and as a pet. Many would think that the Breed Standard has little or nothing to do with these dogs, touching only the rarefied world of the show dog, but this is not so. Remember the GSD Standard is concerned primarily with anatomy and character and is designed to depict the ideal working dog. Adherence to the Standard ensures that the breed will retain its deserved popularity.

USA BEGINNINGS

The first recorded imported GSD into the United States of America was in 1904, but genetically it is of no significance. In 1913 the GSD club of America was founded and in 1915 the first breed show was held, with an entry of 40 dogs. From then onwards the breed really took off. Imports arrived regularly, hence quality and quantity increased but the dogs of those times had no real influence on the present-day population.

Following the First World War more really outstanding dogs were imported from Europe. The German Siegers 1919 to 1923 included International Champion Erich von Grafenwerth, a real pillar of the breed, and Cito Bergerslust who, juding from his photograph, was outstanding for his time and offered great potential. In the ensuing years many all-time greats followed, for instance the great Klodo von Boxberg, his son Utz von Haus Schutting, Pfeffer von Bern, Odin v Busecker Schloss, Troll von Richeterback and many others.

Because of the genetic worth of these sires I have long held the opinion that the USA ought to be able to compete with Germany in terms of quality, but to my mind this is not the case. However, many fine animals have been produced; individuals like Yoncalla's Mike and Lance of Fran-Jo were of excellent type and appealed to me greatly. In latter years a tendency to exaggeration has developed, especially in the hindquarters. Some dogs are over-angulated and presented over-stretched and with an upright stance in front, certainly not the correct GSD type, for exaggeration is the ruination of a working breed. In the US, as in the UK, there is a split within the breed, which is a great pity, for if *everyone* stuck to the Breed Standard, it could well be that the GSD would be of the same type all around the world.

THE BREED STANDARDS DISCUSSED

## 1. GENERAL APPEARANCE

**SV: The German Shepherd Dog (GSD) is of medium size. The height at the withers,**

*The skeletal structure.*
*Line Drawings: Viv Rainsbury.*

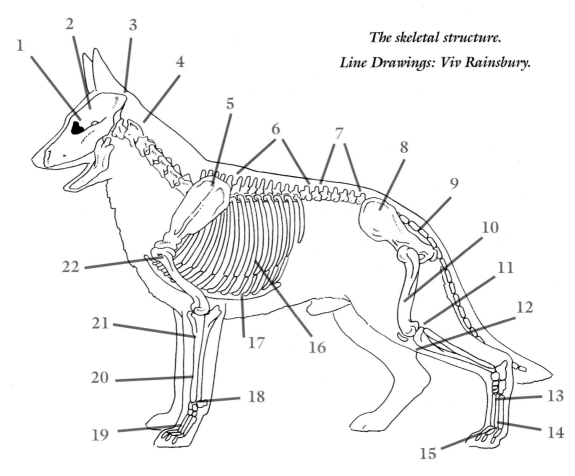

1. *Zygomatic Arch*
2. *Cranium*
3. *Occipital bone*
4. *Cervical vertebrae*
5. *Scapula*
6. *Thoracic vertebrae*
7. *Lumbar vertebrae*
8. *Ilium (pelvis)*
9. *Coccygeal vertebrae*
10. *Femur*
11. *Fibula*

12. *Tibia*
13. *Tarsal Bones (hock)*
14. *Metatarsal bones (hind pastern)*
15. *Phalanges*
16. *Ribs*
17. *Sternum*
18. *Carpal bones*
19. *Metacarpal bones*
20. *Radius*
21. *Ulna*
22. *Humerus*

height of the skeleton with the hair pressed down, should be taken from the withers to the ground along a perpendicular line through the elbow of the dog, the ideal height being 62.5 cm for dogs and 57.5 cm for bitches. A deviation of 2.5 cm either higher or lower is acceptable. Exceeding the maximum or not reaching the minimum height would diminish the utility and breeding value.

The GSD is moderately elongated, powerful and well-muscled, his bones are

*Points of anatomy.*

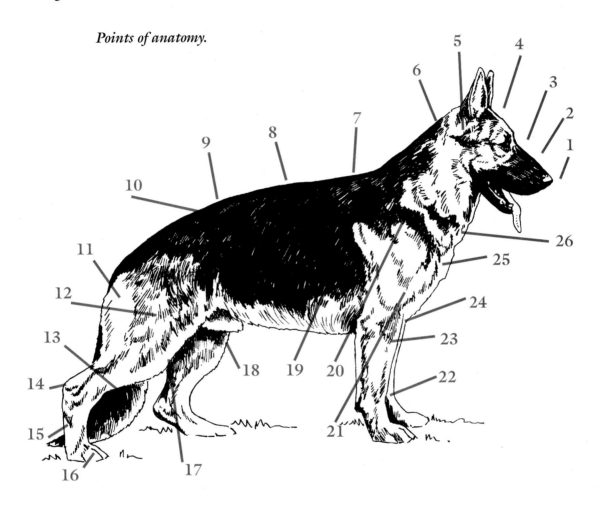

| | | |
|---|---|---|
| *1. Muzzle* | *10. Loin* | *19. Ribcage* |
| *2. Foreface* | *11. Feathering* | *20. Shoulder* |
| *3. Stop* | *12. Upper Thigh* | *21. Upper arm* |
| *4. Skull* | *13. Tail* | *22. Front Pastern* |
| *5. Neck* | *14. Hock Joint* | *23. Elbow* |
| *6. Withers* | *15. Rear pastern* | *24. Forearm* |
| *7. Back* | *16. Foot* | *25. Forechest* |
| *8. Croup* | *17. Second thigh* | *26. Ruff* |
| *9. Tailset* | *18. Stifle Joint* | |

dry and the frame well-knit. The proportion of height to length and the position and placement of limbs (angulation) are so inter-related as to ensure a far-reaching tireless trotting gait. He possesses a weatherproof coat.

A pleasing appearance is to be aimed at but this should not impair the working ability of the dog. The sex characteristics must be well defined, which means that masculinity in the male and femininity in the female must be unmistakable. The GSD, according to this breed picture, conveys to an observer the impression of innate strength, intelligence and agility, with harmonious proportions and balance, nowhere either too much or too little. The manner in which he carries and behaves himself must make it perfectly clear that the healthy body also incorporates a sound frame of mind, therefore providing the physical and mental prerequisites which enable him to be ready for action as a working dog at any time and with great endurance.

Only for the trained expert is it possible to determine the presence of the required working dog characteristics in the GSD. Therefore only a specialist judge should be engaged to assess the dogs presented to him for their temperament including gunshot indifference. Also the grading of 'Excellent' should be awarded only to those GSD which are in possession of a recognised training degree or Obedience title.

With an abundance of vigour he must be easy to manage, must cope with any situation and carry out all given orders willingly and with pleasure. He has to demonstrate courage and determination when it becomes necessary to defend himself, his master or his possessions. He should also readily go into attack at his master's commands but must otherwise be an alert, yet obedient and pleasant member of the household, devoted to his familiar surroundings, mainly to children and other animals, and at ease in his dealings with other people. All in all he should portray a harmonious image of natural nobility and respect commanding self-confidence.

US: The first impression of a good GSD is that of a strong, agile, well muscled animal, alert and full of life. It is well balanced, with harmonious development of the forequarter and hindquarter. The dog is longer than tall, deep-bodied, and presents an outline of smooth curves rather than angles. It looks substantial and not spindly, giving the impression, both at rest and in motion, of muscular fitness and nimbleness without any look of clumsiness or soft living. The ideal dog is stamped with a look of quality and nobility – difficult to define, but unmistakable when present. Secondary sex characteristics are strongly marked, and every animal gives a definite impression of masculinity or femininity, according to its sex.

UK: Slightly long in comparison to height; of powerful, well-muscled build with weather-resistant coat. Relation between height and length, position and structure of fore and hindquarters (angulation) producing far-reaching, enduring gait. Clear definition of masculinity and femininity essential, and working ability never sacrificed for mere beauty.

COMMENT

SV: A rather lengthy description which includes items which I think should have been incorporated under the heading of character, indeed some of them are, which makes for repetition. The fourth paragraph is a contentious one. I agree with the sentiments of the first two sentences, believing that all judges should be trained and tested before they can qualify to judge their chosen breed. However, the Kennel Clubs of England and, I believe, America would never accept this, being heavily in favour of all-breed judges, whereas the GSD fraternity favour specialist judges.

The fifth paragraph dealing with character states "he should readily go into attack at his master's command" etc. This, of course, is not included in the other Standards, nor is it ever likely to be in the foreseeable future. I am sure the relevant Kennel Clubs would never accept it.

US: I like particularly the requirement that the dog "presents an outline of smooth curves rather than angles".

UK: Merely an abbreviated version of the SV.

I conclude, therefore, that there are no significant differences between the three countries' requirements. Insofar as the general appearance of the dog is concerned, my opinion is that the overall general appearance of the dog is very important: it gives the novice an overall picture at which to aim and, for the knowledgeable person, it is something that he or she can base an opinion on immediately. "The whole" is the ultimate, not its constituent parts.

On the question of size, there is no doubt that the breed has got bigger over the last 20 years or so; only rarely do we find a male of genuine middle size figuring in the top awards. A few years ago, at the German Sieger show, in the reports on the dogs their actual size was given (they were measured on the day). My analysis showed that the average size was not the middle size, i.e.

62.50 cm, but 64.00 cm, with the bitches measuring around 58.5 cm. One of the reasons for this is, in my opinion, the promoting of big strong bitches as likely broods – it had to lead to more size eventually.

## 2. ANGULATION AND GAIT

**SV: The GSD is a Trotter. His gait therefore has a diagonal sequence of leg motion, i.e. the fore and hind leg on one side always move in opposite directions. Consequently, his limbs have to be set in relation to each other, i.e. angulated in such a way that he can thrust his hind legs well up to the middle of the body and have an equally long reach with his forelegs, without any appreciable alteration in his top line. With correct proportion of height to length and corresponding length of limbs, it will produce a ground-covering stride which travels close to the ground, giving the impression of an effortless forward propulsion. With his head pushed forward and tail slightly raised, a balanced and steady trotter displays a gently curved topline from the tip of his ears over the neck and level back to the tip of the tail.**

**US: (Gait): A German Shepherd Dog is a trotting dog, and its structure has been developed to meet the requirements of its work.**

**General Impression: The gait is outreaching, elastic, seemingly without effort, smooth and rhythmic, covering the maximum amount of ground with the minimum number of steps. At a walk it covers a great deal of ground, with long strides of both hind legs and forelegs. At a trot the dog covers still more ground with even longer stride and moves powerfully but easily with co-ordination and balance**

so that the gait appears to be the steady motion of a well-lubricated machine. The feet travel close to the ground on both forward reach and backward push. In order to achieve ideal movement of this kind, there must be good muscular development and ligamentation. The hindquarters deliver, through the back, a powerful forward thrust which slightly lifts the whole animal and drives the body forward. Reaching far under, and passing the imprint left by the front foot, the hind foot takes hold of the ground; then hock, stifle and upper thigh come into play and sweep back, the stroke of the hind leg finishing with the foot still close to the ground in a smooth follow-through. The over-reach of the hindquarter usually necessitates one hind foot passing outside and the other hind foot passing inside the track of the forefeet, and such action is not faulty unless the locomotion is crabwise with the dog's body sideways out of the normal straight line.

Transmission: The typical smooth, flowing gait is maintained with great strength and firmness of back. The whole effort of the hindquarters is transmitted to the forequarter through the loin, back and withers. At full trot the back must remain firm and level without sway, roll, whip or roach. Unlevel topline with withers lower than the hips is a fault. To compensate for the forward motion imparted by the hindquarters, the shoulder should open to its full extent. The forelegs should reach out close to the ground in a long stride in harmony with that of the hindquarters. The dog does not track on widely separated lines, but brings the feet inward toward the middle line of the body when trotting in order to maintain balance. The feet track closely but do not strike or cross over. Viewed from the front, the front legs function from the shoulder joint to the pad in a straight line. Viewed from the rear, the hind legs function from the hip joint to the pad in a straight line.

Faults of gait, whether from the front, rear or side, are very serious faults.

UK: (Gait/Movement): Sequence of steps follows diagonal pattern, moving foreleg and opposite hindleg forward simultaneously; hind foot thrust forward to midpoint of body and having equally long reach with forefeet without any noticeable change in backline.

COMMENT

SV: Item number two of the SV is surprisingly "Angulation and Gait". In all there are about 135 words in this section but in fact it does not deal with angulation; it does use the word once, to say that the hindquarters must be "angulated in such a way that the dog can thrust his hind legs well up to the middle of the body". The actual angulation is dealt with under "Fore and Hindquarters". The description of the gait is normal and quite good but in view of the importance attached to the gait one could have expected a much more detailed chapter.

It states "without any appreciable alteration to his topline". In practice, this is not quite correct. At the walk, yes, it is correct; however, when trotting there will be a slight lowering of the body, while when gaiting fast (as described in the AKC Standard), the opening of the fore- and hind-angulations results in the lowering of the whole of the dog. There are, of course, dogs that gait and do not lower the body in this way, but they are the ones that lack the desired length of stride in the front, a common fault today and not likely to be eliminated while "retaining topline" is uppermost in a judge's mind when assessing the gait.

*Movement: Showing an extended trot..*

Another factor to consider is that these days most dogs are pulling hard on the lead when gaiting in the show ring – and being encouraged to do so. This gives a false impression, i.e. the hind legs are "pushing", as if pulling a bag of sand and, in some instances, the front legs are not reaching out as far as is natural to the dog.

US: For me, this is by far the best description of gait, if rather wordy; the reader will learn more from this than the others. It does not, however, mention the fact that the unique angulation of the dog is responsible for this exceptional movement! The main difference between the GSD and other working breeds is, in fact, the angulation of fore- and hind-quarters.

UK: This is rather mean, some 34 words in total. True, it does give the sequence of steps to describing the trotting movement and states "without any change in backline" but there is much more to movement than that. The British Breed Club Standard explains gait much better; it is rather similar to the SV and quite acceptable.

I believe, above all else, that co-ordination is the most important factor and not just length of stride, and certainly not which dog trots the fastest. The Americans speak of "the period of suspension" i.e. a brief moment when all four feet are off the ground, which is very hard to recognise. Ideally, the forefeet should touch the ground at the end of the hind propulsion.

## 3. NATURE AND CHARACTER AND TEMPERAMENT

SV: **Stability of nerves, alertness, confidence, manageability, watchfulness, loyalty and incorruptibility, as well as courage, combative instinct and toughness are the most outstanding characteristics of a pure-bred GSD. They are shaping him in an excellent manner into a utility dog generally, particularly as a watch, companion, guard and herding dog. His capability of scent discrimination, combined with the trotting ability, enables him to work out a trail with his nose close to the ground without physical exertion, making him to a high degree suitable as a tracking and search dog to be employed for a variety of purposes.**

US: The breed has a distinct personality marked by direct and fearless, but not hostile, expression, self-confidence and a certain aloofness that does not lend itself to immediate and indiscriminate friendships. The dog must be approachable, quietly standing its ground and showing confidence and willingness to meet overtures without itself making them. It is poised, but when the occasion demands, eager and alert; both fit and willing to serve in its capacity as companion, watchdog, blind leader, herding dog, or guardian, whichever the circumstances may demand. The dog must not be timid, shrinking behind its master or handler; it should not be nervous, looking about or upward with anxious expression or showing nervous reaction, such as tucking of tail, to strange sounds or sights. Lack of confidence under any surroundings is not typical of good character. Any of the above deficiencies in character which indicate shyness must be penalized as very serious faults and any dog exhibiting pronounced indications of these must be excused from the ring. It must be possible for the judge to observe the teeth and to determine that both testicles are descended. Any dog that attempts to bite the judge must be disqualified. The ideal dog is a working animal with an incorruptible character combined with body and gait suitable for the arduous work that constitutes its primary purpose.

UK: Versatile working dog, balanced and free from exaggeration. Attentive, alert, resilient and tireless, with keen scenting ability.

Temperament: Steady of nerve, loyal, self-assured, courageous and tractable. Never nervous, over-aggressive nor shy.

COMMENT
SV: This gives the necessary requisites, then goes on with almost as many words describing the scenting ability of the dog.
US: This is more detailed insofar as character is concerned but is rather long-winded in listing the signs to look for, which are obvious to any doggy person.

UK: This is an abbreviation of the BBC Standard but quite sufficient.

It is necessary to say that to attain the ideal nature, character and temperament it is essential to socialise and educate the dog during puppy time and adolescence.

4. HEAD
SV: The head should correspond to the size of the body (in length approximately 40 per cent of the height) without being coarse, too fine or overstretched, in general appearance dry. Between the ears moderately broad. The forehead when viewed from front or side is only slightly domed, with centre furrow only shallow if present. The cheeks taper off laterally in a gentle curve without forward protuberance.

The skull (roughly 50 per cent of the head in length), viewed from above, extends from the ears to the bridge of the nose, tapering gradually and evenly, blending without a too pronounced stop into a long wedge-shaped dry muzzle (upper and lower jaw which should be strongly developed). The width of the skull should be approximately the same as the length of the skull, whereby in the male slightly more width and in the female slightly less width would not be objected to. The muzzle is strong, the lips are tight, dry and well closed. The straight bridge of the nose runs almost parallel

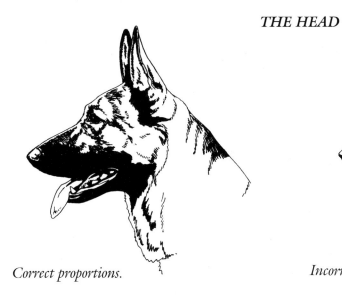

*Correct proportions.*

*Incorrect: The lips are loose and droopy.*

*Incorrect: The muzzle is too short.*

*Incorrect: Turned up muzzle - the muzzle and skull should be parallel.*

*Correct: Firm, tight lips.*

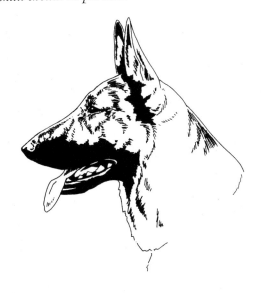

*Incorrect: Lacking stop.*

with an extended line of the forehead.

US: The head is noble, cleanly chiselled, strong without coarseness but, above all, not fine, and in proportion to the body. The head of the male is distinctly masculine, and that of the bitch distinctly feminine. The expression keen, intelligent and composed. Eyes of medium size, almond shaped, set a little obliquely and not protruding. The colour is as dark as possible. Ears are moderately pointed, in proportion to the skull, open toward the front and carried erect when at attention, the ideal carriage being one in which the centre lines of the ears, viewed from the front, are parallel to each other and perpendicular to the ground. A dog with cropped or hanging ears must be disqualified. Seen from the front, the forehead is only moderately arched and the skull slopes into the long, wedge-shaped muzzle without abrupt stop. The muzzle is long and strong with the lips firmly fitted and its topline is parallel to the topline of the skull. Nose black. A dog with a nose that is not predominantly black must be disqualified. The lips are firmly fitted. Jaws are strongly developed. Teeth: 42 in number – 20 upper and 22 lower – are strongly developed and meet in a scissors bite in which part of the inner surface of the upper incisors meet and engage part of the outer surface of the lower incisors. An overshot jaw or a level bite is undesirable. An undershot jaw is a disqualifying fault. Complete dentition is to be preferred. Any missing teeth other than first premolars is a serious fault.

UK: Proportionate in size to body, never coarse, too fine or too long. Clean cut; fairly broad between ears. Forehead slightly domed; little or no trace of central furrow. Cheeks forming softly rounded

curve, never protruding. Skull from ears to bridge of nose tapering gradually and evenly, blending without too pronounced stop into wedge shaped powerful muzzle. Skull approximately 50 per cent of overall length of head. Width of skull corresponding approximately to length, in males slightly greater, in females slightly less. Muzzle strong, lips firm, clean and closing tightly. Top of muzzle straight, almost parallel to forehead. Short, blunt, weak, pointed, overlong muzzle undesirable.

COMMENT

SV: Adequately described.

US: Quite concise, it includes eyes and ears whereas the other two Standards have them under separate headings.

UK: Much more detailed than one might expect and perhaps better than the other two but, on reflection, that may not be so surprising in view of the fact that so many other breeds on the KC list are primarily "head breeds". The GSD, BBC description is by far the best. Note: the old British Standard operated on a points system, of which only five from a total of one hundred were allotted for the head!

It should be noted that 'long' is used in all three Standards: the SV and AKC state "a long wedge shaped muzzle"; the KC says "never coarse, too fine or too long". In recent years there has been a tendency towards heads that are too strong, resulting in loose lips and furrowed foreheads and so not correct or typical of the Breed. We must remember that the Standard caters for both sexes. However, some judges and breeders seem to think that the bigger and stronger the male heads the better, which results in a loss of femininity in the bitches. The correct head of both sexes should be the aim. To exaggerate heads in either sex is detrimental to the other one.

## 5. TEETH

**SV: The teeth must be healthy, strong and complete (42 in all, 20 in the upper and 22 in the lower jaw). The teeth of the GSD act like scissors, i.e. the incisors must grip scissor-like into each other, those of the lower cutting those of the upper jaw. An under or over-shot bite is faulty, also large gaps between the teeth. Faulty is also a level bite when incisors meet in a straight line. The jaws must be strongly developed for the teeth to be deeply embedded.**

**US: See the section on the Head regarding teeth.**

**UK: (Mouth): Jaws strongly developed. With a perfect, regular and complete scissor bite, i.e. upper teeth closely overlapping lower teeth and set square at the jaw. Teeth healthy and strong. Full dentition desirable.**

COMMENT

SV: Precise, and it is the only Standard to list large gaps between the teeth as a fault. It makes no specific mention of missing teeth but, under 'faults', dentition faults are listed. Consequently no dog in Germany can be qualified "Excellent" and would, indeed, be heavily penalised, if the dentition was not complete.

US: Gives the number of teeth etc., like the SV. Then, surprise: "any missing teeth, other than first premolars, is a serious fault" – obviously lenient about missing premolar

ones. Perhaps this explains how a number of their top dogs have incomplete mouths.

UK: Not a very generous description and it ends "full dentition is desirable". The BBC is, again, more precise than the others. The teeth are actually named, i.e. 6 incisors, 2 canines, 8 premolars, 4 molars in the upper jaw and 6 molars in the lower jaw. It also explains the scissor bite: "the incisors in the lower jaw are set behind the incisors in the upper jaw and these meet in a scissor grip in which part of the surface of the upper teeth engages part of the lower teeth."

## 6. EARS

**SV: Ears are of medium size, broad at the base and set fairly high, they are carried erect (parallel to each other and not inward tilted), they taper to a point with the auricle forward placed. Tipped ears, docked and hanging ears are to be rejected. Inward tilted ears have a detrimental effect on the image of the breed. Puppies and young dogs sometimes have their ears down during the teething period up to six months or even longer, or tilted inward. In movement and in lying-down resting position most dogs tip their ears back, this is not faulty.**

**US: See the section on the Head regarding ears.**

**UK: Medium sized, firm in texture, broad at base, set high, carried erect, almost parallel, never pulled inwards or tipped, tapering to a point, open at front. Never hanging. Folding back during movement permissible.**

COMMENT

The SV and AKC Standards are similar, in

# THE EARS

*Correct size and placement of ears.*

*Incorrect: The ears are too large.*

*Incorrect: Soft ears.*

*Incorrect: Low-set ears.*

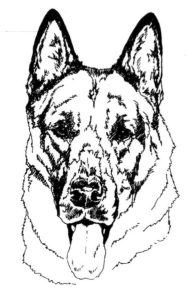

*Incorrect: The ears are too small.*

*Incorrect: The ears are set too high.*

asking for the erect ears to be parallel. The KC Standard states "almost parallel". My view is that the latter is correct; it is the outer edges that are parallel and not a centre line through the ears. All the Standards condemn ears that are not erect. All three Standards stress the fact that it is not faulty for the dog to fold its ears back when gaiting. I am afraid that there are judges who do not seem to realise this. Erect ears when gaiting is attractive but it is over-valued when we consider the wording in the Standard.

## 7. EYES

SV: Eyes are of medium size and almond-shaped, set slightly oblique and not protruding. The colour should compare well with that of the coat of the dog, rather dark. The eyes should project a lively, intelligent and self-confident expression.

US: See the section on the Head regarding eyes.

UK: Medium sized, almond-shaped, never protruding. Dark brown preferred, lighter shade permissible, provided expression good and general harmony of head not destroyed. Expression lively, intelligent and self-assured.

COMMENT

SV: This is an adequate description.

US: As with the SV, and eyes to be as dark as possible.

UK: It could be better worded, but I agree with the view that eyes of a "lighter shade be permissible provided that the expression is good" – a necessary point when considering a dog with an extensive dark mask, where it is

not practicable to require eyes to be darker than the coat colour.

An interesting conclusion reached regarding eye colour was that "light-eyed dogs tend to be more intelligent than dark-eyed dogs" – (Humphrey and Warner of the Fortunate Fields experimental breeding station during the 1930s).

## 8. NECK

SV: The neck should be strong with well developed muscle and without loose and pendulous skin under chin or throat. It is carried at an angle of roughly 45 deg. to the horizontal; it is carried more erect in excitement and lowered when the dog is trotting.

US: The neck is strong and muscular, clean-cut and relatively long, proportionate in size to the head and without loose folds of skin. When the dog is at attention or excited, the head is raised and the neck carried high; otherwise typical carriage of the head is forward rather than up, but a little higher than the top of the shoulders, particularly in motion.

UK: Fairly long, strong, with well developed muscles, free from throatiness. Carried at 45 deg. angle to horizontal, raised when excited, lowered at fast trot.

COMMENT

All the Standards ask for the same, but not necessarily in the same words. The SV and UK Standards stipulate carried at an angle of 45 degrees, raised when excited, and lowered at a fast trot. The UK Standard states, "fairly long"; however, the SV has no mention of the length, which is surprising in view of the fact that they stress the scenting and tracking

*Correct outline.*

*Incorrect: low withers and raised back.*

*Incorrect: Chest too deep, and steep upper arm.*

requirements. One rarely sees a neck too long except in some of the old English bloodlines. Occasionally we see a dog whose neck is somewhat short and stuffy in appearance; this is usually the result of a forward placed shoulder.

The US Standard has a useful addition, i.e. "relatively long proportionate to the size of the head", and "carried forward rather than up but a little higher than the top of the shoulders, particularly in motion". Simply translated, it is as follows – the faster the dog moves, the lower the neck carriage will be, as I have stated earlier under 'gait'.

## 9. BODY

**SV: The length of the body should exceed the measurement of the height, it should be approximately 110 to 117 per cent of the height at the withers. Short, square or high-legged dogs are undesirable. The chest is deep (45-48 per cent of the height at withers) but not too broad, brisket rather long and pronounced. The ribs are well developed and long, neither barrelled nor too flat, reaching down to the sternum which reaches to the elbows. A correctly formed chest allows the elbows free movement while the dog is trotting. A too rounded chest causes hindrance and an outward turn of the elbows, while a chest too flat causes the elbows to be turned in. The brisket extends rather far back so that the loins are comparatively short.**

**The belly moderately tucked up. The back including loins are straight and**

strongly developed, between withers and croup not too long. The withers must be long and set high enough, well outlined in relation to the back, into which they merge gently without interrupting the topline which is sloping moderately from front to rear. The loins are broad, strong and well muscled. The croup is long and gently sloped (23 deg.), the haunch-bone forming the bony base. A short and steep or level croup is not desirable.

US: The whole structure of the body gives an impression of depth and solidity without bulkiness. Chest: Commencing at the prosternum, it is well filled and carried well down between the legs. It is deep and capacious, never shallow, with ample room for the lungs and heart, carried well forward, with the prosternum showing ahead of the shoulder in profile. Ribs: Well sprung and long, neither barrel-shaped nor too flat, and carried down to a sternum which reaches to the elbows. Correct ribbing allows the elbows to move back freely when the dog is at a trot. Too round causes interference and throws the elbows out; too flat or short causes pinched elbows. Ribbing is carried well back so that the loin is relatively short. Abdomen: Firmly held and not paunchy. The bottom line is only moderately tucked up in the loin.

UK: Length measured from point of breast bone to rear edge of pelvis, exceeding height at withers. Correct ratio 10 to 9 or 8.5 Undersized dogs, stunted growth, high-legged dogs, those too heavy or too light in build, overloaded front, too short overall appearance, any feature detracting from reach or endurance of gait, undesirable. Chest deep (45 per cent to 48 per cent) of height at shoulder, not too broad, brisket long, well developed.

Ribs well formed and long; neither barrel-shaped nor too flat; allowing free movement of elbows when gaiting. Relatively short loin. Belly firm, only slightly drawn up. Back between withers and croup, straight, strongly developed, not too long. Overall length achieved by correct angle of well laid shoulders, correct length of croup and hindquarters. Withers long, of good height and well defined, jointed back in smooth line without disrupting flowing topline, slightly sloping from front to back. Weak, soft and roach backs undesirable and should be rejected. Loin broad, strong, well muscled. Croup long, gently curving downwards to tail without disrupting flowing topline. Short, steep or flat croups undesirable.

COMMENT

SV: I have no criticism of this except to say that it could have been extended.

US: This Standard is better in this respect, more explicit and, besides the body, it has headings for Topline, i.e. Withers, Back, Loin, Croup. Yet it fails to give the proportion of chest and leg length. However "carried well between the legs" suggests a somewhat deeper chest than the SV and BBC versions.

UK: This is quite lengthy, almost as long as the SV and of a similar fashion.

The essentials are the same in all the Standards, leaving no doubt about the ideal body shape. At present I hear breeders and exhibitors quoting the proportions of foreleg and chest as 55 per cent leg to 45 per cent chest. This is correct, but the SV and the BBC state that the depth of chest is 45 per cent to 48 per cent of the height at the

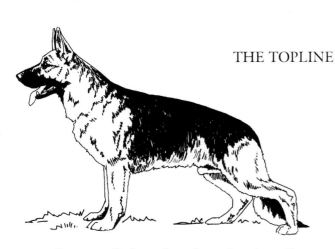

*Incorrect: Body too long, but otherwise well constructed.*

*Incorrect: Body too short.*

*Incorrect: Very steep croup.*

withers. We must remember also that these measurements are of the actual body. To measure the body and leg length of a dog from a photograph can be misleading because the underline, particularly, includes the hair which, on some dogs, can be profuse. In general the dog whose leg length and chest depth appear to be 50-50 is acceptable.

## 9. TOPLINE

**SV: See Body regarding Topline.**

**US: The withers are higher than and sloping into the level back. Back: The back is straight, very strongly developed without sag or roach and relatively short. The whole structure of the body gives an impression of depth and solidity without bulkiness. Loin: Viewed from the top, broad and strong. Undue length between the last rib and the thigh, when viewed from the side, is undesirable. Croup: Long and gradually sloping.**

**UK: See Body regarding Topline.**

COMMENT
Surprisingly all three Standards are somewhat vague regarding this part of the anatomy, and yet judges pay a great deal of attention to it and rightly so, for the firm, harmonious topline of GSD is unique.

Quite often high withers are confused with height at the withers, which has nothing to do with the withers but mostly with long forelegs and steep front assembly. Ideally the withers, consisting of 13 vertebra, should be set higher than the shoulder blades, or at least level, but all too often one can feel a gap between the shoulder blades into which one can put one's fingers. When they are really low, judges will criticise them as flat withers – often accompanied by a raised backline. The

*Incorrect: Soft back.*

*Incorrect: Steep croup and lacking waistline.*

*Incorrect: The body is too long. It is also low to the ground with short legs.*

*Incorrect: Too heavy throughout, although otherwise well constructed.*

*Incorrect: The backline falls away too much.*

*Incorrect: Posed to disguise low withers, i.e. over-stretched.*

ideal topline begins with high withers, sloping down gently into the backline, then sloping, still gently, over the croup to the tail set, giving a smooth unbroken line.

All three Standards state a straight back when, in fact, the back is not really straight because of the shape of the lumbar vertebrae which lessen in size towards the pelvis to give a clean line, so that, ideally, one cannot see exactly where the "croup" starts. Personally, I would like to see this word dropped from our Standards as there is no such structure in the anatomy. We should speak of the pelvis, and all three Standards should agree on what is the ideal angle of it, as with the shoulder blades and upper arms.

In critiques and articles, much is written about the length of the croup and, in my opinion, erroneously so. The pelvis is accepted as the basis of the croup and I doubt if there is much difference in the length of it between individual dogs. We are told that the sacrum has three fused bones on it; I wonder if some dogs have more and some have less? More would give a lower set tail and could possibly be described as a steep croup and less could be described as a short croup when, in fact, both animals could well have a pelvis of equal length.

Again, surprisingly, only the UK Standard describes the croup as gently "curving" which is correct and highly desirable. Sometimes, due to "over-handling", one can only assess the croup when the dog is moving. The theory is that a steep croup allows the dog to put his feet well forward under the body but impedes the follow-through behind, and that the flat croup gives the opposite result, i.e. does not allow the feet to reach as far under the body but produces ample follow-through, even to the extreme of kicking up behind.

## 10. TAIL

**SV: The tail is bushy and should reach at** least to the hock, it should not extend beyond the middle of the metatarsus. Sometimes it forms, at the end, a sideways bent hook which is undesirable. When at rest it is carried hanging down in a gentle curve, with excitement or in motion the curve is more pronounced and the tail is lifted higher, but it should not pass the horizontal. Therefore the tail should never be carried straight or rolled-up over the back. Docked tails are to be rejected.

**US: Bushy, with the last vertebra extended at least to the hock joint. It is set smoothly into the croup and low rather than high. At rest, the tail hangs in a slight curve like a sabre. A slight hook – sometimes carried to one side – is faulty only to the extent that it mars general appearance. When the dog is excited or in motion, the curve is accentuated and the tail raised, but it should never be curled forward beyond a vertical line. Tails too short, or with clumpy ends due to ankylosis, are serious faults. A dog with a docked tail must be disqualified.**

**UK: Bushy-haired, reaching at least to hock – ideal length, reaching to middle of metatarsus. At rest tail hangs in slight sabre-like curve; when moving raised and curve increased, ideally never above level of back. Short, rolled, curled, generally carried badly or stumpy from birth, undesirable.**

COMMENT

The US Standard is similar to the SV, as is the BBC Standard. The UK Standard omits the second sentence describing a sideways hook. I agree with this. On the whole, tails are now longer than is ideal; in Britain, particularly, it is not unusual to see a tail touching the ground when the dog is standing and, during movement, the end of the tail is pointing upwards. Some Germans believe that the dog does this to prevent the hair on the underside of the tail from touching the ground.

## 11. FOREQUARTERS

SV: The shoulder blade is long and set at a slant (gradient about 45 deg.) lying against the body. The upper arm is set on forming an approximate right angle, it should be well muscled, as is the shoulder. The forearm should be straight when viewed from all sides. The bones of upper arm and forearm are more oval-shaped than round. The pasterns are firm and not too steep but not too slanted either (approx. 20 deg.). The elbows neither turned in nor turned out. The length of the legs should exceed the depth of the chest (average 55 per cent).

US: The shoulder blades are long and obliquely angled, laid on flat and not placed forward. The upper arm joins the shoulder blade at about a right angle.

Both the upper arm and the shoulder blade are well muscled. The forelegs, viewed from all sides, are straight and the bone oval rather than round. The pasterns are strong and springy and angulated at approximately a 25 deg. angle from the vertical.

UK: Shoulder blades long, set obliquely (45 deg.) laid flat to body. Upper arm strong, well muscled, joining shoulder blade at approximately 90 deg. Forelegs straight from pasterns to elbows viewed from any angle, bone oval rather than round. Pasterns firm supple and slightly angulated. Elbows neither tucked in nor turned out. Length of foreleg exceeding depth of chest.

COMMENT

All Standards say "the shoulder blade is long and set obliquely", the SV and UK Standards state the angle as 45 degrees, the US Standard does not. This is an important

### THE FRONT

*Correct front.*

*Incorrect: Too wide, feet turning out slightly.*

*Incorrect: Too narrow, feet turning out.*

oversight: in theory this means that the shoulder blade could be laid too far back, say at an angle of 50 degrees and attached to the upper arm at a near 90 degree angle yet not be correct. All ask for the angle to be near right angle (90 degree) but none of them state that the angle should not be more acute than this, nor that the shoulder blade and upper arm should ideally be of the same length to give well balanced forequarters.

We must not forget that the forequarters have a role to play other than movement. I refer to the fact that they support the body of the dog via muscles and ligaments, there being no skeleton formation doing that job – hence the need for high withers.

## 12. HINDQUARTERS

**SV: The thighs are broad with strong muscles. The upper thigh, viewed from the side, is set slanting to a proportionately slightly longer stifle bone which is joined on at an angle of about 120 deg.; without being over-angulated, angulation corresponds roughly with that of the forehand. The hock joint is strong and firm. The strong metatarsus with the stifle bone forms a tight hock joint. The back hand all over must be strong and very well muscled to be able effortlessly to push forward the body of the dog in motion.**

**US: The whole assembly of the thigh, viewed from the side, is broad, with both upper and lower thigh well muscled, forming as nearly as possible a right angle. The upper thigh bone parallels the shoulder blade while the lower thigh bone parallels the upper arm. The metatarsus (the unit between the hock joint and the foot) is short, strong and tightly articulated.**

**UK: Overall strong, broad and well-muscled, enabling effortless forward propulsion of whole body. Upper thigh bone, viewed from side, sloping to slightly longer lower thigh bone. Hind angulation sufficient if imaginary line dropped from point of buttocks cuts through lower thigh just in front of hock, continuing down slightly in front of hind feet. Angulations corresponding approximately with front angulation, without over-angulation, hock strong. Any tendency towards over-angulation of hindquarters reduces firmness and endurance.**

COMMENT

SV: This sets the angle where the two thigh bones meet at 120 degrees but then adds "without being over-angulated, the angulation corresponds roughly with that of the forehand", which, remember, they say should be "an approximate right angle" i.e. 90 degrees!

US: This wording is very different from the SV in the following respect: "The whole assembly of the thigh, viewed from the side, is broad, with both upper and lower thigh well muscled, forming as nearly as possible a right angle. The upper thigh bone parallels the shoulder blade while the lower thigh parallels the upper arm." Now this is matching the forequarters and it is quite specific. It will, I think, result in broader thighs too. This Standard is the only one to state that the metatarsus (i.e. the unit between the hock joint and the foot, often referred to as the hock), should be short and strongly and tightly articulated. There is no warning of over-angulation in this Standard as there is with both the SV and the UK Standard.

UK: It is precise without giving a definite angle.

All three Standards stress the need for strength, and rightly so, for it is from here that the GSD gait begins. They all require broad, well-muscled thighs and strong hocks. After this we find differences; for instance, the SV and UK Standards say that the lower thigh is slightly longer than the upper thigh, while the AKC Standard makes no mention of this.

It is difficult to decide which description of hindquarters is the most efficient. The SV (forgetting the wording of "120 deg. matching the forequarter") and the UK Standard will not be very different. The US Standard is different, with a much more acute angle of upper and lower thigh. Only the testing of gaits could determine which is the more workmanlike hypothesis. My guess is that the AKC ideal could produce a long striding gait, but I feel that there might be excessive stress on the angle in question.

Often I think that the SV should hold a large class of good dogs and judge them solely on movement – with a panel of, say, three top judges. At the end of the judging the dogs should be examined to see if any specific reasons for the better gaits are prominent. We often find that the so-called well-constructed dogs disappoint in movement and, of course, we find dogs that do not impress in stance yet excel in

### THE FEET

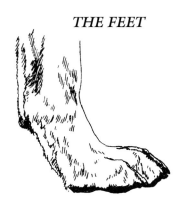

*Maxim. .n angulation of pastern.*

movement. At present we judge on an overall assessment without really putting our theories to the test.

### 13. PAWS

**SV: Rounded, short, well closed and arched. The pads are very hard but not chapped. The nails short and strong, or a dark colour. Dew claws appear sometimes on the hind legs and should be removed during the first couple of days after birth.**

**US: The feet are short, compact, with toes well arched, pads thick and firm, nails short and dark. Dewclaws on the forelegs may be removed, but are normally left on. The dewclaws, if any, should be removed from the hind legs.**

**UK: Rounded toes well-closed and arched. Pads well-cushioned and durable. Nails short, strong and dark in colour. Dewclaws removed from hindlegs.**

### COMMENT

The requirements of all the Standards are similar. My only comments are that, on the whole, feet are not so well-cushioned as they were some 30 years ago, and dewclaws on the hind legs are rarely, if ever, seen these days.

### 14. COLOUR

**SV: Black with regular brown, gold to lightish-grey markings, also with a black saddle, dark sable (black overlay on grey or light tan ground with lighter markings to match), black, iron-grey all over or with lighter or brown markings. Small white markings on chest or very light hair on the inside of legs are permissible but not desirable.**

*White German Shepherds are not shown in conformation classes, although there are clubs which hold special classes for the white GSD. Photo courtesy: Freida Bassett-Shaftoe.*

The tip of the nose must be black on all dogs of any variety of colour (dogs with little or non-existent mask, with yellowish legs, also whitish claws and red tail-end or washed-out pale colours are considered as lacking pigment). The ground hair or undercoat is always light grey except on black dogs. The final colour of a puppy can only be determined after the proper top coat has grown.

US: The German Shepherd Dog varies in color and most colors are permissible. Strong, rich colours are preferred. Pale, washed-out colors and blues and livers are serious faults. A white dog must be disqualified.

UK: Black or black saddle with tan or gold to light grey markings. All black, all grey, or grey with lighter or brown markings referred to as Sables. Nose black. Light markings on chest or very pale colour on inside of legs permissible but undesirable, as are whitish nails, red tipped tails or wishy-washy faded colours defined as lacking in pigmentation. Blues, livers, albinos, white (i.e. almost pure white dogs with black noses) and near whites highly undesirable. Undercoat, except in all-black dogs, usually grey or fawn. Colour in itself is of secondary importance, having no effect on character or fitness for work. Final colour of a young dog only ascertained when outer coat has developed.

COMMENT
The SV and UK Standards are similar with the addition of "white and near whites highly undesirable" and "colour in itself is of secondary importance, having no effect on character or fitness for work". The US Standard states "A GSD varies in color and most colors are permissible. Strong rich colours are preferred." "White dogs must be disqualified." This is the only Standard that refers to disqualification. The nearest we come in the UK Standard is that Blues, Livers, Albinos, Whites (with Black noses) and near whites are highly "undesirable". However, despite these differences I feel sure that in all three countries doubtful colours would not win top honours.

All three Standards are similar regarding colour and what is not desirable. These days the faulty colours are rarely seen. In the old British stock whites were quite common; now occasional blues, livers and tans have cropped up in certain German and British bloodlines. Colour is not always as rich as we could wish but the last few years has seen a big improvement here and, certainly in Germany, some of their judges used to believe that colour was part of type and shunned dogs that were "too dark"! This resulted in many dogs being lighter than was desirable and the black saddle fading away as the dog matured. I think that the future will alleviate this tendency.

## 15. COAT

SV:

**A. The Stock-Haired German Shepherd Dog:**
The outer coat as thick as possible, individual hairs are straight, harsh and close-lying. On the head, including inner parts of the ears, front parts of legs, paws and toes the hair is short. On the neck the hair is longer and thicker-coated. On the back of the fore and hind legs the hair is longer down to the pasterns and hock joints. On the thighs it forms longer breeches. The length of the hair varies, therefore many intermediate forms exist.
A. Too short, mole-like coat is faulty.
**B. The Long Stock-Haired German Shepherd Dog.**
The individual hair is longer, not always straight and most of all not close-lying on the body, mainly inside and behind the ears, along the back of the underarms and mostly around the loin area the hair is noticeably longer, it often forms ear tufts and flags from elbow to metatarsus, the breeches are long and thick, the tail is bushy with flags to the underside. The long stock-haired coat, not being weather-proof as the normal stock-hair, is not desirable; however, if sufficient undercoat is present, it is still permissible for breeding if acceptable by the breed regulations of the particular country concerned.
**C. The Long-Haired German Shepherd Dog.**
The hair is considerably longer than that of the long stock-haired dog, it is mostly very soft and usually parted along the back. Undercoat is not present at all or only in the loin area. Among long-haired GSDs there are frequently narrow-chested ones and narrow, elongated forms of muzzle. In the long-haired GSD this weather-proofing and the proficiency as a working dog are essentially lessened. For this reason the long-haired should not be bred.

US: The ideal dog has a double coat of medium length. The outer coat should be as dense as possible, hair straight, harsh and lying close to the body. A slightly wavy outer coat, often of wiry texture, is permissible. The head, including the inner ear and foreface and the legs and paws are covered with short hair and the neck with longer and thicker hair. The rear of the forelegs and hindlegs has somewhat longer hair extending to the pastern and hock, respectively. Faults in coat include soft, silky, too long outer coat, woolly, curly and open coat.

UK: Outer coat consisting of straight, hard, close lying hair as dense as possible. Thick undercoat. Hair on head, ears, front of legs, paws and toes short, on back, longer and thicker; in some males forming slight ruff. Hair longer on back of legs as far down as pasterns and stifles and forming fairly thick trousers on hindquarters. No hard and fast rule for length of hair; mole-type coats undesirable.

COMMENT

The US Standard has in it a sentence that puzzles me: "a slightly wavy outer coat, often of wiry texture is permissible". What is required is a weather-resistant coat and, apart from the above, the AKC recognises this. Note the list of coat faults. I quote "soft, silky, woolly, curly and open coat"; I think that "wavy" and "wiry" should have been included. The SV and UK versions of the normal coat are similar, and present no problems. It is of interest that whites no longer appear in modern German bloodlines while long coats frequently do so. We were told that both were of the recessive nature – i.e. both parents have to carry the gene. If this is so we should have "bred both faults out" by now and not just one of them.

## 16. FAULTS

SV: Anything which detracts from the usefulness, endurance and working ability of the dog, in particular characteristics not corresponding to the sex or otherwise; a nature contrary to a Shepherd Dog, such as apathy, nervous debility, excitability and shyness; insufficient vitality and eagerness to work; monorchidism or cryptorchidism or testicles too small; soft or flabby constitution and lack of substance; colour paling, blue-coated dogs or albinos (i.e. those lacking all pigmentation, as pink noses, etc.), pure white or near white dogs with black noses.

Furthermore, dogs exceeding the maximum or not reaching the minimum height, stunted growth, high-legged and dogs overbuilt in the front, too short in general appearance, too fine or too coarse in build, soft back, steeply set limbs as well as everything that detracts from ground-covering and endurance-subjected gait.

Also a muzzle too short, blunt, weak, overlong or lacking in strength; an under or over-shot bite and any other dentition faults such as weak or adversely affected teeth. A coat that is too soft, too short or too long and lack of undercoat. Hanging or permanently faulty ear carriage, cropped ears. Ringed, curled or in general badly carried tail, docked tail or congenital bob-tail.

US: Cropped or hanging ears. Dogs with noses not predominantly black. Undershot jaw. Docked tail. White dogs. Any dog that attempts to bite the judge.

UK: Any departure from the foregoing points should be considered a fault and the seriousness with which the fault should be regarded should be in exact proportion to its degree.

Note. Male animals should have two apparently normal testicles fully descended into the scrotum.

COMMENT

SV: This Standard goes to great lengths in listing faults, some of which are not of a disqualification nature but merely a straying from perfection (normal?).

US: This includes "Any dog that attempts to bite the judge"!!

UK: In my opinion this is the most sensible version but, in general, I think all the Standards should list only "disqualifying faults".

# 8 *THE JUDGE'S VIEW*

When you have been involved in the dog showing world for a number of years, you may well feel ready to take on the task of judging. It may be that you have enjoyed a considerable degree of success, and you feel you have something to contribute. Or perhaps you have not been as lucky as you think you should have been, and you see judging as a way of redressing the balance. Whatever your reasons for wanting to judge, you will soon find out that it is not as easy as it looks! It is all too easy to criticise the judge's placings, it is quite another matter to stand in the centre of a busy ring and make calm, rational decisions, based on an in-depth knowledge of the breed, and, most importantly, on the ability to make a clear interpretation of the Breed Standard when assessing living specimens.

JUDGING IN THE USA
In the USA, becoming an AKC licensed judge for any breed is a lengthy process. The AKC is constantly changing their stipulated requirements, seeking to improve the selection of judges with the implied intent of improving the quality of new judges.

An aspiring judge applying to AKC for the first time must meet the following minimum prerequisites:

- Ten years' documented experience in the sport.
- Owned or exhibited several dogs of the initial breed(s) requested.
- Bred or raised at least four litters in any one breed.
- Produced two Champions out of a minimum of four litters.
- Acted as steward at five AKC Member or Licensed Shows.
- Judged six Sanctioned matches, Sweepstakes or Futurities.
- Met the occupational eligibility requirements under AKC Rules.
- Passed a comprehensive 'open book' examination demonstrating understanding of AKC Rules, Policies and Judging Procedures.
- Passed a test on the Standard of each breed requested.
- Be interviewed.
- Provide two references.

To satisfy these and additional requirements requires time, effort, and money on the part of the would-be judge. It is unnecessary to further detail all the convoluted arrangements whereby an applicant is finally approved to judge initially on a Provisional basis, and, after a specified number of assignments, to become a Regular Judge.

The American Kennel Club publishes *Guidelines for Dog Show Judges* which details, in general terms, the required judging procedures. All judges must physically examine each dog, i.e. must open the dog's mouth (or have the handler do so) to check dentition and bite and must check that every male has two normally descended testicles. He/she must go over the dog to determine soundness of back, hocks and coat condition. The judge is required to individually gait each dog to determine soundness, always using the same ring pattern to ensure impartiality.

The interpretation of the Standard is the sole responsibility of the judge. A judge can adjudicate only those dogs which are presented in the conformation ring on a particular day.

## JUDGING IN THE UK

For many years, anyone receiving an invitation to judge at an Open Show was permitted by the Kennel Club to do so. No questions were asked about their suitability to judge the breed, no questions were asked about their knowledge and experience of the breed; provided an invitation could be obtained from a show committee, they were free to take the centre of the ring.

A similar situation also existed with Championship Shows, and, as it takes only three Challenge Certificates awarded by three different judges for a dog to become a Champion, the title could be gained under judges with minimal knowledge of the breed who may never have owned a good Shepherd, or may never have owned a Shepherd of any description.

Gradually the situation improved, and the Kennel Club started to ask breed clubs and the Breed Council for their opinion regarding the experieince of an aspiring Championship Show judge. Although the occasional judge still slipped through the net, most new judges at Championship level had to meet the Breed Council's criteria for experience, which are:

- Ten years active in the breed.
- Ten shows judged, four of which must be Breed Club Open Shows.
- First show to have been judged at least seven years earlier.

## EDUCATION

Now, at long last, the Kennel Club has recognised the need for educating those who award Challenge Certificates, and training schemes for all breeds are being set up. This will mean that judges will have to attend an appropriate training course and pass an exam, as well as meeting the Breed Council criteria. In this respect, the German Shepherd fraternity have been ahead of the game, as they have had a training scheme since 1997.

The Kennel Club itself needs educating. Its system of awards, i.e. First, Second, Third, Reserve, VHC and chuck-everyone-else-out-in-order-to-get-finished-as-soon-as-possible is unhelpful to the owner. The continental system of grading the exhibits, Excellent, Very Good, Good, Sufficient and Insufficient, is much better. If you were halfway down a class of 40, you would obviously prefer to receive a card stating that the judge considers you worthy of a certain grade, rather than being asked to leave the ring to the five or six dogs receiving the award cards. The five or six place cards awarded under the present system could still be given even if grading were to be permitted.

## INTERPRETATION

Whatever the system of judging, the dogs must be evaluated against the Breed Standard. Every judge will swear that they do exactly this, but problems arise in individuals' interpretations of the Standard. The greatest divergence of interpretation of the Standard is the 'back'; and that, along with proportions, is responsible for the arguments that arise between those who support the 'English' type of GSD and those who support the type which is recognised in the country of origin and in most other countries.

While the Standard mentions various faults it does not allow for judges' varying views of the importance of these faults. For example, one judge may not give a second look to a dog with a missing tooth, another may ignore several missing teeth and give it a top award. The differences in evaluating faults added to the differences in interpretation of the Standard prove how essential it is that new judges receive a proper education.

## PROCEDURE
Breed specialist Percy Elliott has been instrumental in setting up training courses, and he sets the following standard for procedure.

"Judging is a subjective pursuit and always will be. Nevertheless, there is no reason why it should not be businesslike and efficient. I have always taught would-be judges to work in a format when assessing a dog. In this manner, nothing is missed.

The handler should bring the dog to the judge on a loose collar and lead. At this stage you can assess the general demeanour of the dog, examine its teeth, and its testicles if male. Once the dog is posed, you can form a general impression of its size, strength, proportions, general harmony, coat and colour.

Move to the front of the dog to assess the head, including eyes, ears and colour, then evaluate the forequarters including the legs, pasterns, feet, and width of chest.

From the side, look at the neck, the withers, the back, the croup, the forechest and the loin. The forequarters, i.e. the shoulder and upper arm, and the hindquarters, i.e. the upper and lower thighs and the hocks, can also be assessed.

Movement must be looked at from the front, the rear, and the side, remembering that ease and enduring movement is more important than mere length of stride. This can best be assessed by taking up different positions in the ring – standing in the centre gives you the same picture over and over again and can make you feel dizzy, especially in a small ring. The best plan is to move from one side and then to the other, and also to stand in a corner. In this way, you can build up a natural impression, for, often during your initial examination, a dog may be pulling hard on the lead, thus distorting the outline.

When judging, remember that you are also being judged. Therefore it is essential to ensure that you see and describe a true picture of every dog. Finally, do not judge in order to please anyone, just please yourself and you will not go far wrong. Good luck!"

## A JUDGING EXERCISE
As an academic exercise, three Championship judges: Sheila Rankin (UK), Fred Lanting (USA), and Percy Elliott (UK), were invited to assess six German Shepherds – three dogs and three bitches – from a series of photographs showing head, profile, forequarters, and hindquarters. The dogs were not named, the judges were merely told their ages.

# A JUDGING EXERCISE
*Photos: Steph Holbrook.*

GERMAN SHEPHERD DOG A:
MALE, 3 YEARS.

## HEAD STUDY

*Sheila Rankin:* "The most classic of the three male heads – masculine without being over-large. The eye is almost almond-shaped and dark; the ears are nicely placed and the right size. The rich tan on his face coupled with his very dark muzzle is attractive, but he should not have the white marking on his chest. His bottom lip ought to be a little tighter."

*Fred Lanting:* "A nearly ideal head, with very good ear size and set. Dark-eyed, expressive and masculine, with good pigmentation."

*Percy Elliot:* "A good, masculine head of medium strength and lively expression. Perhaps a little too much stop, and the forehead is a little too rounded."

## PROFILE

*Sheila Rankin:* " A strong and well-proportioned male. I would prefer him without the slightly raised back which falls steeply to the croup. The right pastern and foot turns out, and he is very slightly sickle-hocked."

*Fred Lanting:* "Medium strong in general appearance. He is slightly stretched, and could have a little more leg length. Good overline to mid-back, but then it falls off at a distinctly different angle before the pelvis. Croup of excellent length and at a good angle (to the portion of the back immediately preceding it). Good underline if slightly deep."

*Percy Elliott:* "A strong dog of very good proportions and firm build. Very good angulations fore and aft, although the lower thigh is a bit short. Good withers, but the back falls away too much."

## FOREQUARTERS

*Sheila Rankin:* "Apart from the turned-out right pastern and the white patching in the fur, there is not much to criticise from this view. It shows correct front development for a male of three years."

*Fred Lanting:* "Normal forechest, and good fore angulation. In good coat condition. Long-bones are straight except the right forefoot is turned out in both poses where it is visible."

*Percy Elliott:* "Correct except for the right foreleg which is slightly out at elbow and pastern."

## HINDQUARTERS

*Sheila Rankin:* "This view shows that he is indeed a little sickle-hocked as well as being rather cow-hocked, but it also shows the strong and muscular body of a mature male."

*Fred Lanting:* "Very good rear angulation, but appears to be cow-hocked.

*Percy Elliott:* "Very cow-hocked, which accentuates the fall in backline. The tail is too long."

# A JUDGING EXERCISE
*Photos: Steph Holbrook.*

GERMAN SHEPHERD DOG B:
MALE, 15 MONTHS.

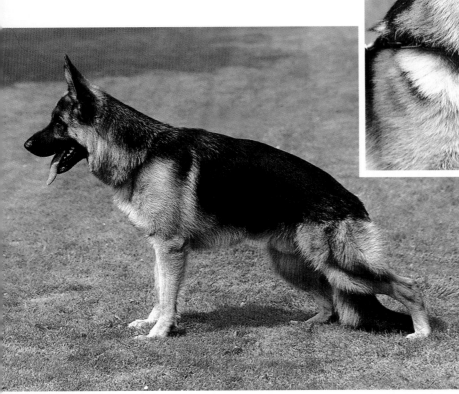

## HEAD STUDY

*Sheila Rankin:* Almost too big, broad and butch, but that is typical of many young males today and it suits the rest of him. The ears are of correct size and nicely set. My personal preference would be for a darker eye, but there is nothing wrong with this tawny colour."

*Fred Lanting:* " The proportions are not ideal. The muzzle could be a little longer and the apparent planes a little more parallel. The right ear appears somewhat overset, not as functional. Medium eye colour, good pigment."

*Percy Elliott:* "Good head. The eyes could be a bit darker, but they are acceptable as the expression is still good. The right ear leans inwards. The skull is slightly domed – it should be nearer parallel with the muzzle."

## PROFILE

*Sheila Rankin:* "This photo shows that he is well-developed for his age; he does not look the junior that he is. He is well-proportioned. Very good hindquarters and, although his upper arm is a little short, I think the angle is probably about right. I particularly like his clean outline."

*Fred Lanting:* "Obviously not yet adult, but a masculine dog with excellent proportions. Very good overline and underline; good croup length and angle from the back. Upper arm could be longer and slightly more inclined. The coat appears to have lost some undercoat."

*Percy Elliott:* "Very pleasing in profile with correct proportions and an impression of strength giving an harmonious overall appearance. Very good withers and back; the croup is a bit steep."

## FOREQUARTERS

*Sheila Rankin:* "The front legs are straight, strong and true with no turning in or out of either pastern."

*Fred Lanting:* "Forechest should improve with maturity. This dog stands straight in front, but the pasterns could be stronger and toes more knuckled-up."

*Percy Elliott:* "Very clean, straight legs, but the pasterns are a bit soft. The upper arm is rather short."

## HINDQUARTERS

*Sheila Rankin:* "Standing almost as true behind as he does in front. This shot confirms that he has a well-developed body for his age but, if compared with Dog A, it can be seen that he is not yet fully mature. I would expect that he moves fairly soundly in both directions and, of the three males, he is the one I would wish to own."

*Fred Lanting:* "Rear angulation is excellent, and stands straight."

*Percy Elliott:* "Very good, broad thighs with excellent angulations. Stands slightly cow-hocked, but this is acceptable in such a well-angulated dog."

# A JUDGING EXERCISE
*Photos: Steph Holbrook.*

## GERMAN SHEPHERD DOG C: MALE, 7 YEARS.

## HEAD STUDY

*Sheila Rankin:* "Although the ears are well set, I do not like the shape of them and the wavy outer edge. The eyes are beautifully dark but rather round and a little prominent, which gives him an uneasy expression. It is nice that at seven years old he shows no signs of going grey on the muzzle, but the under jaw is far too lippy."

*Fred Lanting:* "Very good ears and eye colour. A bit too round (protruding) in the eye, slightly loose in lip and short in muzzle, giving a slightly dish-faced impression and the appearance of too much dome to the backskull. Masculine, just misses being coarse."

*Percy Elliott:* "Quite a good head, but the cheeks should be more filled. The eyes are rather round."

## PROFILE

*Sheila Rankin:* This dog is steep in front, and his hindquarters lack the strength of Dog B. Clean topline with no dips or humps. He lacks chest development. In this shot, his head looks a bit short in the muzzle."

*Fred Lanting:* "Fully-mature, high-withered dog with good pigment and coat. Good height-to-length proportions, but too deep in chest (withers to sternum). Short, steep upper arm with normal scapula layback makes it difficult to tell exactly where the 'stick' would be placed, but wherever, it would show the elbow and whole foreleg to be too far forward. Good overline, good length of croup, but somewhat steep."

*Percy Elliott:* "A tall dog of firm athletic build. High withers, good back and croup, albeit slightly steep. A firm, showy dog looking good for his age."

## FOREQUARTERS

*Sheila Rankin:* "The front legs are straight and true, but he is a bit narrow in chest. His shoulders seem rather undeveloped, but it is probably because he has lost muscle due to his age."

*Fred Lanting:* "This dog stands correctly in front."

*Percy Elliott:* "Steep upper arm of good length. Good, long, straight bones, with good pasterns and feet."

## HINDQUARTERS

*Sheila Rankin:* "He is a little cow-hocked, but the hock bone is straighter than Dog A. His tail hangs correctly. It can easily be seen that, although in excellent condition, he is no longer a spring chicken."

*Fred Lanting:* "Very good rear angulation. From this view, he stands nearly correctly, but he has a slight cow-hocked appearance."

*Percy Elliott:* "Very good hindquarters, better angulated than the forequarters. Stands better than Dogs A and B."

# A JUDGING EXERCISE
*Photos: Steph Holbrook.*

GERMAN SHEPHERD DOG D:
BITCH, 2 YEARS.

## HEAD STUDY

*Sheila Rankin:* This is a lovely head – strong but still feminine. The eyes dark and almond-shaped. The breadth of skull is right, and the ears are the right size and correctly placed. Her under-jaw is just a little 'lippy'."

*Fred Lanting:* "Very good ears. The eyes are a bit close together. On such a dog, I would surreptitiously rest a hand on that portion of the skull while the handler showed me the bite. The lip could be a little loose."

*Percy Elliott:* "Lovely, feminine head and expression, typical of the breed. The right ear is slightly low-set, but I do not think that this would be penalised."

## PROFILE

*Sheila Rankin:* "This bitch has a colour problem – at only two years old her saddle should be a more solid black. I do not like her topline with that bump in the middle and the short croup. Her body is a little short in ratio to her height, and I do not like her over-stretched hindquarters. From the photo, her front angles are good and I like the overall impression of strength."

*Fred Lanting:* "Despite being over-stacked, she has ideal proportions in length, height and chest depth. Good, strong overline but with a distinct hinge midway between withers and tail, over about the last thoracic vertebrae. Croup could be slightly longer, but lies at a good angle to the lumbar portion of the back. Very good underline"

*Percy Elliott:* "Slightly too short, but otherwise good proportions. Good forequarters and hindquarters. A slightly raised back, and falling away into a steep croup."

## FOREQUARTERS

*Sheila Rankin:* 'Her forelegs are strong, straight and true, but she is lacking a bit in chest development. From this view, not so much of her left hock-bone should be visible. Looking through a magnifying glass, I think her nails are light which is another indication of colour-paling."

*Fred Lanting:* "Good forechest, normal shoulder layback, very good upper-arm length and angle."

*Percy Elliott:* "She appears excellent when viewed from the front, i.e. correct width between the front legs, firm elbows, straight legs, firm pasterns and good feet."

## HINDQUARTERS

*Sheila Rankin:* "The left bone from hock to foot is turned outwards which is why it can be seen so clearly from the front view, but there are so many in the breed like this I would not penalise too heavily. I like her body width which is very apparent in this shot – we have too many who are too narrow right through."

*Fred Lanting:* "Very good rear angulation. Cow-hocked in stance. Dry and firm."

*Percy Elliott:* "Very cow-hocked which accentuates the fall in backline. The tail is too long."

# A JUDGING EXERCISE
*Photos: Steph Holbrook.*

GERMAN SHEPHERD DOG E:
BITCH, 2 YEARS.

## HEAD STUDY

*Sheila Rankin:* "This head would sell a million boxes of chocolates, but it does not appeal to me because the sex is not immediately apparent as with the other two bitches (D and F). The ears are a bit too large and may not be as firm as they should be, particularly the left one. The eyes are almond-shaped and dark. Unless it is a trick of the light, there is a large white patch on her chest – a fault which seems to be on the increase in the breed."

*Fred Lanting:* "Definitely not a dry bitch. The ears are slightly large."

*Percy Elliott:* "Very pleasing Shepherd bitch with good expression. The left ear could be firmer, but it is quite acceptable if it remains firm when the bitch is trotting."

## PROFILE

*Sheila Rankin:* "A coat that would be described as "quality" in a show critique, but probably soft and not very waterproof. She has a much better topline than the first of the bitches (D). Her front and rear angles are balanced. I think her tail is a little too long."

*Fred Lanting:* "Plush topcoat. Uran type with pleasing curves, good proportions in height to length, but needs more leg length, less chest depth, even taking hair length between elbows into account. Good croup length but somewhat steep. Upper arm could be somewhat longer. Good underline if rather deep."

*Percy Elliott:* "Very satisfying proportions of 10-9 and very harmonious all through. The back does fall a little and so does the croup, but I doubt if this would be penalised in the ring."

## FOREQUARTERS

*Sheila Rankin:* "This shot confirms the large white patch on her front. Although her front legs are straight and parallel, her chest is far too narrow. Her feet are rather flat and spread."

*Fred Lanting:* "Good forechest. Appears a bit hare-footed, and pasterns could be slightly stronger."

*Percy Elliott:* "Well-anguated shoulder, slightly steep upper arm. Very clean-boned legs with good pasterns and feet. Very narrow in the chest, but as the bitch is just two years old this should not be criticised."

## HINDQUARTERS

*Sheila Rankin:* "Oh dear! With those cow-hocks she could not possibly move soundly, and I bet her long tail would bounce on them and further impede her hind action. This view shows that she is narrow right through and lacks the strength and development of the first bitch (D), who is about the same age."

*Fred Lanting:* "Very good rear angulation, though extremely cow-hocked."

*Percy Elliott:* "Good hindquarters – well-angulated with broad thighs and short hocks. She stands very cow-hocked, which is a pity, and her tail is too long."

# A JUDGING EXERCISE
*Photos: Steph Holbrook.*


GERMAN SHEPHERD DOG F:
BITCH, 3 YEARS.

## HEAD STUDY

*Sheila Rankin:* "Finer in head than either of the other two bitches, but most attractive with those very dark and expressive eyes. She could never be mistaken for a male. Ears well shaped and nicely placed. Although I prefer head D, it would not look right on this bitch."

*Fred Lanting:* "Excellent head with proper muzzle length, strong underjaw, strong ears and dark eyes."

*Percy Elliott:* "Good head and expression – could be a little more filled under the eyes, i.e. *slightly* rounded cheeks."

## PROFILE

*Sheila Rankin:* "My pet hate is a large linked check-chain on a very feminine bitch – it makes her neck look a bit 'stuffy'. Lovely clean outline with good length of croup, though it is a little steep. She is very angulated behind but the front angles do not match them, the upper-arm being rather short and steep. Lacks a bit in forechest. Height-to-length ratio about right."

*Fred Lanting:* "Proportions about 8.5 to 10 in length, and somewhat more than the ideal chest depth as a percentage of height. Very good overline with good length of croup but somewhat steep. Good front angulation, though upper arm could be a little longer. Good ribbing."

*Percy Elliott:* "Very nice bitch type. Very good proportions albeit a trifle short. Harmonious build, falling backline and rather steep croup. Short and steep upper arm, pasterns maximum angle."

## FOREQUARTERS

*Sheila Rankin:* "Stands straight and true and has the right amount of width between her legs. I like the fact that only a little of one hind leg can be seen. Her right front foot turns in a little."

*Fred Lanting:* Stands straight in front with very good breadth of brisket. Pasterns should be stronger, less slanted, and the hare feet are partially hidden from view."

*Percy Elliott:* "Good, straight forelegs, perhaps standing a trifle wide at the right elbow."

## HINDQUARTERS

*Sheila Rankin:* "Even though her left hock is turning in, the hock bones are not as long as those of the other two bitches (D and E), and she is the truest of the three from this view. If all the points that cannot be seen in photos are OK, this bitch would be the one I would most want to own."

*Fred Lanting:* "Very good rear angulation, and good width in the hindquarters. Stands rather cow-hocked."

*Percy Elliott:* "Very good hindquarters, better angulated than the forequarters. Stands better than the other two bitches."

# 9 THE SHOW GERMAN SHEPHERD DOG

We all hope for that day when our dog wins the ultimate major award becomes a reality and all the hard work which must accompany this achievement comes to fruition. Before reaching this pinnacle of achievement, there are many steps and stages to be completed on the way.

## THE POTENTIAL STAR

Many hours of schooling and training are required for both the handler and the German Shepherd Dog. However, the final result cannot be achieved unless we have firstly produced, or acquired, the dog which has correct conformation. Provisionally, the show winner's life is usually decided around six weeks of age. The litter of puppies are observed and, using our knowledge and experience, we choose the pup displaying the attributes most likely to help to ensure a winner in the show ring, a difficult task for most. Conformation is the most important attribute, as this cannot be altered artificially and will develop naturally along with the puppy. Character is also important. Serious thoughts regarding the character are given priority when the parents are matched although, unlike conformation, character can be developed and improved through education.

*The polished performer in the show ring – but to achieve this standard takes a lot of training and hard work.*

*The dog you show must conform as closely as possible to the Breed Standard. This is Int. Ch. Gayvilles Nilo.*
*Photo: Keith Allison.*

*Head study of Gayvilles Voko 16 months, showing male characteristics.*
*Photo: Keith Allison.*

## INITIAL TRAINING

From six weeks to twelve weeks is a very important phase in the life of German Shepherd Dogs. At every opportunity they must be handled. From this exercise they will grow to accept people. During this six weeks' period there is no specific training, the pup should just learn how it feels for human hands to hold it and give it assurance. The puppy should also be introduced to as many people as possible and showered with attention. It is also important that all household items are introduced to the puppy and contact is allowed; this will build and develop the character of the puppy.

After many trials it has become obvious to me that there is not a great deal to be gained from excessive training at breed club training sessions from twelve weeks to six months. This period should be used to socialise the puppy with the other participants at the training club and to introduce a number of important showing techniques regarding the individual presentation.

One of the most important is showing the dog's teeth to the judge, this is the first very important detail to be recorded by the judge immediately after noting the exhibit's number and age. Many would-be aspiring handlers struggle to show the teeth correctly, and it is not unusual for judges to remark on their disappointment at a handler's attempts to present the teeth. Both the handlers and the exhibits must spend time on the skill of showing the teeth.

Some time should be spent on teaching the puppy to walk around the ring under control. It is natural for the puppy to walk by the owner's side. To encourage the puppy to walk in front at the full length of the lead, taking the tension, requires the help of a partner or a friend to coax and encourage the puppy to come to them, walking ahead of the handler around the training ring. Do not continue this exercise continuously, which is the mistake that most make when training the puppy. Spend only approximately five minutes walking the puppy, which equates to

## LEAD WALKING
### Photos: Keith Allison.

*These two young puppies are being trained to walk on the lead. The leader is being encouraged to walk to heel, followed by the second pup who is taking the tension on the lead.*

*As the dogs matures, training can become more strenuous. Here, Voko and Nilo, handled by Davy Hall, are being trained to pull hard. Working together creates natural competitiveness.*

*Nilo training at the walk pulling really hard – this helps the muscles in the back and makes the dog very firm.*

*Control is an essential element in all training. When instructed, Nilo walks out in front without pulling.*

*Free-standing: Nilo is presented for the judge, with no hands-on interference from the handler.*

quarter of a mile – quite enough for a puppy at this early age.

The partner should attract the puppy for two to three laps, then disappear and allow the puppy to do it on its own. When the puppy's interest wanes, reappear and encourage the puppy again for another circuit of the ring, then disappear again. Continue this exercise over the weeks until the puppy requires less and less of the encouragement. When the puppy is four months the exercise can be increased to a half mile, ideally during the time children are going to school. This serves two purposes – character and temperament building; it is also exercising the puppy, gently building and firming muscle tone.

It is important to remember not to overdo or rush the training at this age. The show ring and results are not the most important things at this time; it is only ground work and experience, ready for the most important times that lie ahead. Many top winning puppies do not fulfil their early promise because of excessive training and showing in their early life. With experience and knowledge it will be realised that the most important time for showing and achieving major honours normally starts around eighteen months and can last up to five and six years. You must learn to enjoy the puppy and to allow the puppy to have a puppy's life. The old saying of learning to walk before running is very true and should be followed.

### THE STANCE
Back to the training club. Most of the time, from four months to six months and beyond, should be spent on presenting the stance, sometimes called stacking the dog. First impressions are very important and can go a long way towards determining the final positions at the end of the class and, eventually, the final challenge. There are two methods of standing, one is free and the

*Hands-on: Sasha is presented in the Stand so that the judge can view the overall picture.*

other is "hands on", which can be used to present an untrue picture. In the modern era, the free-standing method is the preferred one. This requires the handler to walk the puppy into the stance at the end of the lead so that the dog is presented naturally; this way the judge sees the true picture and can compare the anatomy against the Standard.

The puppy's attention is held usually by one of the owners, while the handler walks a few paces and stops the puppy in the ideal stance. This usually means practising for ten to twenty minutes; boredom for the puppy can set in after approximately twenty minutes if there is no variation in the training. The handler must practise as much as the puppy; eventually the handler will master the technique given time, although new puppies come onto the scene continuously. Handling is like playing the piano and must be practised to gain the skill.

The "hands on" technique can be very useful in limited space, normally in large classes. Many advantages can be gained from this method and it is useful in hiding particular faults. A skilful handler can mould a puppy by placing the hind legs and then, with a little press in the croup area and a little touch under the brisket creating lift, can really enhance the picture and can deceive the judge. These are the skills professional handlers develop – and this is why the sincere handlers, the exhibitors and, especially, the judges prefer the free-standing method.

## STARTING SHOWING

When the puppy reaches six months of age it is now eligible to compete in the show ring, and this is the time when its future can be developed or destroyed. It is understandable for the newcomer to be very excited about showing their new charge, but we can be on dangerous ground. The very promising puppies will do well at their first attempts in the show ring, and this, in itself, will encourage the owner to enter more shows and, unfortunately, a vicious circle can develop of more training to do more winning. Many top winning puppies do not attain their major titles due to this basic error. All aspects are overdone during the first six months of their show careers and something is lost during this time – it may be simply the puppy's own enthusiasm.

The truth of the matter can easily be observed in the junior and special yearling classes, when the most promising puppies, that had been doing all the winning, begin to drop down the places to third and fourth and even lower. The showing of puppies, and their training, should be very rigidly controlled, so as not to overdo any aspect

and, most of all, to allow the puppy to have a puppy's life and to grow up without undue pressures. Remember that they are puppies until twelve months of age.

Two, possibly three, outings in minor puppy classes, and the same again in puppy classes, would probably be sufficient if you are travelling some distance to the Championship shows. From my experience, puppies from six months to twelve months should continue the socialising initiated between three to six months, continuing to build character and temperament, which is very important. The distance covered during the training sessions could possibly be increased up to three-quarters of a mile, twice a week; the puppy should walk half the distance, gaiting the remainder.

## VARYING ROUTINES

The actual training should be varied. For example, on one occasion the pup could be walked half the distance, turned around and gaited back to the starting point. On another occasion walk the pup two hundred yards, then gait two hundred yards and repeat until the distance and the session is completed. This will prevent the puppy from becoming bored with the same routine at every training session.

When you are at the training club do not fall into the trap of the ritual routines that the training clubs supply. Most training clubs go through the same routines week in and week out – that is, simulating the same requisites as those required on show day when exhibiting in the individual classes. Training clubs are for training, whereas the show ring is for competing, and this is the main difference. This, in my opinion, is where most training clubs fail to supply the benefits for which they are really formed, organised and used.

On training nights converse with the trainer and let him know which particular

PUPPY TRAINING
Photos: Keith Allison.

*This youngster is being trained to stand using the lead only. This shows the very early stages of training.*

*The same pup is presented using the hands-on technique. An experienced handler can mould an animal to create the picture he wants.*

problems you are experiencing in showing the puppy. If, for instance, the difficulty is in showing the teeth, then ask the trainer to demonstrate the correct manner in which to do this and then practise showing the teeth for most of the session until it becomes second nature. The same applies for presenting the puppy free-standing; allow the trainer to teach and demonstrate, then practise for the rest of the session. This applies to any particular problem being experienced. There is no benefit in walking and gaiting around the training ring with all the other members, when most are probably accomplished with this aspect of training.

Practise overcoming any problems. It will always be the problem areas that will prevent the dog from achieving the success that we are all striving to attain. All members should take the opportunity to help each other on training nights. This leads to positive results for all the club members and success for the whole club, rather than the negative results that accompany the normal criticisms directed at each other's animals. It should always be remembered that showing is about the dog and not its owners. Dog shows are for the dogs and the awards are theirs. The improved future of the German Shepherd Dog breed will depend on the breeding of good show-winning animals.

## THE ONE-YEAR-OLD

At twelve months the dogs have reached a very important age, the time when they can and should be X-rayed to determine the degree of hip dysplasia. Prior to this time training should be kept to a minimum to benefit the puppy regarding the development of its hips. Once the dog has been X-rayed the training can be increased. Much emphasis should be placed on the correct development of the German Shepherd Dog and the enthusiast should be reminded that a puppy should look like a puppy, a junior look like a junior, the young adult should look like a young adult, and eventually the adult should look like an adult and be fully developed. The dog should continue to change until fully mature at around four years of age.

At twelve months the GSD will have developed sufficiently, both mentally and anatomically, to allow you to increase the amount of training, and this will again serve two important purposes. Firstly, and most obviously, it will increase the stamina and level of fitness, which is very important when competing in the ring today. Secondly, and just as important, the increased training, and especially the increased distance, will improve co-ordination in the performance of the German Shepherd Dog.

It is important not to have any sudden increases in the training but to do it gradually over a period of approximately six weeks, building up from three-quarters of a mile to as much as two to three miles of gaiting at a respectable pace of about seven or eight minutes per mile. It is not beneficial to train every day; this can destroy the German Shepherd Dog's willingness to please. They are no different to humans in this respect and appreciate the days off. Better performances can be achieved by training every other day. Every German Shepherd Dog must be analysed in training. Most enjoy training in pairs: it is apparent that a natural competitiveness exists, which helps the handler during the training session. However, there are a few German Shepherd Dogs who do not work well in pairs and they must be trained as individuals. These few Shepherds will make the training difficult and awkward and will make it obvious that they are not working in unison.

The training should also be varied and done in different environments; this will keep the German Shepherd's interest high during training sessions. If the interest is lost, the benefits from training will also be lost.

## WEEKLY TRAINING PROGRAMME

Variety of training will keep the mental balance intact, and this will ensure a good performance. One example of an excellent week's training would be as follows.

On the first day take the German Shepherd for a two to three-mile run around your own area, and try to make the route circular; it is not beneficial to return over the same route. The GSD can usually sense that he is on the way home and will pull very strongly; when this happens the control, the co-ordination and the smoothness will be lost. From this session there are many advantages. The dog gains confidence from running among and passing people, children, pushchairs, bicycles and many other everyday objects. He also learns to cope with traffic. Through these experiences you are further developing his character and temperament.

Following a day's rest, a sprint session could be organised. This will entail finding a quiet stretch of roadway and marking off a distance of one-quarter to one-third of a mile. You will need the assistance of someone with whom the dog has a bond. This person travels in a car, or on a bicycle, and encourages the dog to chase them, at sprinting speed in one direction and at a walk in the opposite direction, pulling hard on the lead. The dog and handler steadily improve until they can complete three or four lengths in both directions. These sessions increase the speed of the German Shepherd, build the strength and stamina, and also improve the muscle tone. The sprinting must be controlled by the handler to keep the dog gaiting over the measured distance, and galloping is not allowed.

After another day's rest, the next training session should involve a prolonged gaiting session, again over two to three miles in a different environment, possibly in the park, or in the country, or in fields and woods. This creates a more relaxed atmosphere,

removing some of the pressures. Always closely monitor the training sessions and make observations about the reactions of the dog. If they indicate a lack of response or enjoyment during a particular training session, do not continue the session, stop the gaiting and walk home.

## FINISHING TOUCHES

Continue with the same routine of training through the twelve to eighteen month stage. By eighteen months you will have a super-fit German Shepherd Dog in excellent and healthy condition, capable of competing on the same terms as the older German Shepherds.

From eighteen months to two years there is no great difference in the training regime. During these six months continue the same exercises practised while the dog was a junior, while possibly increasing the number of sprint lengths to four or five, and the distance session to three or four miles – be assured this will be more than enough. This six-month period should also be used to perfect the presentation; this will help to impress the spectators but also, most importantly, the judge. After all the training, the results should be satisfying and the German Shepherd in excellent condition for showing.

## GROOMING

There is one further requirement. Some time should be given to grooming and preparation, ideally fifteen to twenty minutes prior to the start of the class. This will require combing the dog thoroughly before applying a good conditioner, and finishing off with a thorough brushing which will enhance the quality of the coat. Preparing your GSD for the ring starts long before the day of a show. In fact it starts in the kennel with good kennel management. The kennel should be kept clean and hygienic to prevent disease which will affect overall condition and, especially, the coat. Good feeding of a quality food also helps to keep the GSD in good condition. If you are competing extensively in the show ring there will be little requirement for grooming at home in the kennel; the dog will receive sufficient grooming at the show prior to the class and the challenges. Only when the dog is losing coat will it require extensive grooming at the kennel.

Preparation is very important. The well-prepared German Shepherd gives little away in quality to the other competitors and, remember, there are a number of aspects being judged in the final outcome. When competition is at its height, all steps should be taken to reduce any disadvantages that may occur. Realistically, the more affection and attention given to your dog around the kennel and home, the more he will respond by wanting to please you in the show ring, and will give you a more enthusiastic performance. In my experience the German Shepherd thrives on the exercise gained from the training sessions and totally enjoys the involvement with you in the show ring.

THE JUDGES

After all your hard work and preparation and, now, readiness for the competition, the final result rests with the person selected by the committee of the Show Society who has the unenviable task of judging the entry.

We all understand that judges should be comparing the exhibit to the Breed Standard, which describes the ideal and laid-down Standard, then marking accordingly. However, in practice, all judges have their individual opinions and preferences regarding the breed. Overall, the final results are consistent but there will be some minor changes in class positions from show to show, affected by the exhibits themselves, for many reasons. Any dog may have an indifferent

day: they may be heavier from feeding or underweight – it is not always easy to strike the happy medium. There should be consistency – remember the judge is comparing to the Standard and the Standard does not change from week to week.

Undeniably it would be wrong to change the Standard in one's mind to suit any particular German Shepherd Dog that may be competing. However, in GSDs of equal status there may be a preference for the better head, type, topline, shoulder, wither, croup, hindquarter or the movement. All exhibits are not equal in every aspect of their anatomy, but the one who resembles the Standard most accurately should, on most occasions, come out on top. Careful observation of a consistent judge should enable an experienced, successful handler to almost predict the attributes a particular judge prefers and then use these observations to their advantage. The consistent judge who always promotes the correct German Shepherd Dog will gain the respect and admiration of everyone involved.

Just as important is the placing of these German Shepherd Dogs in the correct order; this can have a great influence on which direction the breed will travel. When judging appointments are accepted, the people involved must not forget the responsibility that comes with the job. The judge must be strong of mind and not allow the handlers to take control – this must be retained by the judge. The judge's decision is final and they must have the confidence to make it. Some of the important points to note during the examination are that the exhibit should display definite sex characteristics, correct dentition, correct anatomy and balance, soundness, and a fleeting gait, far-reaching with a powerful drive.

The European judges tend to set the standard for the judges worldwide; the type of German Shepherd Dogs that are promoted

*Correct handling presents a dog off to advantage. Here Ch. Gayvilles Xera is showing off all her attributes – good proportions fore and hind, and correct sloping backline.*

are referred to as the International type. These GSDs can then, if exported, win anywhere in the world, or at home under any visiting International judge. It makes sense to any knowledgeable and intelligent breeder, owner and exhibitor to aim for this type, making the chances for wider success greater.

There are two factions in Great Britain. There is the United Kingdom group, who favour and prefer the old style of presentation and showing – the same style that was used in the seventies and, as I understand it, the same style as the fifties. There are many who believe this group do not feel the need to change or improve, whereas the Progressive group, just as the name implies, are continuously striving to improve, along with Europe and all the other countries who prefer the International type.

Some changes are not always for the betterment of the breed, but they must surely be healthier than stagnating. There is a growing feeling among the German Shepherd Dog fraternity at this time that if both groups came together and debated the future requirements, with ideas from all involved in the breed, Great Britain would be, and would stay, on level terms with the rest of the world. The judges' examinations are of the utmost importance and their decisions will surely determine the most correct Shepherd.

*The correct view from the front.*

*The correct rear view.*

## THE HANDLER

What is required from the handler is assistance to help the German Shepherd display its many attributes and, hopefully, impress the judge sufficiently, which will enable the dog to win the class. However, there are some common handling faults evolving in the show ring which can be infuriating. There is the apparent difficulty in showing the teeth efficiently, to allow the judge an examination to assess the correct dentition. Over-confidence is a contributing

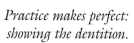

*Practice makes perfect: showing the dentition.*

# HANDLING FAULTS
## Photos: Keith Allison.

The front legs are not in line – a common handling fault.

The handler has placed the front legs too close together.

Standing too short, creating an incorrect outline and a poor, overall picture.

The front legs are too wide apart and the feet are turned out.

The handler is pressing slightly on the hip – this can exaggerate the outline.

Standing too wide when viewed from the rear.

The front legs are stretched too far out, creating the 'rocking horse' position.

The hindlegs are placed too close together.

factor, and the feeling that practice is not necessary. Many of the handlers experience difficulty with the free-standing technique; this fault, again, is due to lack of practice. Control also leaves a great deal to be desired; this comes from a combination of the lack of training by the owner and insufficient practice by the handlers with difficult German Shepherd Dogs.

The most infuriating of all the faults contributed by the handler is the over-running of the other German Shepherd Dogs; this particular undesirable practice makes it impossible for the judge to compare the movement of one dog against another. Unfortunately, in my experience, the majority of judges tend to move up the German Shepherd dog doing the over-running. This does absolutely nothing to discourage the offender; in fact it has the opposite effect. It requires minimal knowledge and intelligence to realise that, by running inside another competitor, the offender is running a shorter distance and may, in fact, not be the best mover. The breed would benefit if the offender were penalised for this action, instead of what appears to be happening at the moment, which is that it is rewarded.

MOVEMENT

The movement of the German Shepherd Dog is unmistakable: it should be far-reaching with a powerful thrust from the hindquarter. The impression it leaves should be undeniably effortless. Too often the opposite seems to be required by the judge and confirmed by the remarks "would have preferred more effort" or, simply, "did not work hard enough", which is a complete contradiction of what really is required. If a German Shepherd Dog is working harder, this confirms, usually, a shorter stride pattern, requiring more steps, than the long-reaching German Shepherd Dog. The shorter stride pattern normally requires a much faster action to cover the required distance of completing one lap of the show ring. This gives the appearance of a much harder, more convincing worker, and a number of judges are leaning towards this preference. The short reach is usually synonymous with the short, steep upper arm and the forward placed shoulder. If this preference continues to grow it will eventually destroy the true workability of the German Shepherd Dog.

There is also a danger of training the German Shepherd dog to take a shorter step. This can be achieved by using running machines, and through not understanding the machine and, hence, the dangers which can develop. Not realising and understanding the speeds at which German Shepherd Dogs can work efficiently over sustained periods is the first danger. The second danger is not recognising when the dog is beginning to tire. Tiredness means the step must shorten: this is fundamental, it has the same effect on all of us. Running machines can be useful in many different circumstances, particularly in building and maintaining fitness, but understanding really is a must, and a great deal of thought in relation to speed and

*MOVEMENT*
*Photos: Keith Allison.*

*Gaiting, under control, at the end of the lead.*

*Showing soundness and true, correct action walking towards the judge.*

*The correct action viewed from behind.*

distance needs to be given. It is normal for the German Shepherd to slow quite naturally when tiring. This is not possible on the machine. While it is in operation the dog must, at all times, keep running at the speed of the machine.

The working or moving German Shepherd Dog is a beautiful sight to behold and we should all do our utmost, in breeding and training, to retain this wonderful sight for future posterity. If we are not always working to improve the breed, then we do it a disservice. This responsibility lies not only with the breeder but also with the owner and, especially, with the judge.

# 10 *BREEDING GERMAN SHEPHERD DOGS*

There are many aspects of breeding, but the first decision to make is whether to breed at all. Hopefully, readers will find enough information in this chapter to help you to decide if you really do want to breed.

## WHY BREED?

Your vet said it would be good for your bitch.

All your family and friends want a puppy.

You parted quite happily with several hundreds of pounds for your puppy and would like some return for your money.

You have seen a dog show on television and you would like to have a go.

You love your Shepherd so much that you absolutely must have a puppy from her for yourself.

It will stop your bitch having phantom pregnancies.

It will improve her temperament.

A man in the park said.....

The above are just a few of the reasons given by people who want to breed but none of these reasons is good enough. There is only one reason for breeding Shepherds, or indeed any other breed, and that is because

*Careful consideration must be given to choosing breeding stock.*

*Photo: Steph Holbrook.*

you love the breed so much and are so fascinated by it that you cannot resist playing God and trying to improve it. Even then you should only have a litter if you intend to keep a puppy for yourself. If this sounds a bit idealistic, then so be it. The activities of some unscrupulous people have caused the general public to regard dog breeders in much the same light as they view second-hand car salesmen, estate agents and politicians; so,

while having ideals and principles may not take you to the top of the show world or improve your bank balance, they will hopefully ensure that people will want to buy your puppies rather than those of the get-rich-quick breeder who cuts corners.

Although many kennel clubs and dog clubs have Codes of Ethics, as yet most do not insist on breeding stock complying with any particular criteria as a condition of registering puppies. However, as the media and the Office of Fair Trading continue to investigate complaints by unhappy puppy purchasers, clubs will eventually be forced to take a more responsible attitude to breeding and will fall into line with their counterparts in other parts of the world. But you want to do what is right for this breed and your puppies, so you will do better than any club requires.

## WHEN?

You should not mate your bitch until she is over two years old, or until her third season, whichever is the later. Some bitches will have had more than three seasons by the time they are two, some will have had less, but Shepherds are slow to mature both physically and mentally so do not be in a hurry.

## TEMPERAMENT

If your bitch is of a nervous disposition, or if she is aggressive, do not mate her. Rearing a litter will not improve her character and she will pass her bad traits on to the puppies. An excitable or hyperactive bitch is not likely to make a good brood either.

## HIPS

Your bitch should have her hips X-rayed before you consider mating her. In Britain the Kennel Club and the British Veterinary Association jointly operate a 'scoring' scheme where the perfect score would be 0 for each hip and the worst 53 for each hip, giving a total of 106. Not many Shepherds have

perfect hips and so the GSD Breed Council's 'Breeders' Charter' includes bitches with a score of up to a total of 35, but obviously the lower the score the better, and, if nearing 35, you must seek a stud known to produce low scores. Australia and New Zealand also use a scoring system but other countries use a grading system for hips, details of which would be obtainable from vets, the Kennel Club or the main Breed Clubs of that country. X-raying and scoring is a costly business, but ask around until you find a vet with a good reputation for producing clear plates at a reasonable cost. It is false economy to breed from unscored stock, for nowadays the general public, who will form most of your purchasers, are swift to take legal action when things go wrong.

## TYPE

The best temperament and the best hips in the world will not compensate for lack of breed type. While your bitch does not have to be a show winner, she should at least look like a decent German Shepherd. Study the Breed Standard and compare your bitch.

## GENERAL HEALTH

Many bitches have an unfortunate habit of losing coat and condition when they are coming into season, but this is transitory. Is she normally healthy or do you spend a lot of time and money at your vet's? Carrying and rearing a litter require a strong physique and sound organs, so a veterinary check-up would be a good idea before proceeding.

## FACILITIES

If you are satisfied that your bitch will produce puppies that are an asset to this breed, there are practicalities to be considered. Where are you going to have the litter? It is lovely to have puppies in your living room for the first couple of weeks but after this it becomes impractical. A utility

*Temperament must be rated a top priority in a brood bitch.*        *Photo: Steph Holbrook.*

room or a conservatory (if shaded) is much better, but it needs to be large enough to accommodate the whelping box and still leave room for the bitch to get away from the pups when she needs to, and room for the pups to play when they are old enough to get out of the box.

You may decide to have the puppies in the garage or garden shed, but these may need a fair amount of converting to make them light, warm and draught-free. Wherever you decide to raise your litter, make sure that it is as far away from your neighbours as possible, for there is usually one puppy in a litter which aspires to be a canine Pavarotti and practises its vocal talents at break of day. This inspires its mates to join in the chorus and there is nothing more likely to upset your neighbours than an early awakening by yowling puppies, particularly if they think that you are making money at the expense of their beauty sleep.

REGISTERING A KENNEL NAME
If you still wish to proceed with your plan to mate your bitch, you should now decide if it is likely to be a one-only litter, in which case you will probably not want to go to the expense of registering a kennel name. If you want a kennel name you should apply before you mate the bitch, as it will take about three months for your Kennel Club to approve your choice. It may sound an easy exercise to choose a name under which to register all your future puppies but there are tens of thousands already belonging to other people and your selection must be different from any of these.

*The stud dog must be sound in mind and body.*

## SELECTING A STUD DOG

The choice of a stud dog for your bitch will not be easy. Ignore the man in the park who offers you a "free" mating to "prove" his dog in return for taking a puppy off your hands. The price of a puppy is worth more than a stud fee to his probably nondescript dog, and it is better to pay a stud fee for the dog most suited to your bitch.

So how to go about it? Study your copy of the Illustrated Breed Standard and note in which respects your bitch is lacking, or could be improved by the right choice of dog. Any tendency to over-compensate by using a male with the opposite fault must be avoided; so, if your bitch is over-long in the ratio of height to length, you will need a dog of correct proportions and not one that is too short and square. If she has a missing tooth you will need the services of a dog that has complete and correct dentition, and do not, as one novice did, use a dog with an extra tooth thinking that it would compensate in the puppies. When it comes to colour, remember that two black and gold parents cannot produce sable puppies – at least one parent must be a sable to do that. Temperament, type and hip-scores should always be more important than colour in your search for a stud dog but, as long as these things are right, it is better to choose a well-pigmented dog rather than one which, although more eye-catching, is rather "paled out".

Having decided where your bitch needs improving you now have to find the male which you hope will do that. The Breed Councils or main Breed Clubs in most countries produce Yearbooks and/or magazines in which stud dogs are advertised. In the UK the monthly GSD National Magazine and annual Survey/Yearbook is published by the GSD Breed Council and you should study the photos against your Standard – but keep in mind that cameras as well as advertisers do not always tell the plain, unvarnished truth. The comments of the Surveyors are far more accurate. You should also attend as many Breed Shows as possible in advance of the season on which you wish to mate your bitch. Buy a catalogue and if any of the exhibits (and not necessarily the winners) catch your eye as being near to the illustrations of the correct Shepherd type, make a note of the breeding. It would also be a good idea to attend a couple of Working Trials as well, because the working ability of the Shepherd should always be a consideration.

If you are lucky you will eventually have a reasonable selection of stud dogs which you think will physically suit your bitch. Some breeders say that "Like (be)gets like" and this is true to the extent that it is rare to get first-class offspring from two indifferent parents. Although the occasional "sport" will turn up as an exception to the rule, physical characteristics cannot be your only consideration; the pedigree must be taken into account.

"Incest-breeding", commonly called in-breeding, is the mating of a closely related dog and bitch, e.g. brother to sister, father to daughter. In-breeding should be avoided at all costs by the novice and, indeed, by the experienced breeder unless they know all there is to know about the common ancestors. In-breeding can quickly bring disaster but it is amazing how many newcomers contemplate doing it.

Line breeding is the mating of a dog and bitch who share a common ancestor further back on the pedigree. It is the less risky method providing you know something about the common ancestor; it is not much use line breeding to, say, a dog that gave soft ears! You will probably need help to learn about the dogs that make up the pedigree, and to extend it back beyond the usual three or four generation stud card. Some breeders think that once a dog is off the pedigree it ceases to exert its influence for good or bad, but this is not the case if there are many lines going back to it. Before proceeding, it is sensible to know what is off the written pedigrees of your bitch and her prospective mate.

## VISITING THE STUD DOG

Having whittled down your selection of stud dogs, you should arrange to visit them on their home ground. Dogs in the show ring are mostly well trained and what may pass for "attitude" may actually be hyperactivity, and the fast gait and pulling on the lead may mask a temperament problem. Most puppies are sold to pet homes, so it is your duty to use a dog with a calm and sensible character and, therefore, you must be able to see the dog at close quarters in his home environment.

There are certain practicalities to be discussed before you finally decide on the dog. How much is the stud fee? Will the owner give more than one mating? And, if the bitch "misses", will he give another mating at the next season without charge or argument? There are some stud dog owners who are most accommodating while there is a fee in the offing but, when a bitch has missed and returns at the next season for a free mating, they become rather less helpful.

## THE MATING

Immediately your bitch comes into season you should notify the stud's owner and hope that ovulation will take place on the "normal" day. This used to be considered as day eleven, twelve or thirteen from the start of the season, but a better indication is when the blood turns to a watery pink, if the bitch turns her tail to one side when you run your hand over her rump, and when the swelling of the vulva has gone down slightly but is still soft and pliable.

Vets and other experts will tell you that, if a bitch is ready for mating, she will willingly accept the stud dog's advances and the mating will take place naturally. This is just not true. Maiden bitches and, occasionally even a more experienced bitch, will often show strong objections to being mated. After all, the stud dog is your choice not hers, and she might well prefer the attentions of some scruffy old mongrel, so be prepared to spend a long time before deed is done.

Introduce her to the dog on the lead and then, if all is well, they can be allowed to romp together, but even if she is keen to be mated, do not be surprised if the dog's owner asks you to hold her head while he steadies her at the back end. Bitches have a habit of sitting down at the crucial moment, particularly if the dog is much heavier than they are. Talk quietly to her all the time the dog is feeling his way and hold tightly to her head when he penetrates her, for now his head will be just behind hers and she could easily take a piece out of his face. Some dog owners will want a fractious bitch to be muzzled to prevent damage to the dog, and you should keep your own face well out of the way because a quick movement from the bitch's hard head may mean a bloody nose or a black eye.

The dog's owner will know from experience if the dog has "tied" (when the glands of the penis have swollen and locked him inside the bitch) and when he is ready to be "turned". It is the dog's instinct to turn himself so that he is back to back with the bitch. It is said that this is so there is a set of teeth facing in each direction and they can

defend themselves if attacked when at their most vulnerable. Some young dogs are impetuous and try to turn before they are fully tied, which results in him slipping out and the semen ending on the ground instead of in the bitch. To avoid this happening the owner of the dog might just remove its front legs from where they are gripping the bitch and place them on the ground so that both animals are facing in the same direction. The owner must encourage the dog to stay in this position for as long as possible before allowing him to turn. Although this position is not so comfortable for the dog, and is at odds with his instincts, there is less risk of him slipping out. If the dog does slip out and the semen is lost, he should be rested for an hour or two before trying again.

It is not really necessary for a tie to take place in order for the bitch to conceive, but most owners prefer to see them tied. The tie can last from a few minutes up to an hour or more, so, if the bitch has been muzzled, the muzzle should be removed as soon as possible. However, you must continue to hold her head and reassure her, as she will soon become restless and try to pull away from the dog, which could injure him.

After they have come apart the dog may immediately try to remount her and, not unnaturally, she may object in no uncertain terms, so be ready to lead her away. Give her a drink and put her to rest in your car while you have a cup of tea with the owner and pay the fee. Remember that the stud fee is for the dog's services, so you must be prepared to pay before leaving. You should have already established what the owner intends to do in the event of a "miss", but it is as well to get this put on the receipt for your fee. Do not allow any other male dog to get near your bitch until well after her season has finished, because the fact that she has been mated will not deter other suitors.

## THE STUD DOG

The advice given so far has been for those who own a female, but there are many owners of male Shepherds who decide that they want to breed with their dogs and I get frequent enquiries on how to go about this.

Unless your dog has a good hip-score, a good temperament and has been blood-tested clear for Haemophilia "A" you should not consider using him at stud. If he meets these three basic requirements you must then ask yourself who is likely to want to use him on their bitch. Is he a well known show or Working Trials winner? If not, you will most likely find that only bitch owners who are breeding purely for profit would consider using him, and your dog's offspring may well fall into the wrong hands or become part of today's unwanted dog problem.

Your dog cannot be hip-scored until he is over twelve months and your vet will give you details. The haemophilia test can be done at any time, but it will be cheaper if you get the vet to take blood while he is doing the hips.

If you are still of the opinion that your dog would be an asset to the breed if he was used at stud, you will need to advertise or ask around for a bitch to "prove" him on, and this should be a steady bitch which has already produced puppies, been hip-scored of course, and with compatible blood-lines.

All owners of males are convinced that their dog is a natural stud and will automatically know what to do. Not true. Some are quite stupid and that is why your dog's first mating must be with an experienced bitch who will teach him, and you, what to do and when to do it. The reason that she should have already had a litter is that if she has not, you will not know if she is fertile and in the event of a "miss" you will not know if the cause is with him or with her.

His first mating must be on his own home ground in a spot where you cannot be overlooked by the neighbours. Do not be tempted to invite all and sundry to watch, as the dog will be put off and the conflicting advice, and the almost inevitable ribald remarks of your friends, will confuse him and you. Let both dog and bitch off lead to play together and she will indicate to him when play is over and the serious business starts. He will probably be extremely silly and try to mount her head. One dog I owned had a foot fetish and wanted to mate her front legs and it took a lot of persuasion from the bitch to get him round to the rear. Even when the dog is at the correct end he may still be stupid and try to enter the bitch everywhere but in the right place, but suddenly the penny drops and he will climb high on her back, clasping her tightly while starting to tread vigorously. If all goes well he will then enter the bitch, tie and turn as previously described.

Most maiden dogs do not wish to be handled during their first mating but you must accustom him to receiving help, in preparation for the occasions when an unwilling bitch is brought to him; so when you are sure that he and she are nicely tied, you should then link your arms around their hind legs, all the time telling him what a clever fellow he is. It is also a good time to allow the bitch's owner to approach and hold her head in order that the dog realises that a mating does not only involve doing what comes naturally.

It is customary not to charge a fee for a dog's first mating. The bitch's owner has risked losing six months out of her breeding life to allow your dog the chance to prove himself, so the most you should expect is "thank you". If the bitch does produce a litter to your dog, you may hope that her owner will offer you the opportunity of purchasing a puppy at a reduced charge – but be grateful if all you get is a bottle of Scotch. If you do expect financial reward for your dog's first efforts then this should be agreed in writing before the mating takes place.

After he has proved himself by producing puppies, you can then advertise him at stud, but, be warned, sometimes a dog that has had a bitch can change from a pleasant companion to a perfect nuisance. Stud work is not easy. Visiting bitches often scream and fight and then your neighbours object, and you need to be pretty strong to cope with a struggling bitch and hold up the dog and bitch together when the bitch is throwing herself all over the place! You will also need to have a spare kennel in case an owner wishes to leave a bitch with you in the event of her not being quite ready for mating.

The stud dog needs special care. He must receive a high-protein, good-quality food and be kept in hard condition by plenty of exercise. You should ask the owners of all visiting bitches to have their vet take a vaginal swab in case she has an infection which your dog could pass on to the next bitch. Following a mating, he should be washed with a mild antiseptic solution and, if there has not been time for the bitch to be swabbed, it might be a good idea to ask your vet to give him a course of antibiotics. All things considered, stud fees are not quite the money for old rope that they may seem on the surface.

## WHELPING AND REARING A LITTER

The normal length of a canine pregnancy is sixty-three days but Shepherds tend to be a couple of days early rather than late. These nine weeks will seem interminable. Is she or isn't she? Some bitches show that they have conceived within a couple of weeks, as much by their smug demeanour as by any physical change, while other bitches keep their secret until quite late in their pregnancy. A vet may be able to feel little "golf balls" at about three

weeks, and even make a fairly accurate guess at the number but, after this stage has passed, he may not be able to feel the whelps until after five weeks. If you really cannot wait until all is revealed by Nature, it is possible to have the bitch scanned and that will tell you fairly accurately how many pups there are.

## THE IN-WHELP BITCH

Many owners will worm the bitch at about five weeks but, if you have regularly wormed her from puppyhood, it should not be necessary to give her this extra stress. Exercise her as normal but do not let her indulge in rough play with other dogs. As the pregnancy progresses let her decide how much exercise she wants to take. She will not need extra food until the fifth week and, if she is on a good-quality complete food, resist the temptation to give additives like calcium. The complete foods are carefully researched and, if you add extras, you run the risk of doing more harm than good.

She will need a whelping box approximately four feet square, with three sides of 18 inches and one side in two removable sections of 9 inches to allow her easy access. There should be a ledge, or rail, about 12 inches from the top to stop her crushing the whelps against the side if one happens to crawl behind her. It is possible to buy a whelping box made of some kind of wipe-clean substance, some even have under-base heating, but they are expensive and I doubt that they could withstand the persistent teeth of a litter of GSD puppies. You will also need an infra-red heater because even on a warm summer night the pups can easily get chilled.

Once the whelping box is installed in the place where she is to give birth, let her spend part of each day getting used to it, because some bitches are worried by the lamp suspended approximately three feet over them. As the big day approaches, watch her carefully to ensure that she does not dig herself into an unsuitable hideaway where you cannot get at her. Nowadays, not many people have coal-bunkers, but if you have one you can be sure that this is where she will choose to make her nest rather than in the place you have so carefully prepared!

You should also contact your vet well before the due date to establish the procedure in the event of a problem occurring, e.g. Who will be on duty? Will they make a night call and, if not, which surgery will you need to go to?

## THE BIRTH

The equipment you will need is newspapers (as many as you can get), a bowl and medicated soap, kitchen scales, a notebook and pen, towels, Nutri-drops (an emergency form of nutrition for new-born pups – ask you vet for advice if these are not available in your area), nail-polish (for identification marks), a cardboard box, scissors, clean soft rag cut into squares, a plastic bin-bag, a low stool, and brandy – to revive pups if necessary and, if not necessary, you should drink it yourself, you will have earned it!

A puppy can survive even if born a full week prematurely but the nearer full term, the better the chances of survival. The bitch will probably become restless as the birth date nears and will start to tear up the newspaper lining the box, in a half-hearted fashion. You will be well advised to sleep on a camp bed near to her box for that last week "just in case", and for a few nights after the birth. If you gently squeeze one of her teats you may find that she has milk, but do not be concerned if she has not, as sometimes it will not come in until after all the pups have arrived.

There are some bitches who do not want human assistance but your bitch will be reassured by your presence and no domesticated animal should be left alone to get on with it. It was your choice to mate her and you must see it through with her. A drop in her temperature to around 98 degrees F will indicate that she will probably whelp within 48 hours and, as the birth becomes nearer, she will become more restless and the paper-tearing will become more frantic. She will puff and pant and lick herself and you will see faint tremors passing down her body. These tremors become contractions and you realise that labour has started.

After a while, if all is normal, there will suddenly be a lot of activity and wetness as the water bag presents and, shortly after, the bitch will push harder and there is your first puppy, still covered in the membrane and attached to the afterbirth. Most Shepherds are good whelpers and know instinctively what to do, but if your bitch fails to remove the pup from its bag and detach the afterbirth, you will need to do it for her. With clean hands remove the membrane and rub the pup quite firmly with a clean towel. This will stimulate the pup to protest and his squeaks will, hopefully, remind the bitch that there is important work to do. In the unlikely event that she still fails to bite the cord you must cut it yourself about three-quarters of an inch from the navel and, if it bleeds a great deal, you may have to bind it with thread (dental floss works well for this). Note the time, sex, and weight in your book and where you have placed the identifying spot of nail polish. Do not worry if the bitch eats the afterbirths. This is nature's way of providing sustenance because, in the wild, there would be no-one to bring her food during the early days when she is unable to leave the puppies.

The birth of the following pups will cause the early ones to become wet again, so some breeders advocate placing each whelp in the cardboard box on a covered hot-water bottle until the whole litter has arrived. If your bitch does not like her pups being placed in the box, do not proceed, but wait until she is occupied with the next birth and then gently move the others to one side. If they do get wet again rub them with a dry towel. Between births offer mum a drink of warm milk sweetened with glucose. If any of the arrivals fail to take breath, you must clear the nose and mouth of mucus, give a vigorous rubbing with a towel and put a spot of brandy on the tongue. If you cannot revive the pup, discreetly wrap the body in paper and put it somewhere where the bitch cannot see it until you have the chance to dispose of it properly.

After the whelping take the bitch out to urinate but be sure to accompany her in case she produces a late arrival outside. Replace all the wet newspapers with clean ones and offer her another drink. See that she is settled and comfortable and the pups are all feeding. Give Nutri-drops to any pups which appear weak or dozy and note which they are from your identifying marks of nail polish. You should sleep on your camp bed for the first few nights; your quiet presence will ensure that your bitch does not become worried by her new responsibilities and, perhaps, tread on a puppy in her agitation.

## THE NOT-SO-NORMAL BIRTH

All whelpings are different and not all are normal. The length of time between the arrival of pups varies but, if nothing happens after an hour, yet you are certain that there are more pups to follow, you must keep a close eye on her. If she is having contractions there may be a puppy in the breech position (hindfeet first). If you can see the pup's hindfeet then it is a breech birth, and you may be able to assist by soaping your fingers and inserting them in the vagina and gently easing out the puppy at a downward angle at the same time as the bitch has her next contractions. Do not pull.

If the contractions have produced nothing after two hours and you cannot see or feel

feet, then it is possible that there is a puppy stuck high up in the birth canal and you should phone the vet. It may be nothing to worry about, but it is for your vet to decide if a caesarean is needed at this stage. It is better to have a caesarean than risk losing the remaining pups and, perhaps, the mother also. If a bitch stops at one or two pups but the contractions are weak, or non-existent, she may have uterine inertia and, again, you must contact your vet, who will decide if an injection of oxytocin will get things going again.

A bitch who has puppies by caesarean has not experienced the birth process and, sometimes, when she comes out of the anaesthetic she is shocked to find these little strangers occupying her bed. Before she is fully awake, squeeze some of her milk on to the pups and do not take your eyes off her until all the pups are feeding and you are sure that she has accepted them as hers. After a caesarean a bitch is usually able to feed the pups but care must be taken that they do not aggravate the wound.

## AFTER THE BIRTH

Call in your vet, who will check to see that there are no more pups to come and no afterbirths left behind. He will probably administer an antibiotic. The vet will examine the pups for cleft palates and other deformities. Hind dewclaws are fairly rare these days but, if present, the vet will probably decide to remove them at about three days. You should draw his attention to any weak puppies and heed his advice about them. There is a difference between a small puppy with a strong will to live which may be pushed off the nipple by its larger litter mates, and the dozy puppy which refuses to stay on the nipple and/or which the mother continually nudges away. The small, vigorous puppy will probably flourish with your help to reach the nipple, but it is distressing for the mother, and for you, if you continually try to force the dozy ones to suck and they will probably die in spite of all your efforts. Your vet may well suggest culling and you should be guided by him.

During the first twenty-four hours after the end of whelping, the bitch should not be given solids but plenty of water, preferably boiled and then cooled. After this she can resume her high-protein food plus a daily addition of some low-fat natural yoghurt. Six or seven puppies are quite enough for a bitch to rear in her first litter so, if there are more, you should help out by the use of a formula made for just this purpose, giving each pup a little to alternate with their turn on the nipple. This is a better idea than feeding some totally on the powdered milk and the others totally on mother.

### ORPHANED PUPS

It is possible to hand-rear orphaned pups on the bottle but it requires two-hourly feeds night and day, plus stimulating the pups to pass urine and to have bowel movements. It is very time-consuming and extremely tiring, but you must be prepared to do it if you plan on breeding your dog. In the terrible event that your bitch dies, you should contact your vet and your local breed club immediately. One of them may know of an available foster

mother. Conversely, if you lose all, or most of your litter, you should notify the same people that you have a foster mother available.

### FROM BIRTH TO SELLING

After the first few days the pups should be put on synthetic bedding. This will keep them clean and sweet-smelling, but remember to change the newspaper underneath frequently, as the urine goes through and the paper becomes just as wet and unpleasant as newspaper used alone.

Your friends and neighbours will want to see the new arrivals but it is not fair to the new mother to allow all and sundry to disturb her. It is also not safe for the pups.

At the end of the first week phone your Kennel Club and take care of the paperwork you need to register your litter.

### TOENAILS

At ten days cut the pups' toenails. Just remove the little 'hooks' from the end of each nail to prevent them making the bitch sore, and continue to do this weekly. Their eyes will begin to open anytime now and you may begin to notice that some of the coats are of a different texture and some of the heads look a different shape. Note which these are, as they may be long-coats.

*Weaning can be a messy business...*
*Photo: Steve Nash.*

*...It is not long before the pups get the idea.*
*Photo: Steve Nash.*

*During the weaning process, the puppies will still suckle from their mother.
Photo: Alan Jones.*

*Most German Shepherd bitches enjoy playing with their puppies.
Photo: Alan Jones.*

*A puppy-run is a useful item of equipment as it keeps the puppies safe, and the mother is free to come and go.
Photo: Alan Jones.*

## WORMING

Most pups have worms even if you do not see evidence of them, but if you have followed a worming regime for your bitch since puppyhood the infestation should not be too heavy. Nevertheless, you must worm the litter between two and three weeks after their birth, either with a preparation from your vet or a tried and tested proprietary product. They will need to be wormed again at four to five weeks and at seven to eight weeks.

## WEANING

If the dam starts to regurgitate partly digested food, do not be alarmed; this is her way of weaning the pups and, once you take over, she will stop this rather revolting but totally natural process. These days very few breeders use the scraped meat / milk / biscuit / vitamin-additive method, so, assuming that you will use a complete food formulated especially for puppies, choose a premium brand, but stick to one that can be easily obtained by your puppy buyers, because the puppies should not have to face a change of diet at the same time as the trauma of going to a new home. A complete food does not need additives, but the inclusion of a small amount of low-fat natural yoghurt is very beneficial to their digestive systems and will keep their motions firm.

Weaning is a gradual process so, unless it is a very small litter, you should start it at about three weeks. The puppies will need four meals a day and it is easier if you move the bitch away for half an hour before each meal, putting her back after they have finished. You must watch the pups feed to see that they are all getting their share, and to make sure that none of them vomits after eating solids, because, if this happens to a puppy more than once or twice, it may indicate a problem with the oesophagus.

*The puppies learn social skills while playing with each other.*
*Photo: Alan Jones.*

At four weeks the mother will be away from the pups half the day, at five weeks she is away all day and back at night, and at six weeks she will be away from them all night as well. There is no harm in letting her visit them for short periods if she wants; they will still try to suckle from her – she will not stay long.

## SOCIALISING

Once the pups have their eyes fully open and are starting to climb out of the box, visitors should be welcomed as part of the very important early socialising, but only if you are sure that they have not been in contact with other dogs. It is surprising how many adults will casually drop a pup on to the floor when it wriggles, so never leave visitors unattended with your litter. Children are great for socialising but they can be clumsy, so do not allow them to play with the pups unless closely supervised, nor should they be allowed to hold the pups unless they are sitting on the floor. Puppies that have early contact with children usually grow up to be totally trustworthy with them and there is no nicer sight than a child with a Shepherd. Normal household noises like washing machines and vacuum cleaners are all part of socialising, so allow the pups some time in the house, if possible.

## SELECTING YOUR PUPPY

If you intend to keep a puppy for yourself you will not make your final choice until the litter is eight weeks old but, from the time they start getting out of the box, you should be watching them very carefully. If one particularly catches your eye, note which one it is from its identifying spot of nail polish and, if this same puppy keeps impressing you as you watch them at play, then it is probably the one you should keep. Some breeders spend hours pushing and pulling puppies

*In no time, individual personalities become apparent.*

into a show stance, but it is better to make your choice from how the puppy looks naturally. Until you are more experienced, it is as well to ask the stud dog's owner, or some other knowledgeable person, if he agrees with your choice.

From about four weeks onwards you may be able to tell if the pups you thought had different textured coats are actually long-coats. It can be quite difficult to be certain, as the hair of a puppy which will end up with the luxuriant coat much favoured by exhibitors is not much different in length from that of the puppy which will grow to be long-coated.

## ADVERTISING AND SELLING

You should notify your breed club that you have puppies for sale. You should also

*A beautifully reared litter, ready to go to their new homes. Photo: Steph Holbrook.*

advertise in the canine press. Do not advertise in the regular newspapers. State the name of the sire and dam, their qualifications if any, and their hip scores. Give the date of birth of the pups, their colours and sexes and your name, address and telephone number. Do not make exaggerated claims. Do not ask inflated prices, but neither should you sell too cheaply.

You should be prepared to answer any questions – but it is just as important for you to question the would-be purchasers and so establish their suitability to own a Shepherd. Ask them to visit more than once and to bring all the immediate family. Never sell to a husband who wants a pup as a surprise present for his wife (or vice versa) as it is more likely to be a shock. Do not sell at Christmas time. Do not sell to flat dwellers unless they are on the ground floor and have access to a garden, and ask if the landlord permits pets.

You must let them see the mother with the pups, but note their reaction to the dam. If, for any reason, you have doubts, then do not be afraid to say that you have changed your mind about selling. You must state quite clearly what the price includes – for example, if you are insuring the pups or having the first inoculation done – but do not allow the purchaser to haggle on the price. It is as well to stress that Shepherd puppies are very destructive if left to their own devices and to warn purchasers with children that the first teeth are like needles and that the pup will "mouth" a lot until the second teeth are

through. Be honest about which puppies are pet quality and which have potential show quality. And be firm about which should not be bred.

## HAEMOPHILIA TESTING AND TATTOO MARKING

At six weeks the male pups will be big enough to have their haemophilia tests, which you can arrange through your vet. Tattoo marking in the ear should be done before the puppies leave you for their new homes, so ask the tattooist to call on you when they are seven weeks old. Some pups will make a little fuss, some hardly notice the momentary pain, but so many lost dogs have been reunited with their owners because of their tattoo number that it is really worth having done.

## TIME TO GO

Your puppies will be ready to leave for their new homes when they are eight weeks old. They should take with them a bag of food, an information sheet which gives full details of the diet, worming, and training classes etc, and a folder containing pedigree, registration certificate, haemophilia certificates (males only), tattoo certificate, and a receipt for the purchase price. If there has been a hold-up with any of the documents, you should put on the receipt that these are to follow. Follow up your pups with regular phone calls during the first few weeks, and encourage your buyers to call you with any questions.

# 11 BEST OF BRITISH

That the German Shepherd Dog has grown significantly in popularity over the last twenty-five years is not in doubt. The Kennel Club registration figures underline the fact. In 1972 Kennel Club registrations for the breed numbered 15,078. By 1996 the figure had soared to an impressive 25,690. And this at a time when the two main rivals of the breed in the working group, the Doberman and the Rottweiler, showed a decrease in the number of dogs registered over the same period.

## DIVERGENCE IN TYPE

But the last quarter of a century has been significant for other reasons too. Inevitably,

some old-established kennels have disappeared and new ones emerged. This period has seen closer contacts between breeders and enthusiasts here and those abroad, particularly in Germany. It has seen the development of two distinct types of German Shepherd in the UK, each with its own staunch adherents. It has seen important advances in measures to deal with hereditary diseases and the introduction of breed surveys. Fashionable stud dogs have predominated for a time, then lost influence as others emerged. But behind it all are people. A breed's evolution in a country like the UK is not shaped by an influential group or a strong individual as in Germany, where

*Ch. Laios van Noort: German bloodines have become increasingly significant in the UK.*

the president of the SV has enormous influence over which males are promoted as future studs; it is determined by the innumerable decisions made by large numbers of individual and independent breeders, all 'doing their own thing'.

But the freedom enjoyed by breeders here and the relative lack of any directing control over breeding decisions, means that breed development will be an unpredictable matter and very much influenced by the vagaries of chance and fashion. It is here that the impact of judges is important: they will elevate certain animals in the show ring and breeders will attempt to breed dogs that will satisfy the current crop of judges. Over the last two decades or so, many breed judges have interpreted the Breed Standard in line with that of breed experts in Germany, the home of the German Shepherd. Other judges have avoided such influences, preferring their own, often idiosyncratic, interpretations. This has resulted in the "two types" controversy. Most breed clubs organise shows and invite judges that will attract the type of Shepherd satisfying the requirements of the international expert whose understanding of the standard is based upon the SV blue-print. A small number of breed clubs and a significant number of all-breed shows promote the so-called British type or 'Alsatian'.

At the beginning of the 70s such a split in the breed did not exist. Crufts Dog Show attracted a large entry from the breed as a whole, irrespective of which judges officiated. Today, the same show will attract one type or the other depending on the judges. In 1971 Ch. Ramacan Swashbuckler, a product of mostly 'British' breeding based on the Lindsays' well-established Brinton bloodlines, went Best in Show, while the Bitch CC winners, Ch. Karenville Ophelia CD Ex., was the daughter of a German import.

## KENNELS OF THE 70s

During the early 70s a number of long-established kennels were beginning to fade in importance. Mrs Barrington's famous Brittas kennels, based in Co. Meath, Ireland had dominated bloodlines immediately before and after the Second World War. Her kennels produced many outstanding dogs including several international Champions. She herself was a personal friend of Herta von Stephanitz, the daughter of the breed's founder. Her breeding proved the foundation of many successful kennels including Letton, Kentwood, Vikkas av Hvitsand, and Southhaven. The Brittas kennel was one of the few that developed a recognisable type. Mrs Barrington's breeding programme was based on judicious line-breeding within her own family. She rarely used fashionable winners from the mainland such as the top sires Ch. Avon Prince of Alumvale and Ch. Ludwig of Charavigne, preferring occasional infusions of fresh 'blood' from Germany. A similar uniformity of family type was evident in the Kentwood dogs over several generations, and in the Letton animals that were more immediately based on Brittas foundations.

## INFLUENTIAL SHOW DOGS

The 60s had been dominated by the influence of the popular show dog Int. Ch. Asoka Cherusker and by the offspring of Ch. Ludwig of Charavigne. Bred by Peggy Litton from a Vikkas-bred Ch. Avon Prince daughter, Asoka Cherusker had a dazzling career in the ring handled by one of the few successful professional handlers of the time, Eric Gerrard. Cherusker bore no resemblance whatsoever to his sire or dam, which makes it more surprising that he was able to stamp his own general appearance upon so many of his offspring. A richly pigmented, lavishly coated, very well angulated dog, he dominated every class he entered through sheer showmanship. He produced very good forehand angulation but some short front legs and over-deep briskets, together with some looseness in ligaments. He produced 13 CC winning progeny, 11 of whom achieved a Championship title throughout the sixties.

Ch. Ludwig was to prove the other successful sire during this period. Mrs Iris Dummett of the Charavigne kennels, breeder of Ch. Dante before the Second World War, had made visits to the German Sieger Show with a mere handful of enthusiasts at that time and eventually imported Cent v.d. Fünf Giebeln, a very rich red-tan and black dog who passed this striking colour to his son, Ludwig, which in part accounted for the latter's show popularity. He, like Cherusker, was also out of an Avon Prince mother, Halla of Charavigne, and inherited the erect 'showy' carriage from that side of his pedigree. The German influence shortened his general proportions somewhat and gave good length of foreleg. Ludwig produced twenty Champions who won 101 challenge certificates so that his genetic influence was widespread.

The Brinton kennels of Brian and Dorothy Lindsay mated Vanity of Brinton, a daughter of their good bitch, Happy of Charavigne, who was altogether better balanced than her litter sister, Halla, to Cherusker and produced Ch. Archer and Ch. Ailsa of Brinton. Ailsa was an excellent animal of correct type who won a Res. CC under Dr Funk, the then president of the SV and breeder of the famous Haus Schutting Shepherds – proof positive, along with other examples, such as Ch. Allegro of Seacroft and Ch. Empress of Peadron, that the best animals produced by 'British' lines could satisfy foreign experts. Ch. Archer went on to perpetuate the Cherusker influence, while that of Ch. Avon Prince was still transmitted through Hella (Ludwig) and Happy.

Ch. Archer was the second most-used dog

of his time, siring 183 litters with six CC winners. His influence was strong during the 70s through the use of his son, Ch. Vondaun Ulric of Dawnway and later by Ch. Ramercon Swashbuckler who was line-bred to Archer. Like Archer, Swashbuckler was widely used, producing five Champions, including the top-winning Ch. Spartacist of Hendrawen who won 35 CCs and was a popular stud. Spartacist carried four lines to Archer, though his dam was by a German import. Many of the so-called 'British' type of animal shown today have several lines going back to Spartacist. The top-winning Lornaville kennel, in particular, has perpetuated the extravagant proportions and angulation of this line in their current Champions.

Ch. Ludwig's influence was to persist through the 70s via his grandson Hendrawen's Charade of Charavigne, who in turn produced the well-known winning Champion Eclipse of Eveley for May Tidbold, whose Eveley kennels had been continuously successful throughout the late 50s and 60s. Mrs Tidbold always demanded 'glamour' in her show-stock and, whatever their anatomical limitations, the Eveley dogs were always flashy and colourful.

GENETIC BOTTLENECK

Eclipse carried no fewer than ten lines back to Ch. Avon Prince and typified the prevailing problem at that time – too much amassing of that famous dog's name at the back of many pedigrees. Eclipse and Spartacist embodied the prevailing fashion of the day: the picture was of an over-long dog with extreme length of neck and stifle, tending toward exaggeration but presenting an impressive picture when manipulated into an artificial show pose. Eclipse produced five Champions, including Ch. Tarquin of Dawnway who possessed his sire's rich colouring and glamour. Tarquin was to be held up as a model by those breeders who found little to like in what was emerging as a type more akin to that demanded by German judges.

The growing number of animals of a less exaggerated construction, with greater emphasis placed on general firmness and gait, was a feature of the 70s and 80s. More of our judges were visiting the annual Sieger show, and German judges officiated far more regularly in British rings. Their awards and gradings were highly coveted by breeders aiming for a more 'International' type without the excesses produced by the concentration of Avon Prince – Archer – Ludwig – Spartacist lines.

INTRODUCING NEW LINES
To avoid that genetic bottleneck, breeders needed new lines and thankfully a handful of breeders had quietly worked to provide them. Nem and Percy Elliot of the Vikkas av Hvitsand kennels played an important role in this respect. They had visited Germany regularly since the early 60s and were zealous advocates of the merits of Shepherds produced in the homeland of the breed. In the 60s they imported Ilk von Eschbacher Klippen and Dux von Braunschweigerland and though, like many imports, their influence was not so positive in their immediate progeny, they are to be found in many pedigrees throughout this period through the widespread use of the Ilk grandson Int. Ch. Rossfort Premonition and of the Dux descendant Ch. Delridge Erhard, both top winners in their day.

When Molly Hunter of the Rossfort kennels brought out Premonition, a young black and red-tan puppy at the BAA Championship show in 1969 to win best puppy under Herr Steenbock of Germany, many admired him but probably few could predict how important a part he was to play in breed development over the decade ahead.

Although his dam, Vondaun Belissima of Brinton, was bred from the rather lengthy, low-legged Archer line, the influence of Ilk and of the other import in his pedigree, Roon von den Sieben Faulen, gave him more correct proportions. He was successful under a variety of judges including Dr Rummel, the then President of the SV, who awarded him the CC and graded him excellent at the BAA Championship show in 1975. He won 27 CCs and sired 276 litters in Britain before being exported to New Zealand, producing 14 Champions here and 21 in New Zealand.

His popularity as a stud was in part due to the fact that more breeders were aiming at a firmer, less exaggerated type while still retaining the 'glamour' associated with the established British show lines. A significant shift in perception of what constituted good type was developing, and the 1970s saw the separation of the breed into two camps: those wishing the British Shepherd to evolve more closely to the pattern set in Germany and those who, for a variety of reasons, resisted such a development.

OPENING UP THE BLOODLINES
Oddly, a decision made on the other side of the world in 1974, was to have considerable repercussions on breed development here. In that year the Australian Government lifted a ban on the importation of German Shepherd Dogs. There was obviously a market there for someone to exploit and one commercially astute enthusiast, Malcolm Griffiths, of the Bedwins' kennels did just that. He was one of the first breeders to realise the potential of a quarantine kennel on his own premises and, importantly, to forge close contacts with Germany. He could import and export to considerable advantage. In so doing he was to bring several dogs into Britain that played a great influence in kennels up and down the country. Interest in German sires increased as more and more people visited the German

Sieger Show and studied the bloodlines there. A brief look at some of the more successful kennels of the last decade or so later in this chapter will reveal how important a foundation of imported bloodlines was.

After Ch. Rossfort Premonition's departure for New Zealand in 1975 he left the breed fairly well saturated with his blood. There seemed few alternative studs available that did not carry the Cherusker – Archer – Vondaun lines or the Ludwig influence through Eclipse. Progressive breeders wished to avoid an over-concentration of these lines. Fortunately a young male appeared with the masculinity and type that appealed. Ch. Delridge Erhard attained his title in 1976 and though he carried one line back to Archer, he was strongly influenced by his line-breeding on the Elliot's import, Dux von Braunschweigerland. Both British and foreign judges appreciated him and he won 23 CCs in all, siring nine Champions. Although Erhard was an outstanding dog, he did not prove as dominant a sire as Premonition had been, his progeny being rather varied in type. His most famous son, Ch. Royvons Red Rum, who won 46 CCs, was widely used by breeders preferring the 'British' type, and sired six Champions.

## CITO VON KONIGSBRUCH

If the 70s had been dominated by Premonition and his descendants, the 80s were to see the emergence of an imported male who was to prove the most widely used dog in the history of the breed in Britain. Paul Bradley, of the Vornlante kennel, purchased a young dog, Cito von Konigsbruch, after watching him gain a good placing in the youth class at the Sieger show in 1980 where he finished 18th. Paul writes: "I remember standing at the side of the ring on the Friday, I was really taken by this dog, he impressed me by his rhythm of movement and his absolute firmness and dryness of body. Totally a one piece dog that demanded your attention."

He achieved his title in May 1982 and it became clear from his first puppies that breeders would see in him a stud who could produce the 'International' type that many were seeking. As a son of the important German sire, Nick von der Wienerau, he was bred to breed on. He produced 17 Champions and very many consistent Championship winners. Like Premonition before him, his blood dominates the pedigrees of his era. Most of the current producing males have Cito somewhere behind them. The Vornlante kennel, having established its reputation with Ch. Cito, continued to enjoy success, particularly with the quarantine-born Ch. Catja of Vornlante, the CC record holder for bitches in the UK. Catja is behind the Scottish Champion Cotchees Digger and Ch. Peterwell Wasp among others.

## THE ROTHICK KENNELS

In recent years several relatively new kennels have gained prominence in the show-ring. Most of them have based their breeding on contemporary successful German bloodlines.

In the mid-70s Audrey Ringwald of the Rothick kennels imported the bitch, Esta v.d. Maiwiese, in whelp to the VA German sire Gundo von der Klosterbogen. One male, Ezra, remained in her kennel and was hardly shown. A litter brother, Echo, was purchased by the Sandersons in Lancashire who exhibited him extensively with fair success. Ezra was subsequently mated to Mrs Ringwald's other imported bitch, Mona v. Adeloga, with line breeding on the outstanding stud and pillar of the modern breed in Germany, Quanto von der Wienerau. A resulting male, Invictor, achieved his title. As his breeding suggested, he excelled in forehand angulation, a feature which most breeders of the time feared was deteriorating in many animals.

Invictor was used successfully by the Iolanda kennels, siring Ch. Iolanda Britta. Invictor's sister, Ilona, was the foundation bitch of the Frabern kennels in Northern Ireland. Mated to the excellent producing bitch Ch. Judamie Nevada, he produced Ch. Kemjon Biene who, in turn, was the dam of the excellent Int. Ch. Kemjon Lex. Interestingly, Nevada was a daughter of the imported Barry vom Status Quo, a widely used, unshown import brought into the country by Malcolm Griffiths and subsequently exported to Australia. The Kemjon kennel mated Ch. Nevada to Rothik Atilla, which resulted in Ch. Kemjon Inca. The Kemjon success underlines the importance of a good brood bitch to a kennel.

Nevada seemed to 'click' with the Rothick males and this was doubtless in part due to the fact that both Invictor and Nevada were grandchildren of Gundo von Klosterbogen. Sensible line breeding paid off. A repeat mating of the Rothick 'I' litter produced Vinobe who, though not widely used, sired two excellent Champion offspring in Ch. Labrasco Paco and Ch. Deshwar Marshadesh of Nidebed. Paco himself came from a kennel whose success was founded on an outstanding bitch, Ch. Labrasco Chico, a Premonition daughter, whose son by Barry Status Quo, Labrasco Fidelio, was also to prove a useful sire during this period in the Longvale and Janshar kennels.

## THE KURTRIDGE KENNEL

Another kennel that enjoyed outstanding success from a dominant brood bitch was the Midland Delridge establishment. Breeder Beryl Budd was lucky to have bred Delridge Camilla, the dam of Ch. Erhard and his very good brother Echo, subsequently exported to Australia where he gained his title. Mated to Ch. Druidswood Consort she produced Ch.

Delridge Indigo and a good sister, Iona. Iona was mated to her half-brother, Echo and the result was Kurtlee Minnesota of Delridge, bred jointly with Margaret Lee, who owned Erhard. Minnesota, inbred to Camilla, was to prove herself an outstanding brood bitch in Australia, where she, together with Fairycross Clickety Click, a Scottish-bred Erhard daughter, founded the top Australian Karlrach kennel from which came many outstanding winners down under. Camilla was also the dam of Australian Ch. Delridge Joll and his good Res. CC-winning sister, Jola, who did not seem to prove as good a producer as the inbred Minnesota.

For a while the kennel went into abeyance but found a new direction after Beryl Budd and Margaret Lee amalgamated their kennels to form the new prefix of Kurtridge. Once again they were fortunate, as were so many breeders at this time to profit from imports brought in by other people. In their case they managed to purchase the quarantine-bred Greenstan Elkie, a granddaughter of the outstanding German sire, Uran v. d. Wildsteigerland. Elkie was a born show girl and won her title in 1989.

In mating her they looked for a substantial male from the Quando v. Arminius line which they knew had suited Uran bitches in Germany. In her first litter she produced the good winning Ch. Kurtridge Quando, purchased by the Videx kennel and exhibited in their ownership. The dam of Elkie was then taken back to Germany to be mated to the full-brother of Elkie's sire. A bitch from this mating, Greenstar Otti, has produced well in the Kurtridge kennel, being the dam of Ch. Kurtridge Dino and the good male Kurtridge Joll, a dog of grand character who already has two offspring working as guide dogs. Currently the kennel has progeny based on Elkie and Otti, both of whom have produced Champion sons – a good foundation for future progress.

*Ch. Novem Volka (Zack v. Adeloga – Novem Xenia).*

*Ch. Novem Adagio of Silkenwood (Arko v. Huhnergrab – Novem Xenia).*

### THE NOVEM KENNEL

The Novem kennel, owned by George Woods, is one of the oldest in the breed today. It housed the sable Champion Riot of Rhosincourt who won two CCs at Crufts, beating Ch. Avon Prince of Alumvale in the 50s. Later, during the Ludwig 'boom', it made up his son Ch. Takleway Rock of Novem, and, using Premonition, bred the lovely Ch. Novem Bolero. Recently it has achieved success based on imported

producing bitches. From Xenja v.d. Baiertalestrasse came Novem Xenia, a good bitch who needed slightly more length of foreleg. Mated to Zack v. Adeloga for improvement in this respect she produced the good Champion Novem Volka.

Later George saw the outstanding bitch Kindi v. Haus Beck at the Bygolly kennel of Sue Hadley. He knew she was just the bitch he needed for Volka but she was not for sale. Using his considerable powers of persuasion he managed to buy a share in the bitch and the Volka mating was effected. George's intuition proved sound, for the result was the beautiful Music Man of Novem who, unfortunately, was not campaigned in the show ring but who could certainly have made his title. Music Man sired Ch. Kurtridge Dino. Xenia was then mated to a similar large, scopy male, the Quando v. Arminius son, Arko v. Huhnergrab, imported by the Bedwins kennel. The result was Ch. Novem Adagio of Silkenwood, a good winner and popular stud who sired the consistent Ch. Middross Xaver, and the excellent Ch. Copybush Quant.

### CH. SHOTAANS BIANCA

While watching a class of the heavy, low-legged type being judged at a Championship show in Wales, I saw a young bitch of quite different type discarded with the also-rans. I advised her owner to show her under judges who valued the 'international' type of Shepherd. He did so with considerable success and she eventually became Ch. Shotaans Bianca, Best of Breed at Crufts. She was subsequently bred from and produced excellent animals in practically every litter which strongly mirrored her type. Similar uniformity of type emanated from the Cito daughter Karikburg Barbel at Amondahl, resulting in bitch Champion Melissa for the Amondahl prefix, strongly mirroring her type.

## MOONWINDS

The Moonwinds kennel, owned by Pam Meaton, enjoyed consistent success through the 80s making judicious use of the best contemporary German bloodlines. Here again the importance of a good producing bitch was evident. Miss Hopkins, Pam's assistant at Moonwinds, had managed the famous Rozavel kennels for Thelma Gray. The latter had appreciated some of the bitches produced by the import Derby v.d. Schinklergrenze and from him bred the all-black dog, Rob Roy of Rozavel. He was to sire an excellent, strong vigorous bitch in Moonwinds Golden Showers, who was an important foundation for later success. Mated to Emmevale Zaroff, himself from a German sire line to Archer bitch breeding, Showers produced Ch. Moonwinds Golden Cumulus, whose litter sister Cloudburst was mated to Ch. Cito. This mating gave Ch. Moonwinds Golden Harrier and her sister Ch. Moonwinds Golden Mirage. These good animals all showed the influence of Showers in their general appearance.

Mated to the German sire Eiko v. Kirschental, Mirage was the dam of the litter brothers Ch. Moonwinds Golden Mahdi, who sired Ch. Moonwinds Fanta and Ch. Moonwinds Golden Emir. The Moonwinds kennel continues to explore the potential of modern German sires and are probably looking for another Golden Showers, with whom they certainly struck gold.

## EVOLUTION IN TYPE

During the period under review the Amulree kennel in Scotland, now re-established in Belgium, demonstrated the evolution in type that was evident in most 'progressive' kennels. During the early 70s their breeding was based on the prevailing Ludwig – Archer bloodlines which they soon realised were not going to yield the type they sought. Two bitch Champions were the outcome at that

*Ch. Amulree's Heiko: Winner of 47 CCs. Photo: Jack Oliver.*

time but Isobelle and Harry Anderson were determined to do better. Using Premonition lines they produced the outstanding show dog Ch. Amulree's Heiko who won 47 CCs – a testimony to his appeal to all judges, both British and foreign. Heiko was not widely used but did produce four Champions.

A clear indication of the Andersons' determination to improve type was the purchase of Rintilloch Havoc of Amulree, a daughter of Emmevale Zaroff who exhibited his virtues of correct proportions and pronounced withers. Heiko was mated to Havoc, who had gained her title, and produced his best son, Ch. Amulree's Hassan, who was very much like his dam in type. Often the animals that resembled Heiko were inclined to be too low-legged and deep.

In recent years the Andersons have consolidated type by using good imported sires and by sending their best bitches to be mated in Germany. Using Ch. Cito they bred the good sable Ch. Amulree's Sindy, and a Cito son, Ch. Longvale Octavius, gave them the excellent Ch. Amulree's Tisn't. She was mated to Tony v.d. Wienerau, a son of the Sieger Zamb v.d. Wienerau and produced Amulree's Tulyar whose son, Josalka Barracuda, has one CC at the time of writing and looks a certain Champion. A litter sister to Tulyar is the dam of Ch. Markoy Eiko at Jemness. Another excellent Tisn't son, Amulree's Ideal, was a very promising youngster and would probably have earned a title had he not been killed in an unfortunate road accident.

Other excellent Scottish kennels include: Jonal, who produced two good male Champions from Cito breeding in Ch. Jonal Basko and his son, Ch. Xaran of Jonal; the Stanhope kennel, breeders of Ch. Kassi; the Cotchees' kennel, based on modern imports, who bred Ch. Cotchees Digger; and the Graloch kennels, who have sustained a home-bred bitch line over several generations culminating in the good male, Ch. Graloch Domingo.

## THE VIKKAS KENNEL

The late Nem Elliot and her husband, Percy, having had great success with Brittas-bred bitches after the war (they made up the first Champion in peace-time), shared Mrs Barrington's understanding of the Shepherd as a natural, balanced, workman-like animal without exaggerations. Their Vikkas kennel has continued to be influential throughout the last twenty-five years. Many successful kennels were founded on bitches bred by the Elliots including Takleway, Asoka, Rossfort, Jacnel, Ronet, Delridge, Norwulf, Letton, Mynstonmoor, Sheracyn, Innsbrook and several others.

As regular visitors to the German Sieger Show since the mid-60s, the Elliots followed a policy of importing young sons of outstanding sires, thus making available alternative bloodlines to the British breeder. To promote these dogs in the early days, when they seemed markedly different in type from the popular show dog, Nem and Percy had to quietly and persistently attempt to school the eye – of those prepared to see – to the virtues of their imports. Thus began that shift of perception that has resulted in a generally correct type now being exhibited at most specialist German Shepherd Shows. Percy Elliot, as a successful dog and pigeon breeder, takes pride in being a practical stockman; show ring reputation comes second to the fascination and challenge of breeding. Many good Vikkas dogs have not been campaigned or were retired after initial wins, but they have been available as stud dogs to those who wished to take advantage of Percy's experience.

*Vikkas Rasputin: One of a long line of top-quality Shepherds.*

*Sagaro Xigi.*
*Photo: Jack Oliver.*

*Ch. Sagaro Gobi.*

## THE SAGARO KENNEL

In recent years young kennels have emerged to produce dogs that fulfil the exacting standards of both British and German judges. It is to their credit that SV judges assert that our best dogs could compete with the best on the Continent successfully.

Adrian and Jill Miller founded their Sagaro Kennel in 1983. Adrian's father was a bookmaker and keen racing man, who won enough money on the triple Ascot Gold Cup winner Sagaro during the seventies to buy

their first Shepherd dog – hence the prefix! Within eleven years the Sagaro kennel attained the pinnacle of show ring success by winning both dog and bitch Challenge Certificates at the Two-Day National show in 1994, with home-bred and trained Shepherds. Yet again the story is of intelligent enthusiasts benefiting from the importing done by others. The Millers had appreciated animals produced by Gundo v.d. Mordschau out of Alf v.d. Quengelbach daughters. Alf was one of the more influential Bedwin imports of the time. They took a long-coated daughter of Alf to Gundo and produced their first Champion, Sagaro Danzak, a powerful, impressive male who won well under all judges. He was only out of the cards once in the whole of his show career and has produced good winners and many excellent working animals in the police-force and in trials.

His best daughter, Sagaro Xigi, won the Bitch CC at the National. Wishing to continue breeding the 'international' Shepherd, the Millers imported the bitch Diva von der Freiheit Westerholt, a typical daughter of the VA dog Fando vom Sudblick, whom they much admired. She had his brilliant tan colouring and quality coat, the icing on the cake of good type and construction. Mated to a young dog emanating from another up-and-coming internationally-minded kennel, namely Middross Panto, a son of the popular Gorbi von Bad-Boll, Diva produced the outstanding Champion Sagaro Goby, who took the dog CC at the Two-Day National in 1994, where he won his title at just 20 months of age, and again in 1995. Goby has appealed to judges of all persuasions, being singularly free from many of those features that some imagine are typical of the 'German' type. The Millers have recently imported another very good young female which they hope will further their breeding plans.

## THE ROSEHURST KENNEL

If Annette Broadhurst of the Rosehurst kennel had not owned a video-player, the history of the breed over recent years might have been different. Annette had never been to a Sieger show but she had watched the video film of that great show and was impressed by the progeny of the 1984/1985 Sieger Uran von Wildsteigerland. Uran had established himself as one of the greatest sires in Germany ever, and Annette was looking for a suitable dog to mate to her Ch. Cito granddaughter, Rosehurst Ramona.

Annette and two friends, in a car that broke down on the journey, began the long trek to the Wildsteigerland kennel in Southern Germany. Driving through the beautiful countryside, they spotted a man working in the woods. A beautiful Shepherd splashed about in the stream nearby. "That's Uran and his owner!" exclaimed one of Annette's companions and soon the dog was loping home behind a tractor for the planned assignation with Ramona. The resulting

quarantine-born litter produced the great stud-force Int. Ch. Rosehurst Chris, through whom the influence of Uran was widely disseminated in contemporary successful breeding.

I first saw Chris as a chunky, wobbly puppy at just six months of age at Bolton Championship Show where he won the Minor Puppy class. He was beautifully angulated and an obvious future star. Just four-and-a-half months later I acted as an interpreter for Herr Kirchhoff of Germany, who judged males at the West Yorkshire GSD Championship Show, when an outstanding puppy won his class. The transformation in Chris in that short time was amazing. He had completed his height growth, developed a very pronounced wither and moved round the ring with flair and drive. After Herr Kirchhoff had been informed that the Challenge Certificate should be awarded to the best male, he astounded everyone by handing that coveted award to Chris's handler. The decision was naturally controversial but Chris went on to justify Kirchhoff's assessment of him by attaining his title at 22 months of age and proving the most influential sire of the 90s. Until his death, aged nine-and-a-half years in February 1996, he had dominated the show ring in the UK and produced, among his many winning progeny, six British and five Irish Champions.

## LINDANVALE

Int. Ch. Rosehurst Chris was influential in many kennels but no where more so than in the Lindanvale kennel of Linda and Danny Wilson. But, like so many successful kennels mentioned in this chapter, the Lindanvale winning Shepherds emanated from a good foundation bitch. Malkris Fenya was a daughter of the striking Bedwins import Ch. Alf von Quengelbach who won his title in

*Int. Ch. Rosehurst Chris.*
*Photo: Swan.*

three successive shows and was responsible for converting many an enthusiast to the modern German type. Fenya was mated to yet another import from the Bedwins kennel, Ch. Lauser von Hasenborn, a beautifully pigmented, shapely male with lots of quality. This mating produced Bedwins Tosca of Lindanvale and the repeat mating gave Becky of Lindanvale.

Both bitches were to be influential in the Lindanvale kennel. Tosca, mated to Makris Axel of Lindanvale, produced the good bitch Lindanvale Stella. Becky was mated to Int. Ch. Chris and produced Ch. Lindanvale Vegas, sire of many good winners, including Jemness Atlas, who is already perpetuating this line successfully. Vegas mated to Stella, thus doubling up on the original Lauser-Alf combination, has produced a certain Champion in the beautiful Lindanvale Rena. Tosca was mated twice to Int. Ch. Chris, resulting in Int. Ch. Lindanvale Odessa, the CC-winning Odin, Irish Ch. Lindanvale Hurricane, a dog unlucky not to be campaigned on the mainland where he would certainly have gained a UK title, Hell's Angel, and the good bitch, Helena.

Tosca's litter sister was also mated to Chris and gave Ch. Vorhanden Aphrodite. The Lauser – Alf combination had been successful when Danny mated Bedwins Uta, an Alf daughter, to Lauser, producing the first Lindanvale Champion in the bitch, Banja. Understandably, Danny has stuck to his winning formula and, with the aid of Int. Ch. Chris, has bred within the family, producing a recognisable Lindanvale type in Rena and her full brother Simply Red, a consistent winner under SV judges.

## THE BEDWINS KENNEL

The great influence of Bedwins imports on contemporary breeding has been a recurring aspect of breed development in the last decade or so. The Bedwins kennel soon

*Bedwins Gildo.*

established itself as a top-producing establishment with Ch. Bedwins Pirol and Ch. Bedwins Siegaro, together with recent imports such as Arko von Huhnegrab being popular studs. Breeding from exclusively German lines in recent generations, the kennel inevitably produced a type that satisfied most visiting SV judges. In the skilful hands of ace-handler Malcolm Griffiths, the Bedwins' exhibits are always a force to be reckoned with at breed shows. The kennel is justifiably proud of its success at the Sieger Show. It has exhibited home-bred animals there and won top gradings in stiff international competition.

## THE MIDDROSS KENNEL

Dave and Wendy Middleton founded their successful Middross kennel on the Bedwins import Ch. Alf von Quengelbach after being hugely impressed by him at the GSD Club of Essex 1983 where, in the hands of outstanding handler Tony Howson, he won the CC under me. As was the case with the Lindanvale and Sagaro kennels, the Middletons were lucky to find an Alf daughter, Kuma of Rosetown, who proved a dominant influence in succeeding generations. She is behind every Middross animal to date and she has been line-bred in successfully. Mated to the import, Gundo von der Mordschau, she produced Champion Middross Sonny and his excellent sister Sassy, a Res. CC winner. Mated to Ch. Lauser von Hasenborn, Kuma was the dam of Champion Middross Mica, and two males from the litter gained titles abroad. Sassy produced the excellent CC-winning Vicky, sired by Ch. Bedwins Pirol, who was the mother of the Res. CC-winning Arunfield Gabel.

Sassy was subsequently mated to the 1990 youth Sieger Gorbi von Bad-Boll and produced the good-winning Middross Panto, the sire of the National winner Ch. Sagaro Goby, and the outstanding Ch. Sagenhaft Tamara. Another good Kuma daughter, Middross Rena, by Vopo von Kirschental, was the dam of Ch. Middross Xaver, Best of Breed at Crufts 1996. Line-breeding back to Kuma has produced the Res. CC-winning Middross Kris.

## THE JONIMAY KENNEL
A dog on the way from Germany to Australia, and spending the statutory time of residence in the UK at the Jonimay kennels of Lilly and Terry Hannon, proved influential there. Condor v. Arminius was to be an important stud down under and, although little used here, he produced a daughter whose grandson was Ch. Jonimay Shannon, while a son, Gero of Jonimay, sired Ch. Jacnel Nacale, the dam of Ch. Kassieger Tamil of Alatrack who, in turn, produced Ch. Alatrack Banma – yet another example of the latent genetic potential of imports successfully exploited by UK breeders.

*Ch. Quaxie vom Haus Gero and Ch. Laios van Noort.*
*Photo: David Warne. Kind permission of the Kennel Club.*

## THE ARDENBURG KENNEL
Wendy and Graham Stephens have long enjoyed the ownership of good imported males, with the emphasis always on outstanding temperament. After their first Shepherd in 1966 proved to be unreliable in temperament and subjects to fits, they were lucky to be offered Ferdl v.d. Eschbacher Klippen, full brother to Ilk, owned by the Elliots. Ferdl embodied all they hoped for in character and stimulated their interest in German dogs. They began attending the Sieger Show in 1968 and have not missed one since! They imported several males which were very rarely shown because of increasingly demanding business commitments.

Then, in 1981, after purchasing the Arden Grange quarantine kennels, the Stephens had the chance to develop their own breeding programme. In 1987 they imported a good bitch, Alfa v. Steigerhof, a daughter of the Res. Sieger Tell v. Grossen Sand who, to the German sire Fando v. Sudblick, produced Ch. Ardenburg Fina who won her title in 1992. By this time Graham and Wendy were well

*Ch. Quant vom Kirschental.*

and truly bitten by the showing bug and had imported the striking Laios van Noort, a widely used sire and top male GSD in the UK in 1992. After gaining his title in that year, he went on to win 14 CCs. Laios was widely admired not only for his glamour and striking head but also for his superb character. 1992 also saw the outstanding bitch Ch. Quaxie vom Haus Gero win her title. The following year was dominated by Ch. Quant vom Kirschental, a superbly moving dog who thrilled the ringside by his flying gait. He is also a dog of excellent working ability, popular with breeders of working trials dogs.

Wendy's comments on Ardenburg's aims are worth quoting. "Since our introduction to German Shepherds was with a poor temperament, our aim has been to import dogs from Germany of good type with positive attributes that we felt were needed in the UK at that time, but most important of all, with extremely good temperament and character. For us that has to be the number one consideration. What worth is a VA or a Champion dog that you cannot confidently share your life with, or that will pass on either nervous or aggressive traits to their progeny, most of which go into pet homes? Our wish would be for everyone to be able to experience the joy that a good-temperament Shepherd can bring into your life. Show wins, CCs and Champion status are purely a bonus (albeit a very enjoyable one) and should be kept in that context."

## THE GAYVILLES KENNEL

Davy and Joan Hall's Gayvilles kennel is probably the most consistently successful establishment in recent years. They registered their prefix in 1968 when their chosen breed at that time was the Springer Spaniel, a decidedly 'gay' breed, full of bounce and enthusiasm. From the beginning they were successful with German Shepherds. Their first litter in 1975, sired by Ch. Spartacist of Hendrawen out of Numarks Minnet, produced the winning pair Gayvilles Ambition and Allacante. The highlight of their careers was in 1978 at the West Yorks GSD Club Championship Show when they both won the CC.

Exhibiting continued with home-bred stock over the next few years, but Davy and Joan were beginning, like many at that time, to admire the progeny from the famous Ch. Cito v. Konigsbruch. Mated to Gayvilles Lorraine, retained exclusively as a brood bitch, Cito produced perhaps his best daughter, Ch. Gayvilles Canti, and New Zealand Champion Gayvilles Celli. Canti was an outstanding bitch, gaining eight CCs and six Res. CCs, and embodied completely the harmonious, clean-lined athletic type aimed at by progressive breeders.

In 1984 the Halls purchased a beautiful rich sable bitch, Trethvane Barbara Anne. Mated to the imported Ch. Meik v.d Talquelle, she gave Ch. Gayvilles Dixie and New Zealand Ch. Gayvilles Dingo. Dixie and Canti kept the Gayvilles flag flying during the

matings where one partner scores in features that the other lacks and keeping an informed eye on the progeny of prospective studs.

## CONCLUSION

The central development in the past decade has been the shift towards a more 'international' type, and a significant part in this progession has been played by some of those kennels which have bred top animals through three or more generations, demonstrating the intelligent use of imported bloodlines.

The preoccupation with stud dogs from abroad has, however, had its drawbacks. Breeders too often rush to use the latest import, regardless of whether he will suit their bitch or tie in with her pedigree. Home-bred dogs of outstanding merit are often denied the opportunity to prove their breeding worth. Ch. Aromwood High and Mighty, thought by most to be Ch. Cito von Konigsbruch's best son, was little used because some breeders disliked his 'English' mother-line. Consequently, the chance to perpetuate Cito's influence through his best son was lost.

Similarly, three Muscava male Champions, all with outstanding movement, were not exploited in breeding. Ch. Muscava's Flint, Ch. Rocky and Ch. Arnie did not have the best bitches brought to them because of their largely English lines. Nevertheless, British breeders can be proud of their success in producing German Shepherds which can compete with the best anywhere.

90s. At this time it was decided to introduce new blood from Germany. A male, Cello v. Aschera, has proved very influential and is behind several good winners both in the UK and in Ireland. Mated to the very good imported bitch Ronnie v.d. Berghutte, he produced Ch. Gayvilles Xera for the Halls. Xera, who won 19 CCs and 10 Res. CCs, not only distinguished herself as a show bitch, winning the bitch CC at the National Two-Day Show in 1993 and 1995, but proved her worth as a brood by being the dam of Int. Ch. Gayvilles Nilo and Ch. Gayvilles Natalie by Ch. Rosehurst Chris.

Nilo looks set to be a successful stud, having already produced a Res. CC winner in Shotaans Fella. In addition, Cello produced Gayvilles Yana who won 4 Res. CCs. Another imported bitch, Quirli v. Friedenspark, in whelp to Laios van Noort, gave Ch. Gayvilles Astra who won the Schutzhund National trial in 1994. The Halls are justifiably proud of their success: top kennel in 1993, 1994, and 1996, with six UK Champions and six overseas Champions carrying the Gayville prefix. They have tried to breed type to type, with complementary

# 12 THE GERMAN SHEPHERD DOG IN NORTH AMERICA

To catalog and chronicle the major breeders in the US is like trying to carry sand in a sieve. The picture changes so quickly that today's news is tomorrow's history, which is to say that today's majors may be gone by the time you read this. Despite the size of the North American continent and the number of German Shepherd Dog breeders, there is marked similarity in the type of dog that is produced and some kennels could be regarded as branches of the kennels they bought foundation stock from. This is not an adverse criticism, it is just saying that the pioneer component is not great. As examples, many breeders, large and small, used the combinations of the Troll Richterbach grandson, Lance of Fran-Jo, with Bernd Kallengarten, or the other line to Axel Deininghauser Heide coming through Llano-Estacado's Gengis, or with the other sable line, the K-litter of Waldesruh. Less used, but still quite popular, was Lance with Caralon's Hein (more Axel and R-litter OsnabruckerLand).

Other names in the sport are known more for their handling, or perhaps importing or owning a number of highly successful dogs. Others are in that overlapping or transition area, gradually gaining recognition for their own lines. For the above reasons, I will group some major breeders together.

Remember, size or activity is not necessarily proportional to quality. It is also worth noting the number of breeders who supply German Shepherd Dogs to the police, the security services and to guide dog schools, showing that temperament and trainability remain a strong point in the breed. The German Shepherd has always excelled in the discplines of Obedience, Tracking and Agility, and this is reflected in the activities of many of the top kennels today.

## COVY-TUCKER HILL

Two ladies in the Southwest US bred GSDs for some years until one of them, Cappy Pottle, moved to California and teamed up with Gloria Birch in 1971. They utilized a mix of bloodlines, using a combination of Lance of Fran-Jo with some Bernd Kallengarten, and added Gauss vom Stauderpark with heavy influence from the R-litter OsnabruckerLand. They came up with several very beautiful bitches, including the mostly German, fantastic, Gauss daughter Angelique.

One of their best-known successes was Covy-Tucker Hill's Manhattan, the first GSD to win Best in Show at Westminster, the most prestigious show in America. 'Hatter' was a flashy, well-pigmented, close-coupled dog of very good temperament and full of personality and showmanship. Impeccably

*Gen-Eve's Padrino v. Salix UD: A 'Manhattan' son pictured at ten months of age.*

groomed and trained by leading GSD handler James Moses, and owned by Jane Firestone, Hatter was a pleasant sight for eyes grown tired of extreme rear angulation and poor temperament. He brought the Shepherd in America back into public favor as no other dog in recent times was able to do. His show record included 201 all-breed Best in Shows and 332 Herding Group firsts. He was the top winning German Shepherd male of all time, and was named Show Dog of the Year at the Tournament of Champions. He won BIS at the AKC Centennial, Chicago International, Santa Barbara KC, Houston KC, Westchester KC and the Canadian Show of Shows. Sired by Covy's Flanigan of Tucker Hill out of Ch. Covy's Rosemary of Tucker Hill, Hatter was used at stud and produced many Champion offspring

Misses Pottle and Birch also utilized Sundance Kid (Bear), who was line-bred 2-2 on Doppelt-Tay's Hawkeye. This was strong Lance-Bernd line-breeding. Bear founded a

dynasty carried on by his son, the 1987 Grand Victor (Crunch) and Crunch's sons, 1988 Gr. V. Polo and 1991 Gr. V. Nestle's Quik, the latter being owned by Cappy and Gloria.

## FRAN-JO

The grandson of Troll v. Richterbach, named Lance, provided Fran and Joan Ford with the beginnings of a change in America. They, and many others, bred a number of bitches to Lance. The show lines that had Lance in their near pedigrees included Abraxas, Alator, Amber, Anton, Apfelsine, Ausgang, Ben-Jo, Brentaryl, Campaigner, Clayfield, Cobert, Cypress, DuChien, Eko-Lan, Falkrigia, Fircrest, Halcyon, Hoheneichen, Jo-San, Ken-Delaine, Kenlyn, Kismet, Kubistraum, Landaleigh, Langenau, early Merkel, Mirheim, Noroda, Peddacres, Pinebeach, Proven Hill, Rittara, van Cleve, von Saar, Scher-Lo, Stuttgart, Wellspring, Winaki, Windwalker, Woodhaven. These and many others owed most of their raison d'étre to Lance or his sons and grandsons. There are many others, not as well known, or no longer very active.

## CARALON

Scootie Sherlock and Pat Parsons struck black gold when they produced Caralon's Hein v. d. Lockenheim out of two imports. For a

*Three generations of AKC Champions with the GSDCA title of Grand Victor. Pictured (left to right): Stuttgart's Sundance Kid, Rio Valle's Nestle's Crunch and Piper Hill's Polo.*

long time this was known as the premier kennel for normal hips and nice-looking dogs with dark pigment and general soundness. They also used other imports and the Yoncalla's Mike lines to good advantage. They have been successful Corgi breeders as well. Scootie helped the New Skete monastery dog breeding and training program get on the right path after they experienced too much HD in their early lines. The Caralon dogs also provided much of the foundation for such kennels as Mari-Fiori, LeBarland, and Judeen.

## SCHOKREST

For many years Lorraine Schowalter has been one of the foundations of West Coast quality, and in 1996-97 gave good examples of her work with such dogs as San Diego, Denver, and the fantastic mover and deeply pigmented, select-quality bitch, Triumph, admired by many at the 1996 National Specialty.

## VON NASSAU

Ann Mesdag's personal history as a WW II prisoner of war is fascinating, and she brought her indomitable spirit to the sport of breeding and exhibiting, as well as activity in the GSDCA. She owned the 1972 and 1995 Grand Victors as well as many other notable animals. She did not limit herself to American lines; rather, she was one of a very few in the national or parent club to import fairly frequently. Ann made her kennel into a commercial producer of dogs on a grand scale.

## WYNTHEA

Primarily known for her Obedience dogs and her teaching of Obedience training, Winifred 'Wynn' Strickland also turned out more than two dozen AKC Champions, some of whom were imports. She used mostly German lines but bred to Lance, Noah (K-Waldesruh, Llano-Estacado's Gengis), and other famous American dogs. Wynthea dogs are fairly

*Pictured (left to right): v. Salix's Phantasie (dam of Ch. Luno v. Haus Link), her daughter Jade (sired by Ch. Jo-Lor's Navaroon of Riverdell), Phancie's dam v. Salix Felicia of Rebelhaus, owner and Obedience judge Sharon Crossman, Trommel Hyrue Houston as a pup, and Wynthea's Dakota UD. Photo: Kathy Simonette.*

uniform in style, being substantial, well-pigmented, pleasant, responsive workers. No-one else has put as many dual titles on GSDs, or perhaps any breed, as far as we can determine. Her dogs have spread across the US and Canada, they have won in Obedience, Tracking, and Agility, and they work in sheepherding, therapy, and police occupations. Of more than 170 Obedience titles, at least 40 were perfect scores, and she won the National Obedience Championship for five consecutive years with three dogs.

## TROMMEL AND JENDHI SHEPHERDS
I combine these in the same paragraph because of their similarities. Dr Lynn Graves blended Yoncalla's Mike and Tellaheide's Gallo lines with good East and West German dogs and turned out many handsome von Trommel dogs, some of whom earned

Schutzhund titles. Don Kille, of Jendhi Shepherds a long-time handler and breeder, also used Bernd Kallengarten extensively to produce many Champions, including Select at the GSDCA National. He helped to break old patterns by entering and winning third Open Dog with an imported Mark Haus Beck son at the 1994 National. Several excellent German dogs were entered that year, (because I was the judge and their owners knew that the international style dog would be on an even footing). Don later purchased Jaguar van Noort, to continue the successful blending of domestic and imported lines.

## TOTANA-PIPER HILL
Piper Hill kennel did very well in combining domestic lines. This was Barbara Woelfel's kennel, and when she married Frank Lopez, it became Totana-Piper Hill. Frank and Barbara combined have, for a long time, had a successful East Coast kennel with numerous litters and much blending of German and American lines. Frank had imported Yasko v. Zenntal, who was undefeated in the US and was 1958 Grand Victor the first time he was shown in this country. He also owned Atlas Piastendamm, sire of the famous Raps, at about the same time. Between the two of

*Landa v. Hasentanz: A Sieger-Uran dam, owned by B. & R. Impellizzeri.*

them, they finished over 35 AKC Champions, including two Grand Victors and one Grand Victrix.

## WELLSPRING AND AMBER
Both East Coast breeders, Rosalind Schaefer (Wellspring) and Barbara Amidon (Amber) using similar bloodlines, such as Sundance Kid, and sometimes each other's dogs, produced many show winners in the three decades leading up into the 1990s.

## RECENT GERMAN INFLUENCES
There was a hiatus in the influence of imports after 1965 when Gr. V. Brix Grafenkrone figured so prominently in American show kennels. Imports did not make much of a dent until the 1980s and 1990s.

At the 1994 National show, several imported dogs were entered which could

*Regalship Destany: Linebred Ernemond Gold Lancer, Dunmonaidh Junker and Sieger Axel Hainsterbach.*

have been rated excellent, and a couple very good. Reserve Winners Dog was First in Open, Kimbo Bisschofsheim from Holland, and V-3 in Open was a Czech son of Mark Haus Beck. There were three East German dogs, or offspring of East Germans, that would have ranked high-SG (very good). The other import that fared well was Bill Leonard's Dingo Haus Wurdemann.

Several kennels contributed to the gene pool, albeit in a more diverse way, and usually with the blending of German and American lines. Ernie Loeb was a very successful handler and importer on Long Island, and his fellow East-coast contemporaries Julius Due and Joe Bihari also did much to elevate the status of the import with the show crowd, though against the tide at the time. Joe, especially, blended lines to great advantage, while the other two did more importing and judging. Totana, Darby-Dan, and Haus Link also became known for good import lines for the show rings, and successful blending with American lines.

Others who contributed to the welfare and health of the breed include: Jim Cusick, Connie Berkhardt, Carmen Battaglia, Mary Ellen Kish, Don Smith, Jim Moses, Dave Ranke, Mary Gattone, Sam Lawrence and

*Representatives of the Steffen-Haus kennel (pictured left to right): Cayla v. Steffen-Haus, Elan v. Steffen-Haus, Halle v. Steffen-Haus and Ozzie v. Steffen-Haus.*

Linda Workman. Their focus was on soundness of mind and structure, which they achieved using bloodlines from Germany and the United States. Each of the above have bred and exhibited top winning German Shepherd Dogs. Emphasis has been primarily on American bloodlines for health and trainability.

## WILHENDORF

The Henkel family, with support from Ron Harris, established an international beachhead on American shores as had not happened since the early days of the breed here. They bought Jello v. d. Wienerau from Walter Martin after that dog had already produced quite well in Germany, and brought over the VA-3 bitch Wanni Wienerau, as well as a few other superstars. The von Wilhendorf kennel shot to the top in kennel group, progeny class, and individual USA

*Bravos v. Steffen-Haus: 1994 Vize Jugendklasse Sieger.*

## STEFFEN-HAUS

Jane Steffenhagen of Wisconsin has been involved in breeding German Shepherd Dogs for over 50 years. In 1994 her own home-bred V-1 Bravos vom Steffen-Haus SchH-3 was shown at the International World Sieger Show in Germany, and from a class of 397, Bravos earned the title Vize Jugendklasse Sieger, becoming the first American-bred dog to win this international award. The kennel had another notable first with a progeny group at the German Sieger Show (Karlsruhe, 1996) sired by Bravos v Steffen-Haus, and including offspring from Norway, South Africa, Denmark, Germany, and America. Jane also had the first American kennel group entry at that show. She has produced good-looking, healthy dogs that represent the breed well at shows.

Interestingly, Steffen-Haus also has a kennel located in Germany, and the best dogs enter a training program at 12 month of age and compete for titles in Gemany set down by the German Verein fur Deutche Schaferhund (SV) and WUSV. To date, over 263 Steffen-Haus dogs have achieved their full titles (Schutzhund and Show) in Germany.

*Gotcha v. Steffen-Haus.*

Sieger Show competition with many very beautiful dogs. Jello's son Lars (ex Hilla, a Hoss Hasenborn sister) was the first VA dog bred in America in USA Sieger Show history, and his sister Lussi made VA here a year later. Lars was the first VA in the GSSCC (Canadian) Sieger Show in 1996, too.

## TYSON-WITMER

This northern California working-dog kennel has imported and bred many fine animals for police departments, Schutzhund sports enthusiasts, and personal protection. While they concentrate on the utilitarian aspects of the breed, they have entered dogs in the show ring, including several USA Sieger Shows since the first one in 1990, where Randy Tyson-Witmer was the principal organizer. She imported Vize-bundessieger (second-place in the German Schutzhund championship trial) Cliff v. Huhnegrab as well as USA Sieger Illo Bergmannshof. Cliff has a good record in producing dogs with normal hips as well as good looks, and very good working dogs.

## HAUS LEDDA

Adrian and Rita Ledda began in 1983 to breed for Guide Dogs for the Blind in California. Out of their first six litters, one was for themselves, and a couple of dogs from this D litter did well in Schutzhund and FH in German and American trials, one of them becoming the highest-rated American-bred 'V' bitch in the USA's first Sieger Show; from the G litter came the highest-scoring

*Vopo v. Sendberg, owned by Bob Eby.*

bitch at the Schutzhund-3 Championships the same year. In 1996, V-rated Nichole, SchH-3, was the highest placed bitch at the USA Sieger Show (bred, trained, and handled by Rita). To date, more Haus Ledda dogs have competed in working dog trials than dogs from any other American kennel, and Rita is one of only a handful who have won the Stufe Sports medal.

## VALKYRE

Rebecca Rodgers became a professional AKC show handler in 1974, got her first GSD in 1981, and produced her first litter in 1984. In the short time since, Becky has become known for quality in both show and working dogs. She supplies dogs for many police officers, even though she intentionally keeps her kennel to an easily manageable size. Her vet tech background helped mold her emphasis on good hips and general health, and her attention to anatomical perfection makes her a formidable competitor on the showgrounds as well.

*Am. Ch. Neumann's Jim: An example of good East German lines combining show and working characteristics. Note the substance, bone, pigment and masculinity. East German lines are well-known for good lips, color, boldness, health and working ability.*

## OTHER KENNELS OF REPUTE

Mack-Zwinger (Karen MacIntyre) in New Hampshire is one of several kennels with a good reputation for breeding toward a balanced show-working dog, such as her 1991 Canadian Siegerin and several Schutzhund dogs. Another respected NH breeder and importer is Mike Pinksten, who has supplied many police and Schutzhund enthusiasts with excellent working dogs.

Malka Nagel consistently breeds good dogs from good lines, using the Alcazar-Zwinger kennel suffix. Her foundation bitch was sired by a working dog linebred on the B, F, and G Lierberg litters, bred to a female from show lines with Lasso, Mutz, Marko, and Dingo background. Malka sells several of her dogs to police officers and departments, and has exported to Germany and Mexico. Egon Vollrath and son (von Etzal) have been well represented in Schutzhund. Medlenhaus (Richard Medlen of Kentucky) has done a respectable job in breeding and trialing. Spezialblut in Texas (Carla Griffin and Mary Coppage) have been known more for their imports.

My own von Salix lines have supplied protection, police, estate, and show dogs to Americans and Canadians and have formed the foundations for several other kennels. My early lines were twofold: one being the Lance-Bernd show line and the other being the show-and-working lines of Lierberg and Caralon's Hein, and I have long been a advocate for blending German and American, with major emphasis on the former.

Valiantdale is the kennel name used by Kathy Watson of Tulsa, who has a private training business, and although she does not exclusively target the Schutzhund market, she has produced dozens of dogs who have earned those titles.

Johannes Grewe (Sunland), Inger Olavson, Jim Hill, Wiesenberg, Waldberg, Fenwald, Lundborg, Bach im Tal, Sunrise, Nadelhaus, Haus Ventura, Westerland, Nord Rasen, Elizabeth Klause, Drei Sonnenseen, Neuen Welt, Dondar, Haus Miller, Saxon, Vollkommen, Von Kohs, Mimosenweg, and Leerburg are additional names that are associated with breeding recent import lines, for show or sport or both.

## CANADA

In Canada there are two GSD national breed clubs. The GSDC of Canada is affiliated with the Canadian Kennel Club (CKC) but not quite in the same way as the GSDCA is connected with the AKC. In Canada, individuals are members of CKC, but in the US only clubs can be members of AKC. The German Shepherd Schutzhund Club of Canada (GSSCC) is a full voting member of the WUSV and, as such, is entitled to hold Sieger Shows.

It is impossible to draw as distinct a line between Shepherddom in Canada and that in the United States as governments have done with borders. Canada's human population is 10 per cent of that of the US, and it can be expected to have about that much difference in numbers of dogs and breeders. Because of particular breeders' locations, rather than any geographical influence, much of the German influence is to be found in the western provinces, primarily British Columbia. American influence is most strongly felt in populous Ontario and Quebec and, since the Canadian National is usually held near Toronto, their Grand Victors etc. are often in GSDCA Select classifications, and vice-versa. In many kennels, the dogs and their ancestry are indistinguishable.

## BLACKCREST

One of Canada's premier breeding establishments, located in Nova Scotia, is J. Blois Boyd's award-winning kennel. For more than 40 years, Blois has worked tirelessly for the breed, using the best

*1992 Canadian Sieger Putz Glanerhove, owned by Ann Mesdag.*

German, American, and Canadian dogs to develop a Canadian strain that well represents the international style. He once used Bodo Lierberg effectively, and in later years has used such excellent dogs as Kimbo Bisschofsheim and Quai v. Tronje to produce great offspring and hold up examples for the rest of Canada to emulate. Blois is a multi-breed CKC judge.

## CRYSTARIDGE

On the opposite end of the country is the other of Canada's big award winners (the Pedigree Top GSD Breeder award for 1993, 1995 and 1996), Sylvia Clark. Tucked away on Vancouver Island, overlooking Victoria, the city known for its flowers, this kennel has performed extremely well. The only access to the island is by air or by a very long ferry ride, and competing elsewhere is an expensive endeavor requiring much dedication. Sylvia has primarily used the same bloodlines most popular in the US and, in spite of the barriers, has excelled at winning in the ring and producing healthy dogs with a high rate of orthopedic soundness.

## BULLINGER

Some Canadian kennels truly do distinguish themselves in producing good working-quality show dogs. One example is Tracy Bullinger McCulloch's efforts in BC. Hers is the only kennel in North America to have bred seven dogs that were V-rated at USA Sieger Shows up through 1996, and she has won the Kennel Group on occasion. Tracy's dogs always seem to impress everyone with their combination of beauty and wonderful showing in the courage tests.

## BRUCELEE

Paul Rousseau near Quebec City has produced many dogs that have been on the Canadian WUSV teams and has titled many more himself. His high-drive dogs generally conform well, anatomically and temperamentally, to the Standard.

## SUNSHADOW

Barry and Cathy Gay of Saskatchewan have been breeding since the mid-1980s and from forty-some litters have titled about 75 in Schutzhund, many of them competing at the national level. They also have supplied police with service dogs, and in 1987 had the Canadian Siegerin.

Of course, there are many others who could have been named, some with long histories and spectacular dogs. But I have chosen the above examples to give a broad picture of the breed in North America and to highlight representative kennels.

208

# 13 THE HOMELAND OF THE GERMAN SHEPHERD DOG

This chapter deals with the last twenty-five years of the breed's history in Germany by looking at some of the leading animals in both the show and trials fields. This is done by splitting the work into three periods, the seventies, the eighties and the nineties; then by commenting on the leading dogs in each of those periods by reference to the main breed show (Bundessiegerhauptzuchtschau = HZS), the main trials event (Bundessiegerprüfung = BSP) and the main tending performance (Bundeshauptleistungshüten). The Deutsche Meisterschaft für Diensthundführer has been ignored, mainly because the competition is not restricted to Germany Shepherd Dogs, though it must be stressed that the breed still provides the vast majority of service dogs.

In a relatively short chapter it is not possible to mention every title-holder in the fields outlined above. As to why working dogs are included, it should be noted that, while there are only about 200 or so breed shows every year, there are about 10,000 trials events! Would that we had the SV system of sports badges in the English speaking world. Show dogs achieve their ratings and placings by subjective tests, whereas trials dogs are objectively placed according to marks obtained. The HGH test for herding dogs is marked out of 100, while the Schutzhundprüfung Stufe 3 (SchH3) is marked out of a total of 300, broken down into A (tracking) = 100, B (obedience) = 100 and C (protection work) = 100.

In this chapter I refer to winners of the main breed show as Sieger; to winners of the BSP as Leistungssieger; and to winners of the tending Championship as Hütesieger. For a female the word siegerin is substituted for sieger and the plurals are sieger (no change) and siegerinnen. I apologise for the fact that, as an aid to presentation, the prepositions vom, von der etc. have been omitted from the narrative. Readers will also note several references to "register dogs". These are animals which, for one reason or another, cannot be entered into the SV studbook. If they gain working qualifications, however, they are recorded in the special registers for working dogs.

## THE SEVENTIES

The Sieger title was abandoned in 1938 and replaced by the VA (Vorzüglich-Auslese = Excellent Select) system. A handful of the top dogs were to be graded VA and deemed to rank equally with each other. It was hoped that a broader breeding base would be facilitated by this innovation. This system continued – except for certain years during the war – but in 1946 the VA animals began to be ranked VA1, VA2 and so on. In 1955 the Sieger title was restored with the VA system remaining in place. It has always struck me as odd that certain breed icons, e.g. Rolf Osnabrücker Land and Axel Deininghauserheide should be VA1 but not Sieger. Poor Lido Friedlichenheim was VA1 twice (in 1952 and 1954) but never Sieger!

In 1974 the Sieger title was again discontinued. The VA system was retained but it reverted to the earlier arrangement whereby all animals ranked equally. For whatever reasons, the Sieger title was restored in 1978 and VAs were again ranked in order. It is from this time that one began to hear the term 'VA inflation', which referred to the fact that the annual count of VA gradings was usually almost double that of the sixties.

When the Sieger titles were restored in 1978, the first winners were Canto Arminius, a Canto Wienerau son, and Ute Trienzbachtal, a Hero Lauerhof daughter. Ute was Siegerin again in 1979, when the Sieger was Eros Malvenberg (VA2 in 1978), a Canto Wienerau grandson. The "perceived wisdom" of the seventies, seen from the perspective of main breed show placings, and especially from VA gradings, was that four males in particular came to be looked upon as both great sires and the outstanding influences in the breed. I refer to Marko Cellerland, Mutz Pelztierfarm, Quanto Wienerau and Canto Wienerau. These four came to be known in the English-speaking world as The Big Four. Within a few years Marko had been downgraded and virtually written out of the story, and we were left with just The Big Three.

Marko Cellerland was Sieger in 1972 and VA on three other occasions. Quanto Wienerau was also VA four times, including VA2 in 1971. Mutz Pelztierfarm was VA2 in 1970, while the highest that Canto ever achieved was V1 in 1971. It should also be mentioned that Canto was originally Körklasse 2 (selection class 2); that his

character was not ideal; and that he undoubtedly had Haemophilia A which he transmitted to all his daughters. Hardly the stuff of greatness!

But the really important point is that the Big Four were so defined not by research and quantification but rather by the perceived wisdom of a few individuals. A little thought will show that the relative status of a dog as a sire can only be judged objectively by statistical evidence and none was produced, basically because it requires research. In similar vein, it should be clear that the status of a dog as a breed influence can only be judged by the sort of pedigree analysis (using Galton values) carried out by Humphrey and Warner for early German dogs or the magistral work by Malcolm Willis relating to British dogs. Perceived wisdom, of course, is just totally inadequate for both elements.

In 1994 I published research details which dealt with the standing of a sire by reference to the percentage of progeny which passed the breed selection process. The data showed that, far from being the least effective as a sire, Marko had 15.82 per cent of progeny through the process, with Mutz at 14.84 per cent, Canto 13.07 per cent and Quanto 12.19 per cent. Vello Sieben-Faulen was also included in the survey because many of his matings were to non-angekört (non-selected) females and he ought to have scored less well than males which had better mates. In fact, 15 per cent of his progeny passed the selection process.

Since 1996, the SV itself has published data for VA and top 20 males at the Sieger show, born in 1988 or later, and covering Körbucher entries 1992-1996. More than 20 sires exceeded 14 per cent and though the breed average for selection process passes is undoubtedly a little higher for the nineties than for the seventies, the figures say something about classing certain animals as "great" without proper quantification. For three recent winners of the Sieger title the progeny pass figures were: 16.8 per cent for Kimon Dan Alhedy's Hoeve; 21.8 per cent for Ulk Arlett; and 18.9 per cent for Visum Arminius.

During the seventies some 70 to 80 leading trials dogs qualified each year for the BSP. This grew to 90 or so in the eighties and is over 100 nowadays. The seventies threw up a number of animals, first-class workers themselves, who became noted for the working ability which they tended to produce in their progeny. Pre-eminent was Bernd Lierberg, especially as he bred on through his son Ignaz Oberscholvenerweg – renowned particularly through the Haardblick kennels – and his daughter, the double Leistungssiegerin Betty Bonsdorf! Betty produced the famous 'A' litter Neffeltal (Apoll, BSP 1973 = 7th; Arx BSP 1975 = 2nd; Ari BSP 1977 = 3rd), much respected for breeding trials dogs. Bernd himself competed at the 1969 BSP and came 21st with a V rating! Breed Sieger Bodo Lierberg went to America when he was six, but he left behind a number of top trials dogs including Amor Dürener Land, sire of the 1975 Leistungssieger, and Heck Godewind, runner-up in 1970!

Arguably as important as Bernd Lierberg was Enno Antrefftal, the superb Leistungssieger of 1974. A son of the tough Frei Gugge, Enno produced many workers, including both Drigon Fuhrmannshof and Falk Eichendorfschule. Much though I admire Enno, I believe that quantification by pedigree analysis will show Drigon to be even more influential than his sire. Both Enno and Drigon were handled by Fritz Biehler, who also won the BSP in 1970 with the register dog Drago (Biehler).

The Bündeshauptleistungshüten brings together the top tending dogs actually in service with the flocks; anything from 12 to 18 making up the trials. Mostly the shepherds use two dogs, a 'chief' one and a 'supplementary' one (the beihund). For obvious reasons, relatively few kennels are involved with the breeding of herding dogs but the following should be noted from the seventies; Kirschental, Stammherde Ramholz, Haus Knufken, Küchenthal, Ruine Schönrain, Ahrends Berg, Drohnenberg, Paarquelle, Sumpfbach and Haus Böge. Of these, Kirschental stands apart, because the fusing of top show or trials 'blood' with the HGH bitches seems to be the hallmark of Kirschental breeding.

Witz Stammherde Ramholz, who won his third title in 1975, came from along line of HGH dogs and his sire, grandsire and great-grandsire were all hütesieger! This chain was extended even further in 1976 when Edo, a Witz son, took the title. Edo's dam, Ulli Kirschental – a top trials bitch herself – was sister to Ubo Kirschental, runner-up in 1974 and sire of Nixe Haux Knufken. Nixe, on her dam's side, was a grand-daughter of Erlo Stammherde Ramholz, sire of Witz. Both Dasso Ruine Schönrain and Loni Ahrends Berg were sired by Jordan Kirschental, son of Mike Bungalow (a source of good working 'blood') and Pleya Kirschental of the famous 'P' litter.

## THE EIGHTIES

From the show point of view it can be said that the eighties consolidated the position of the Big Three, where they appeared constantly as the animals being inbred to in the pedigrees of leading show stock. It is less clear that this is so in general terms, because many pedigrees of so-called working lines carry few examples of inbreeding to them. The matter will only be resolved when the Körbucher, or better still, the Zuchtbucher, are analysed in the manner of Sewall Wright for Shorthorn cattle. What a subject for a doctoral thesis!

Quanto Wienerau was grandsire to Axel

*Dingo vom Haus Gero: Sieger 1983, Frankfurt, with handler Dennis Vessey. Photo: Jack Oliver.*

Hainsterbach via Lasso Val Sole – arguably Quanto's best son – and appears in Natan Pelztierfarm through his son Reza Wienerau, though Natan was actually inbred on the older Lido Wienerau and Klodo Eremitenklause. Uran Wildsteiger Land, said by some to be the greatest sire of all time (more perceived wisdom?), was inbred on Quanto with three lines to him. Quando Arminius, a Xaver Arminius son out of the leading show dog producing bitch Palme Wildsteiger Land (sister to the 1982 Siegerin) was inbred very closely on Wilma Kisselschluct and, rather less closely, on Quanto. The Uran son, Eiko Kirschental, was also inbred on Quanto, with further Quanto in the sixth generation.

Dingo Haus Gero, he of the floating movement, was inbred 2-3 on Canto Wienerau. Eiko Kirchental was also inbred on Canto, with further lines off the pedigree through Asslan Klämmle. Similar comments apply to Iso Bergmannshof. Perle Wildsteiger Lane, a Nick Wienerau daughter, was inbred on Canto with further inbreeding to Canto's grandsire, Fix Sieben-Faulen. Senta Basilisk, the Swiss-bred bitch, carried four lines to Canto, three being through her dam.

Tina Grossen Sand, twice Siegerin and sister to the twice VA Tall, was inbred on both Quanto Wienerau and Mutz

Pelztierfarm. Pischa Bad-Boll, an Irk Arminius daughter, carried three lines to Quanto, Senta Basilisk, mentioned above, was inbred on Lasso Val Sole and Wilma Kisselschluct through the litter mates Xaver and Xandra Arminius. My abiding memory of 'bloodline' charts for the late eighties is the apparent importance of Dingo Haus Gero (for Canto Wienerau) and Lasso Val Sole and Uran Wildsteiger Land (for Quanto Wienerau).

In terms of trials dogs, the eighties saw the continuing influence of Bernd Lierberg as a source of inbreeding and via his sons Ignaz Oberscholvernerweg and the East German-bred Pushkass Haus Himpel. Enno Antrefftal bred on through his sons Cyras Weinsbergtal and Roland Wohrabrücke, but especially through Drigon Fuhrmannshof. Drigon produced a number of top trials dogs including the litter brothers Uwe and Uran Kirschental, both of whom turned out to be important sires in the trials field. Valet Busecker Schloss and Mike Bungalow were still being inbred to, aided in this by the increasing influence of the 'A' litter Neffeltal for Valet and the rise of Greif Lahntal for Mike.

Both Greif and Mike stood at the Busecker Schloss kennels as stud dogs, as did Ebbo Astener Moor and Arko Haus Buch.

*Eiko vom Kirschental: Sieger 1988, Bremen. Photo: Jack Oliver.*

Arguably, however, the most important single influence was Racker Itztal, Leistungssieger in 1971 and son of Pirol Kirschental of the famous 'P' litter. Django Castell 18 was a Racker grandson; Dunja Greifenstein was inbred on him; Bona Waldwinkel carried him; Boris Steckelsberg was inbred on him; and Iwo Lauterstein also carried him. Tail-male 'bloodlines' charts do not do Racker justice, because so much of his influence comes via his daughters.

The Kirschental kennels maintained an important standing in the herding trials of the eighties, fusing HGH with other 'blood' as previously mentioned. Sara was sired by the powerful Kai Silberbrand, son of Marko Cellerland. Hanny was sired by Argus Aducht, a VA show dog. Her dam was the tough Fenga Kirschental, daughter of Racker Itztal and grand-daughter of Bernd Lierberg! Vaso had HGH parents but Argus Klämmle (show) and Ebbo Astener Moor (work) as grandparents. Even Hexe Bösen Nachbarschaft had a Kirschental dam, her sire being Anderl Kleinen Pfahl, a Mutz Pelztierfarm son and Bernd Lierberg great-grandson. Anderl was a noted source of fine temperament and working ability.

Manfred Heyne, of Stammherde Ramholz fame, also left his mark on the eighties tending scheme with his three times Champion Fax (Heyne), a register dog. Fax was by Wotan Stammherde Ramholz, brother to Witz, out of Elfe Stammherde Ramholz, a Witz daughter. Georg Krieg also had three

wins; two with his register bitch Anja and the other with Ursel Schäferstamm, a son of Hexe Bösen Nachbarschaft, winner in 1982. Anja (Krieg), though sired by a register dog, was out of a Dick Adeloga daughter.

THE NINETIES
In relation to the HZS in the nineties it can be said that the influence of both Canto Wienerau and Quanto Wienerau is now rather greater than that of Mutz Pelztierfarm. For all three, of course, the influence comes more through the inbreeding to descendants than through direct inbreeding to them, for they have begun to 'fall off' five generation pedigrees. The Canto influence comes through Tell Grossen Sand and Fanto Hirschel; through Fedor Arminius via his sons Folemarkens Jasso and Kimon Dan Alhedy's Hoeve; and through lines to Argus Aducht and Dingo Haus Gero.

Quanto comes via Lasso Val Sole through his son Xaver Arminius and the Xaver son Quando Arminius. Quando is especially important via his son Odin Tannenmeise, sire of both Jeck Noricum and Zamb Wienerau. Odin also sired the 1991 Siegerin while Jeck produced Visum Arminius, and was grandsire to the 1996 Siegerin. Zamb Wienerau sired both Vanta and Nathalie Wienerau. The Quanto line is also continued through Uran Wildsteiger, especially via Eiko Kirschental to Yago Wildsteiger Land, sire of Palie Trienzbachtal and Ulk Arlett.

The influence of Mutz Pelztierfarm appears

to come mainly through the Jonny Rheinhalle sons Jupp Hallerfarm (to Cello Römerau) and Kuno Weidtweg (to Fanto Südblick). The Kuno son Nick Wienerau was the sire of Palme Wildsteiger Land, with all that entails for the inbreeding to Palme!

More important than lines of descent are details of inbreeding, and I must admit that I view the leading show animals of the nineties with some degree of trepidation in this respect. Basically, this is because of the inbreeding to Palme Wildsteiger Land, not least through the Q litter Arminius, and to Lasso Val Sole, not least through the X litter Arminius (Xaver Arminius and Palme Wildsteiger Land sired the Q litter, Arminius and Lasso sired Xaver). Palme herself was inbred 3-4 on Canto Wienerau with further inbreeding to the Canto grandsire Fix Sieben-Faulen. Xaver was inbred 5-4 on Jalk Fohlenbrunnen and Quando thus Wilma Kisselschluct 2-4, Quanto Wiernerau 3-5 and with increased inbreeding to Jalk off the pedigree. Suffice it to say here that inbreeding to Palme is shown by the Siegerinnen of 1991, 1992, 1994, 1995 and 1996 and by the Sieger of 1993, 1994, 1996 and 1997. Inbreeding to Lasso is shown by the Siegerinnen of 1992, 1993, 1994 and 1995 and by the Sieger of 1992, 1993, 1995 and 1997. In many cases the inbreeding to Palme is through the Q litter Arminius, while the same is true for Lasso and the X litter Arminius. Inbreeding such as this can bring an unrealised increase in individuals off the pedigree as witnessed by recent revelations in Britain that some animals (in 8 to 10 generations) carry 20 to 30 lines to Canto and the same to Quanto!

By the late eighties and into the nineties a number of kennels were producing top trials

*Ulk vom Arlett: Sieger 1995, Hamburg.*

*Fanto vom Hirschel: Sieger 1990, Frankfurt and Sieger 1991, Karlsruhe.*
*Photo: Jack Oliver.*

dogs on a regular basis. Kennels such as Bösen Nachbarschaft, Haus Anja, Karthago, Körbelbach, Lechrainstadt, Wolfendobel and Zeuterner Himmelreich spring to mind. Inbreeding, not usually close in trials dogs, is still mainly based on Bernd Lierberg, Enno Antrefftal, Racker Itztal and, to a lesser extent, Anderl Kleinen Pfahl and Eros Busecker Schloss, a Mike Bungalow son. Individuals appearing on pedigrees relatively frequently also included Greif Lahntal, Uwe Kirschental, Wicko Meran and Oldo Starken Eiche. The last named is brother to Olf Starken Eiche, sire of the great producing bitch in the Karthago kennels, Afra Stoppenberger Land. The nineties will also be remembered for the new leading sires in

the trials field, namely Harro Lechrainstadt, Fero Zeuterner Himmelreich, Xento Maineiche, Arec Bunsenkocher, Arek Stoffelblick, Mink Haus Wittfeld, the East German-bred Lord Gleisdreieck and so on.

A number of new herding kennels came to the fore in the nineties, although Kirschental continues to be important. Amie Kirschental was by Sieger Eiko out of a Fenga Kirschental daughter. Amie herself produced Xiewa who was inbred on Sieger Uran Wildsteiger Land. Dago Steffanberg, inbred on Ebbo Astener Moor, was also out of a Kirschental bitch. In the case of Blanka Reischactal, both of whose parents were HGH, it was her sire who carried the Kirschental name. Manfred Voight, who won with Blanka, also won with Alice Dolderbrunnen, who he bred himself. Alice's sire was mainly of trials breeding, being inbred on Mike Bungalow and Bernd Lierberg and carrying both Greif Lahntal and Racker Itztal. Frauke Teuchelwald was inbred on Greif Lahntal, with further inbreeding to Mike Bungalow and the Bernd Lierberg daughter Seffe Busecker Schloss. Both Busecker Schloss and Bungalow still try to produce soundly structured animals with first-class working ability. The Holzheimer Linde bitches, Lucy and Ista, were of mainly show type breeding and inbred on Uran Wildsteiger Land. Strangely, they both had Kirschental grandsires who were not HGH; Vopus for Lucy and his brother Vagus for Ista.

*Lasso vom Newenberg: Sieger 1997, Dusseldoff.*

## CONCLUSION

As the SV approaches its centenary it can look back on a job very well done. For many years, indeed for most of the century, the Germany Shepherd Dog has been the leading service dog in the whole world. The emphasis on the working aspect of the breed was especially dear to the heart of Rittmeister (Cavalry Captain) Max von Stephanitz, founder of the SV, though proper tribute must be paid to those who followed him as SV presidents – Dr Curt Roesebeck, Caspar Katzmair, Dr Werner Funk, Dr Christoph Rummel, Herman Martin and the present incumbent Peter Messler. SV members have a number of guiding principles (Leitsatz) which stress the work aspect. For example: "No breeding without performance and no performance without breeding"; "Improve the performance if you want to serve the breed"; "To breed a shepherd dog is to breed for work". It is around thoughts such as these that the SV breeding system – the shows, the trials, the selection meetings and so on – is really built.

*Oll vom Bergmannshof showing the outstanding gait that is typical of the German Shepherd Dog. Photo: Jack Oliver.*

## Winners of the Sieger Title (Male) 1978 - 1997

1978  Canto v Arminius SchH3

1979  Eros vd Malvenburg SchH3

1980  Axel vd Hainsterbach SchH3

1981  Natan vd Pelztierfarm SchH3

1982  Natan vd Pelztierfarm SchH3

1983  Dingo v Haus Gero SchH3

1984  Uran v Wildsteiger Land SchH3 FH

1985  Uran v Wildsteiger Land SchH3 FH

1986  Quando v Arminius SchH3 FH IP3

1987  Quando v Arminius SchH3 FH IP3

1988  Eiko v Kirschental SchH3 FH

1989  Iso v Bergmannshof SchH FH

1990  Fanto v Hirschel SchH3

1991  Fanto v Hirschel SchH3

1992  Zamb vd Wienerau SchH3

1993  Jeck v Noricum SchH3 FH

1994  Kimon v Dan Alhedy's Hoeve SchH3

1995  Ulk v Arlett SchH3

1996  Visum v Arminius SchH3 FH

1997  Lasso v Neuen Berg SchH3

## Winners of the Sieger Title (Female) 1978 - 1997

1978  Ute v Trienzbachtal SchH3

1979  Ute v Trienzbachtal SchH3

1980  Dixi v Natoplatz SchH3 FH

1981  Anusch v Trienzbachtal SchH3

1982  Perle v Wildsteiger Land SchH3

1983  Tannie v Trienzbachtal SchH3

1984  Tina v Grossen Sand SchH3

1985  Tina v Grossen Sand SchH3

1986  Pischa v Bad-Boll SchH3

1987  Senta v Basilisk SchH3 FH

1988  Ronda v Haus Beck SchH2

1989  Inka vd Eichwaldhutte SchH3

1990  Inka vd Eichwaldhutte SchH3

1991  Yolli v Kreuzbaum SchH3

1992  Vanta vd Wienerau SchH3

1993  Palie v Trienzbachtal SchH3

1994  Vanta vd Wienerau SchH3

1993  Nathalie vd Wienerau SchH3 FH IP3

1996  Quena v Haus Sommerlade SchH3

1997  Connie v Farbenspiel SchH3

## Winners of the S.V. Bundessieger Prufung 1973 - 1997

1973  Gero v Porzenacker SchH3

1974  Enno v Antrefftal SchH3

1975  Cherry v Durener Land SchH3

1976  Drigon v Fuhrmannshof SchH3 FH

1977  Eck v Charlottenhof SchH3

1978  Falk vd Eichendorffschule SchH3

216

1979  Vargo v Seebachtal SchH3 FH

1980  Rex (Kappenberg) (Register Dog)
SchH3 FH

1981  Boy v Grawenhof SchH3

1982  Drechsler v Warnautal SchH3 FH

1983  Django v Castell 18 SchH3

1984  Perry v Beilstein SchH3 FH IP3

1985  Karlo v Johanneszwinger SchH3 IP3

1986  Aco vd Burg Esch/Dunja
SchH3 FH IP3
and vGreifenstein (Jointly)
SchH3 FH IP3

1987  Bona v Waldwinkel SchH3 FH

1988  Boris v Steckelsberg SchH3 FH IP3

1989  Iwo v Lauterstein SchH3

1990  Xando v Karthago SchH3 FH

1991  Brix v Kapfwald SchH3

1992  Blacky v Neuen Lande SchH3

1993  Okar v Karthago SchH3

1994  Gotthilf vd Kine SchH3

1995  Agbar Bethme SchH3

1996  Dax v Baumberg SchH3

1997  Quaid vd Hegewiese SchH3 FH1 IP3

## Winners of the S.V. Hauptleistungshuten 1973 - 1997

1973  Witz vd Stammherde Ramholz HGH

1974  Dasso vd Ruine Schonrain HGH

1975  Witz vd Stammherde Ramholz HGH

1976  Edo vd Stammherde Ramholz HGH

1977  Nixe v Haus Knufken HGH

1978  Ursa v Kirschental HGH

1979  Loni v Ahrends Berg HGH

1980  Sara v Kirschental HGH

1981  FAX (Heyne) HGH (Register Dog)

1982  Hexe vd Bosen Nachbarschaft HGH

1983  Hanny v Kirschental HGH

1984  Fax (Heyne) HGH (Register Dog)

1985  Fax (Heyne) HGH (Register Dog)

1986  Vasko v Kirschental HGH

1987  Anja (Kreig) HGH (Register Dog)

1988  Anja (Kreig) HGH (Register Dog)

1989  Ursel v Schaferstamm HGH

1990  Amie v Kirschental HGH

1991  Dago v Steffenberg HGH

1992  Blanca v Reischachtal HGH

1993  Alice v Dolderbrunnen HGH

1994  Xiewa v Kirschental HGH

1995  Lucy vd Holzheimer Linda HGH

1996  Frauke v Teuchelwald HGH

1997  Ista vd Holzheimer Linde HGH

# 14 THE GERMAN SHEPHERD DOG IN AUSTRALIA

Australia, even though it is thousands of miles from Europe, has not been impeded by distance in its search for success. We have produced, over the last decade, German Shepherds of world standard quality. The three prime reasons for this are that we have dedicated breeders; that the German Shepherd Dog National Council initiated far-reaching breed improvement schemes; and that people have been willing to spend large sums of money to acquire imports carrying bloodlines which will continue to develop and improve the breed in Australia. This chapter should provide an overview of the contemporary German Shepherd in Australia.

## INFLUENTIAL MATERNAL BLOODLINES
*Researched and written by Malle Morley of the Karlrach Kennels.*

It is becoming well recognised that, while a stud dog most certainly has more influence on the breed due to the volume of progeny he is able to produce, it is nevertheless the well-bred brood bitch which spells the success of a kennel. The prepotent brood bitch, consolidated by strong sound line-breeding enabling her consistently to reproduce her type, is invaluable to any kennel. And further, if the successful brood

produces an ongoing son, that kennel and its successful maternal line will have an enormous influence on the breed.

In Australia it has become increasingly evident that a number of kennels have put that very principle into action – to name a few, Denargun, Hasenway, Karkrach, Hagenstolz and Iniff. All these kennels have a very strong bitch line and each produces quality stock performing consistently well nationally and recognisable as the breeding of that specific kennel.

The most influential and prepotent dams in the last two decades have been Kurtlee Minnesota (imp. UK), Ambala Lovely Lady, Dina von Restrauch (imp. Germ.) and Duval Royal Velvet. These four bitches have made a significant impression on the breed in Australia, appearing on the pedigrees of the most successful dogs currently being shown. Their prepotency and their ability to withstand inbreeding determines their position in the hierarchical stakes. Often they appear in the same pedigrees linking their genes. In effect, they are the maternal cornerstones of the breed in Australia.

However, the value of any animal, as one to be considered uniquely significant, must be measured by his or her ability to withstand linebreeding and come up 'trumps'. That is to say, when linebred closely (in-breeding) and if the resultant offspring are sound (i.e. free of major genetic faults) and are phenotypical of their valued individual parent, such an animal must be considered as being one of major significance. And further, if this animal has been bred with demonstrable success, such an animal would be well defined as a cornerstone of the breed. Kurtlee Minnesota was one that conformed to this definition.

## KURTLEE MINNESOTA

Kurtlee Minnesota was imported to Australia in 1979, yet her presence is still evident in the contemporary German Shepherd of Australia. This was seen at the 1996 Main Breed Evaluation Show, where Minnesota prepotently appeared in the pedigrees of the winning first four bitches through the lines of Landrina Magic Melody and her daughters. The sire in each case was equally a dog of great value, Dorsten Monte Cito, whose bloodlines have been highly successful when combined with those of Minnesota.

Minnesota was imported from the UK to Australia by Karlrach Kennels. A black and gold bitch of very good type with a pronounced wither and particularly firm in ligamentation, hocks and elbows, she possessed an excellent character. She was shown sparingly, yet successfully, but her value lies in the prepotent gene base making her impact on the breed in Australia nothing short of spectacular. She was the daughter of Delridge Echo and Delridge Iona, mirroring closely her grandmother Delridge Camilla on whom she was inbred 2:2. And here lies the strength of Kurtlee Minnesota.

Her most influential litter was from her mating to the Reza von Haus Beck son Liakar Satan, with whom she produced the winning and prepotent lines of Karlrach Kentucky Lad (triple National Medallist) and his sister Karlrach Wyoming Belle (National Gold Medallist and vice-Siegerin). Although not negating the Satan influence, nevertheless

*Aust. Ch. Landrina Magic Melody.*

*Aust. Ch. Hagenstolz Draw Card.*

*Karlrach Curtain Call.*

both brother and sister mirrored very closely their mother.

She also produced well with her first litter in Australia to the German dog Enno v.d. Hoheneiche, Karlrach Utah Annie and brother California Joe being most notable. While California Joe was a particularly lovely animal and had enormous breed potential by his phenotype, he had little opportunity as he was campaigned sparingly and retired early from the show ring.

A number of kennels have had substantial success with Minnesota bloodlines and one of particular note is Hagenstolz kennels via Landrina Magic Melody. She is a Kentucky Lad/Duval Royal Velvet daughter, who mirrors closely her breeding. The most notable of her progeny is the very lovely, anatomically well-constructed and well-bred (sired by Dorsten onto Cito) Hagenstolz Draw Card (triple National medallist, 1994 reserve Siegerin and Siegerin in 1996) who, when further linebred to Kentucky Lad/Wyoming Belle 4:3 via Iniff Vagrant, produced the shapely bitch Djuenen Class Action. This is not to ignore the significance of the linebreeding of Edlenblut Orkan 3:4 which exists in Class Action, all contributing to the final outcome.

The measure of the breed-worth of any animal is significant when it can withstand the scrutiny of close linebreeding, namely inbreeding. A number of breeders have adventurously and, more often than not, successfully doubled further on Minnesota creating 4 x Delridge Camilla.

This has been most successfully and prolifically utilized over the years by our Karlrach kennels. This kennel continues breeding with the Minnesota influence currently via their producing bitch Karlrach Curtain Call and her sister Bit o' Fun. Both bitches are inbred 2:2 on the Kentucky Lad/Wyoming Belle combination, making them 3:3 Minnesota, and most importantly

they mirror their maternal line.

Denargun kennels, whose success stems from a sound prepotent foundation, take the honours as Australia's top winning kennel. Their foundation bitches carry the Minnesota phenotype with their two Kentucky Lad daughters, sisters Denargun Chardi (Excellent Select) and Charisma, who have subsequently produced well.

Denargun kennels have utilized double Minnesota through the Kentucky Lad/Wyoming Belle combinations via Iniff Vagrant, notably Denargun Silhouette, Brass Razoo and Fandango, and produced winning results to validate their selection. But, of more importance, Denargun kennels as a result have established a strong, sound mother line for future outcross breeding.

Iniff Kennels, whose foundation bitch was Karlrach Wyoming Belle, the most utilized Minnesota daughter either directly or indirectly, not only had enormous success in the show ring, but have produced progeny which has maintained Iniff kennels as one of Australia's most valued. Her best daughter Iniff Trapeze, National Gold Medallist and twice VA, mirrors her mother most strongly. However, the most influential of Wyoming Belle's bloodline – albeit she is the great-grandmother, and not ignoring the fact that he does not mirror Kurtlee Minnesota – is Sieger Iniff Vagrant. Iniff kennels have utilized Vagrant to further linebreed on Wyoming Belle via her daughter Iniff Sonata, producing the double 'D' litter. It is, nevertheless, through Vagrant that many breeders, already carrying the lines of Minnesota, are able to continue the further use of her valuable prepotent genetic make-up.

## KARLRACH KENTUCKY LAD

This dog was the most important dog to access the valuable line of Kurtlee Minnesota. He was undoubtedly Minnesota's best son,

*Aust. Ch.
Karlrach
Kentucky Lad.*

producing with regularity his phenotype. His father was the Reza v. Haus Beck son, Liakar Satan, who corrected Minnesota's pigment, leaving Kentucky Lad a rich black and gold dog.

Kentucky Lad, shown relatively sparingly, had nevertheless considerable success in the show ring, bringing home three National Medals, although he never cracked the Gold. He was not shown at the Main Breed Show but undoubtedly would have been well worthy of his VA classification. He was a high-withered, medium-sized, medium strong dog with much glamour and he always demonstrated a great joy in performance. Of particular relevance to his presence in the breed was that he had the gene base which made him a highly prepotent sire, mirroring his mother line most strongly. He has been valued for the tightness of his elbow and hock joints, a characteristic which Kentucky Lad passed on with great predominance – a virtue he inherited from his mother, Kurtlee Minnesota.

It is evident, a decade and half later, that Kentucky Lad's influence is still present in our current show dogs in 1997, making him a major significant influence in the breed. This honours him as a truly important cornerstone in the breed in Australia and a strong foundation for future outcrossing to new imported bloodlines.

AMBALA LOVELY LADY VA B.S. CL.1'A'
Ambala Lovely Lady, purchased by Dorsten Kennels, graded Excellent Select at the 1990 Main Breed Show, reinforces the justification of her award by her valued presence in the breed. She is the daughter of Vinberg Grey Nina (who in turn is the daughter of one of the more important dogs in Australasia, Dunmonaidh Junker) and the valuable sire Edlenblut Orkan, VA and twice Sieger. Lovely Lady mirrors Orkan, inheriting his type, dark eye and, of particular value, his very good ability predominantly to reproduce excellent hips.

Lovely Lady's influence is felt most strongly through her son, Dorsten Monte Cito, the triple National Gold Medal winner and triple Australian Sieger winner. He is a dog of much substance and type and he, too, has offered much in the areas of soundness in

*Aust. Ch. Hasenway Wild Knight.*

*Aust. Ch. Lindendale Strike Force.*

and with excellent hip results. Both he and Hagenstolz Draw Card are Sieger/Siegerin and Gold Medallists. Both animals are of the highest merit.

The best daughter of Ambala Lovely Lady is Dorsten Sinitta (sired by Quincito Awol), herself a lovely bitch, though of paling pigment which curtailed her show career, but she has not passed this on to her more outstanding progeny. Sinitta produced two sons of note, the strikingly well-coloured red/black dog VA Lindendale Strike Force, a Silver and Bronze Medallist winning dog, and Lindendale Thunder Bolt, a Vagrant son, who in turn sired VA Iccara Hard Rock, Excellent Select. He, in turn, is starting to produce some exciting progeny, albeit they are still very young.

It is evident, through the lines of Monte Cito, Strike Force, Thunderbolt and Hard Rock, how their presence in the breed will continue to position Lovely Lady as an important brood in Australia. The challenge now is to linebreed on Lovely Lady and cement her producing capacities and establish her phenotype, so that future outcrossing to imported lines can be attempted with confidence.

## DINA V. RESTRAUCH B.S. CL.1 'A' (IMP. GERM.)

Dina was a daughter of Argus v. Aducht and Alfa v. Restraugh. She was imported by the small, yet highly successful, Hasenway Kennels and has been a valuable asset to the success of this kennel. She was a very lovely, firm and dry bitch who was a National Gold Medal winner. Dina, when mated to the German import Condor v. Arminius, produced the highly influential dog Hasenway Putz VA and three times vice-Sieger, whose influence and name appears on many current top winning show dogs.

From Putz came the lovely multi-National Gold Medallist and dual Siegerin Darkana

hips and elbows. He has been used widely and highly successfully, particularly with the lines of Landrina Magic Melody, the most notable being Hagenstolz Draw Card and Craisan Mortisha. As a result, the influence and presence of Lovely Lady will be ensured in many generations of Australia's top animals.

Monte Cito's best son is the very impressive Hasenway Wild Knight who is producing, in his own right, valued progeny

*Condor v. Arminius: Imported from Germany.*

Burg Hausbrunn, and behind Darlegen Fiery Scandal through Darlegen Elusive Lady mated to Edlenblut Orkan.

From her litter to Iso v. Friedenspark, a Karo v. Aschbacher Land son, Dina produced Hasenway Rina, mother of Hasenway Truly Ruly, 1993 Siegerin, a bitch of much type and harmonious anatomical construction. It is evident that Dina has passed the test of longevity within the breed and her value will be perpetuated via Monte Cito and his daughters, and the younger Hasenway Wild Knight.

## DUVAL ROYAL VELVET

Royal Velvet is the daughter of Parouke Mystical and Volscain Jester, who was an English import and a Gold Medallist at the 1978 Australian National. Jester was an attractive dog with a firm character and of stretched type with very good movement.

Royal Velvet was structurally an animal who inherited the best virtues of her parents, and has left, to her credit, a commendable number of highly graded animals. She consistently produced stock showing good improvement in the croup and upper arm regions. She also has contributed very successfully in the area of hips and with a very high percentage of Breed Survey Class 1 animals.

However, most of her influence is felt through the lines of her daughter Landrina Magic Melody and her son Landrina Cassius Clay, a dog who excelled in type and harmony, sired by Karlstadt Tumblin' Dice coming down from Masuta Piaute and Tandina Red Star. Both have been graded

Kalani, a harmonious, balanced bitch of beautiful type. She was a bitch who represented the ideal and an animal to whom breeders could aspire. Of equal quality, Putz also produced one of the most major influential sires in Australia, Dorsten Monte Cito. It is through Monte Cito, with a stud career stretching over many years, that the lines of Dina will be felt for many generations. The current highly awarded, impressive-moving dog 1996 Sieger Hasenway Wild Knight is from the same prestigious lines. (Strictly speaking, all German Shepherds are linebred to one another by the very definition that they are of the same breed.)

The mating of Dina to Condor was done three times, with the most successful and influential being the litter which produced Putz. However, while the 'O' litter was not as successful as Putz in terms of show, the bloodlines have come to the forefront with the subsequent resultant offspring in their own right having performed well but, more importantly in terms of breed progress, having produced well.

The Hasenway 'O' litter was behind Siegerin Kantenna Love Match through Cabernae Inspired, who was mated to Heiko

Excellent Select. Magic Melody, a Karlrach Kentucky Lad daughter, has been one of the most important dams in the country, where her influence and prepotency is evident well into the late 1990s. When crossed with Dorsten Monte Cito lines she has produced outstanding progeny which, no doubt, will continue to breed on.

## INFLUENTIAL SIRES

*This is a summary of influential sires at the Main Breed Show, judged, critiqued and written by Louis Donald.*

The basis of the structured development of influential sires in Australia was via the Main Breed Show first held in 1987. This event ran along similar grounds to the Sieger Show in Germany. Sires were selected and then, via the breed survey scheme, promoted. Importantly, sires were selected in a very precise order and promoted in a very selective way, particularly in relation to their inter-relationships and the sequence of their inter-use.

The first step in the chain was the selection of a dog called Edlenblut Orkan. He was five years old when he was made Sieger and, while he had made a few wins at shows, he was not a major winner or a dog of high status. There were other dogs who were considered to be, by many, a better prospect. Orkan had, though, attributes the others did not have, and primary among these was his ability to pass on a phenotype that carried more needed traits than did the other possible sires. In other words, there were a few dogs who had possibly better progeny than Orkan on the ground, but these tended to be less than phenotypical and were very mixed in their type. None carried the prime requirement of a long upperarm and long croup.

Importantly two other, still very young, dogs had caught my eye and these dogs, Prima Zorba and Quincito Awol, were considered to be able to work well with Orkan in a general sense, but more importantly in the specific sense of the upperarm and croup.

In effect, at the first Main Breed Show, the next three Siegers were selected in such a way as to keep the other two, relatively lesser, positioned in order that the appropriate sequence would be followed by the breeders This concept of having an ideal, with a clear plan on the sequence of achieving it, is critical to any success.

## EDLENBLUT ORKAN VA B.S. CL.1.'A'

This was a 62.5 cm stretched black and gold dog with a lightish mask. He had lovely dark eyes at a time when light eyes were a problem in the breed. He had high withers and a straight firm back and, at the time, a very good croup. His forehand angulation was very good, the upperarm could have been a bit better laid, but it was long. He had pronounced hind angulation and very good chest formation; however, the pasterns were not firm. In movement he showed a very good ground-covering gait and was basically quite firm in the joints other than the wrists.

*Edlenblut Orkan.*

His temperament was outgoing, confident and trustworthy. The virtues he passed on were middle size, overall typy appearance, good croup and forehand, even though the upperarm should have been better laid, firm temperament, very good colour except a number of progeny did have a light mask, very good bones and expression. The greatest attribute was the ability to produce, with consistency, an overall higher than average type and the advantage of his progeny to 'click' with the other primary sires that were to follow.

### HASENWAY PUTZ
Putz was a very valuable dog for his breeding potential but not a dog that would become a Sieger, yet he was Reserve Sieger for three years. He lacked that special, and sometimes indefinable, presence both when standing and running. He did not have the length of croup and upperarm that I saw as critical for a Sieger, yet he was a dog of very good proportions and had lovely strength and substance.

He stood at 63.5 cm. with a lovely masculine head, strong jaws, just medium-coloured eyes, moderate hind angulation and a slightly short upperarm and croup. He was a harmonious dog with good, as opposed to exceptional, movement and straight short back, short croup, firm joints, good withers and balanced chest formation. He stepped cleanly and had very firm hocks.

Putz brought to his progeny a phenotype, lovely proportions and strength, lovely substance and overall firmness, with great masculinity and harmony. Importantly, he carried forward many of the attributes of his sire Condor von Arminius, that is, praiseworthy proportions and balance, medium size, very good colour and short firm backs. There did exist a tendency to some low set ears. However, the high level of good hips is important and the fact that Putz 'clicked' beautifully with Orkan.

### PRIMA ZORBA
Zorba was structurally a much superior dog to Orkan and Putz. He was a large 65.0 cm, handsome, decidedly masculine, powerful, robust and substantial dog with impeccable temperament and sound character. He was a well-coated grey with an excellent head, strong bones and a stretched dog with high withers, a straight back and good length of croup. He had a truly excellent forehand with a long well laid upperarm and very good hind angulation with broad thighs. He stood clean in front and, while his elbows were firm, the hocks were a little loose as were the ligaments over the back. His movement was very good indeed, with a powerful drive and very good groundcover. He brought to his progeny the Dunmonaidh Junker qualities of great masculinity, substance, groundcovering movement, typy appearance, strong bones, outstanding forehand and hind angulations.

Zorba both complemented and built upon Orkan, Putz and later Awol. A great bonus was the high level of hip scores in his progeny and he can be credited with

*Hasenway Putz.*

completely reversing the forehand problem in Australia.

## QUINCITO AWOL

Awol was the most structurally correct dog of all the Siegers. He was a very handsome, charismatic and noble dog of lovely colour and great presence.

A 64.5 cm dog, he was as impressive in stance as he was in movement and was a major show winner in Australia for many years. He was not as strongly boned as Zorba or Putz, but he was absolutely masculine, with dark eyes, a lovely neck, high pronounced withers, a firm tight back and slightly short but well laid croup. He had a clean over and underline with excellent chest formation, a forehand that was on a par with the forehand of Zorba, and a hindquarter that was pronounced; he had long limbs and was quite typy to his sire Heiko v.d. Burg Hausbrunn. Unlike Zorba, he did not have a full type coat but nor was it short. He had a lovely dark mask that enhanced his very noble, handsome appearance and expression. In movement he was impressive, although not always enthusiastic, yet, when enthused, he was spectacular in walk as in gait.

Awol complemented Zorba, Putz/Condor and Orkan very well and was an excellent dog to consolidate their virtues. He tended to produce just medium-boned, dry, firm, large, typy, medium-coated, well-angulated, showy, expressive dogs.

## DORSTEN MONTE CITO

Monte Cito was in many ways, very typy to Putz/Condor, particularly in relation to his proportions, substance, masculinity and harmony.

He was a 65.0 cm dog that was in most respects very correct and free of any form of exaggeration – a black and gold, well-coated, medium-strong dog with good withers, a firm straight tight back and a slightly short but well-moulded croup. He had a dark mask, dark eyes, strong neck of medium length, good chest proportions, a good forehand and very good hind angulation. He had the inheritance of Orkan with the wrist strength and should have stood more correct in front. He was in all other respects a dog with very good bone connection and overall firmness. This was a dog who gave a very good impression in stance due to his overall very good structure and balance, but this was further enhanced by his very good movement and, particularly, the harmony and continuity of it after prolonged gaiting. Of all the Siegers this is the one that came closest to the ideal insofar as balance, harmony, lack of exaggeration and consistency of presentation are concerned.

He gave to his progeny his excellent proportions, very good strength and substance, balance, and medium eye colour. There were mixed withers, clean firm toplines, slightly short croups, good angulations but, in overall summation, he gave a depth and standard of quality that few dogs are able to do. This was a dog of considerable breed value that blended extremely well with main line sires and who gave Australia much depth and material for future years.

*Quincito Awol.*

## INIFF VAGRANT

This was a 64.0 cm dog who had an outstanding show career from a very early age. A dark-eyed and darkly coloured, fully coated, evenly tempered, masculine, well-proportioned dog with very good fore and hind angulation.

Like Monte Cito he was very well-balanced and was free of any form of exaggeration. He had a very masculine, well-coloured, darkly pigmented face with very strong jaws, a powerful neck, straight firm backline and very good length and lay of croup.

The thighs were broad and powerful and he showed very good firmness in his steps and stance. The chest proportions were very good despite the fact that he appeared short in foreleg due to his heavy coat. And, as with Awol, his movement was exceptional when enthused.

Vagrant brought to his progeny a phenotype that was characterized by dark colour, very good proportions and balance, full coat, much strength and substance, dark eyes, good fore and hind angulations, short straight backs, slightly short steep croups – and a few not standing quite straight in front. In all respects a very influential and successful sire.

## KARDIN CHATS CHAMPION

This was a very substantial, well-boned, masculine, powerful, well-coated, reasonably pigmented but well-coloured black and gold dog, who, structurally, was the best Zorba son and had a very good show career. He was a 65.0 cm noble and very handsome, just slightly deep-chested, dog with an extrovert nature that won him many fans.

He had a very powerful jaw formation, a powerful neck, pronounced wither, firm straight back and slightly short croup. He had very good fore and hind angulation with powerful thighs and a fully developed fore and underchest with strong bones.

As a young dog there was looseness in the joints; however, these firmed considerably by the time he was four years of age. He was criticized because of his light eyes. He brought to his progeny the lovely strength and substance, light eyes, pronounced withers, good toplines, slightly short croups and upperarms not quite as good as his own. The early joint problems he exhibited were not really seen in his progeny.

## THE FUTURE

In recent years there has been a remarkable influx of German bloodlines. Some of the bloodlines are new to Australia, others already exist. The arrival of these animals will be of major significance, even though their value at this early stage is unknown. Certainly breeders are keen to take advantage following the long drought of new blood in Australia. Thus, it will be of particular interest to keep track of the resulting offspring and see how the lines will marry with the existing bloodlines. These imported dogs will broaden the blood base , which has always been a problem due to the enormous costs involved in importing dogs, and of Australia's isolated geography.

# 15 *HEALTH CARE*

For the dog's comfort, and in order to have a responsive working dog, it is essential to maintain a dog in as good health as possible. A dog that is undernourished or anaemic will tire easily and be unwilling to perform too many tasks. Similarly, the dog with aching hips, or a dull but constant pain from bad teeth, will become bad-tempered and quick to turn if it thinks that, by being touched, the pain will intensify. The veterinary surgeon will want to co-operate with you, as the owner of the German Shepherd, in keeping the animal well for as long a natural life as possible, but the dog must be handled well when brought into the surgery to allow a full examination to be made. With large breeds the collection of blood samples for disease screening may be impossible unless the dog is first muzzled or well sedated, as the person withdrawing blood from the dog's forearm is placed in a very hazardous situation. Some veterinary surgeons prefer to collect samples from the jugular vein at the lower side of the neck and this is especially useful when larger volumes of blood are needed for analysis. Co-operate with your veterinary surgeon by attending for the annual booster vaccines, and remember it is beneficial, on these visits, to allow the dog to be inspected for early signs of disease. Visits early on in life, when there are no painful procedures and when rewards can be

offered by the veterinary staff for good behaviour, will make future visits all the easier.

Between visits, you should inspect your dog for any changes in coat condition, for breath odour or for any unusual lumps or swellings. Daily brushing and grooming helps you to get to know the dog and pick up any early signs of disease. Improved diet and preventative vaccinations are contributing to a much longer life for all domestic animals. The dog's weight should be watched, and weighing at three-monthly intervals, if suitable scales can be found, helps to detect any gradual change in condition.

SELECTING VETERINARY CARE
The choice of a veterinary surgeon may be based on accessibility, especially if you like to walk your dog to the surgery. Dogs excited by car travel may be frustrated if, after a journey, they are deposited in a waiting-room full of other dogs' odours and no opportunities to work off their pent-up energy. If there is no practice nearby to which the dog can be walked, some people make enquiries from other German Shepherd owners they meet before deciding which veterinary practice will have the greatest sympathy to their dog and their requirements for veterinary care. Treatment prices will vary and it is fairly easy to phone around and

grooming, especially at times when they are moulting. Knots in the coat are easier to remove when they have only been present for a short time rather than having been left for weeks or more. Grooming your dog is an ideal time to inspect the body closely, to look for any unexpected abnormalities and assess the general condition. The sooner a health problem is noticed, the quicker the vet can be asked for an opinion, and the better the chance of a full recovery in a progressive disease or a tumour.

The German Shepherd puppy should be groomed from the earliest age so that the puppy will learn to consider such handling to be a pleasurable experience. Procedures will be easier to carry out if this is started early in life. If a dog is used to being handled in this way, it will be far easier for a veterinary surgeon to make an examination, and a visit to the surgery becomes less stressful for the owner as well as for the dog. Before you start to groom the dog, carry out a thorough physical examination to check for any abnormalities. Always start at the head end, as the hands are cleaner when looking at the orifices on the head, before handling the dog's feet and the anal region.

EYES: Inspect the eyes first for matter or discharges in the corner. There should be no excessive watering and the white of the eye should be briefly looked at to see that it is not red or discoloured. The surface of the eye should be clear and bright and the expression one of alertness. There are specific diseases that affect the eyes, so any abnormal signs should be noted and reported to the veterinary surgeon if necessary.

enquire the cost of a booster vaccine, or the cost of neutering, in order to judge the level of charges, especially if you are new to an area. Facilities in practices are not all the same, so a practice or veterinary hospital with 24-hour nursing staff residing on the premises and equipment for emergency surgery, will have to charge more than the smaller surgery, which adequately provides for vaccination and other injections but requires you to go elsewhere for more complicated procedures.

## GENERAL GROOMING AND HYGIENE
German Shepherds have relatively easy coats to maintain but they do require daily

EARS: A painful ear can be a very irritating complaint for your dog, so the prevention of ear problems is important. If there is a noticeable build-up of wax in the ear canal, this can be easily removed by first softening the wax with an ear-cleaning fluid and then wiping gently with cotton wool. The use of cotton-wool buds in the ear is discouraged and all cleaning should be the most gentle possible. There is a range of ear cleaners suitable for the German Shepherd and the vet will advise on the one most appropriate for routine use.

If there is an excessive amount of wax in the canal, or if the ear is hot, reddened or swollen, this is an indication of infection or inflammation and veterinary attention should be sought quickly. Should an infection be left untreated, the dog will scratch the affected ear repeatedly, often introducing other infections carried on its soiled hind toenails. Oozing, and the multiplication of harmful bacteria in the moist discharges, will make the ear much worse and treatment becomes more difficult. In some dogs ulcers will be seen in the base of the wide open ear and any cold wind, or inadvertent touching of the ear, may make the dog cry out, having experienced a sharp pain.

MOUTH: Check your dog's gums each day for redness or inflammation. This can develop as the tartar builds up on the teeth and food particles get caught at the gum margin. The decaying food will produce breath odour if not removed and mouth bacteria can produce even worse halitosis. The teeth and gum margins have pain receptors, so any tartar build-up can lead to a disease which puts the dog off its food and even causes bad temper. With some German Shepherds it may be almost impossible to examine the condition of the back molar teeth until the dog is given a general anaesthetic or a deep sedative.

Canine toothpastes are now available, which can be used to help prevent a build-up of tartar. If the dog's teeth are cleaned regularly, you will avoid a state of dental neglect so advanced that your German Shepherd needs a general anaesthetic to have the teeth scaled and polished at the veterinary practice. Start brushing a dog's teeth at about four months of age but avoid the areas where the permanent teeth are about to erupt. At first, the puppy will want to play but, little by little, will become used to having all its teeth cleaned while young and small – rather than you waiting until you have a fully-grown dog before you start teeth-cleaning, because the dog will then object to the procedure.

Puppies lose their milk teeth between four and six months and sore gums will be apparent at that age. Massaging the skin just below the eye will help when the molar teeth are about to erupt. While grooming the older dog, look for signs of abnormalities such as mouth warts, excess saliva or white froth at the back of the mouth.

NOSE: Again, remove any discharges and look for cracking or fissuring. There is little point in worrying about a 'cold wet nose' as a health indicator.

SKIN AND COAT: Examine the whole of your dog's body when grooming. Tell-tale black dirt or white scurf may indicate a parasite infection. Patches of hair loss, redness of skin and abnormal lumps may first be found during grooming. Your German Shepherd's coat will normally have a slight shine, and oil from the sebaceous glands will give it water-proofing grease that gives the smooth feel as the hand is run over the hair.

NAILS AND FEET: Nails should be worn short, as over-long nails may splinter painfully, especially in cold weather when the nail is brittle. If the dog is regularly walked on hard surfaces such as concrete, paving stones or rocks, the nails will wear down naturally. Tarmac and grass do little to wear nails down at exercise times. If the nails are left to become too long, they are difficult for the dog to wear down; the heel takes more of the weight of the leg and the nails may split, with painful consequences.

Clipping nails is a delicate task. If you cut too short, into the quick, blood will flow and the dog will find it painful. The dog may then become very wary of anyone who tries to get near its feet with nail clippers held in the hand. Exercising the dog on concrete may be safer for the beginner than attempting to cut across the nail with new, sharp clippers.

Make a habit of feeling the area between the toes, where tufts of hair attract sticky substances. Clay soils can form little hard balls between the toes, and tar or chewing gum can be picked up on a walk with equally damaging effect. You will notice any cuts and pad injuries when handling the feet for grooming.

PERINEUM AND GENITAL AREA: Check for swollen anal sacs or unexpected discharges. Segments of tapeworms might be seen near the rectum. The bitch's vulva should not discharge except when signs of her being on heat are present. The prepuce of the male dog should have no discharge and the penis should not protrude, except if the dog is unwisely excited during the grooming or handling.

GROOMING: Once the first physical examination has been carried out, a grooming routine for the German Shepherd should be followed. Here is one I recommend, based on a large kennel which trains dogs:
1. Using your finger-tips, massage the coat against the normal backward lie of the hairs.

This will loosen up the dead hairs and encourage the skin to secrete the sebum oil that gives the healthy shine.
2. Use a bristle brush to pick up the hair you have loosened, again working against the lie of the coat.
3. Using a metal-toothed comb, you can now work your way in a methodical order over the dog's body, combing with the lie of the coat, paying particular attention to the feathering down the hind legs, tail and around the neck and ears.
4. Finally, to finish, bring a shine to the coat; use a bristle brush down the back and limbs. Brush the neck and head, praising the dog or offering a small food reward.

## PREVENTATIVE CARE – VACCINATIONS

The use of vaccines to prevent disease is well-established for human as well as animal health. The longer life expectancy of the animal, and the comparative rarity of puppy disease and early death, is something that has been taken for granted in the last 40 years. Yet many older dog breeders remember the very ill puppies that died of distemper fits or were left twitching with chorea for the rest of their lives; so the appearance of parvovirus in 1979 was an unpleasant shock to those who thought that veterinary treatment could deal with all puppy diarrhoeas. There were then many deaths in puppies under 12 months old until the new vaccines gave protection. Some died of sudden heart failure caused by the parvovirus damaging the heart muscle. Immunity later protected the puppy, either through the mother's milk, or by the early use of vaccines to stimulate the puppy's own body defences as they became old enough to respond to an injected vaccine.

The vet is the best person to advise on the type of vaccine to use and at what age to give it, since vets have a unique knowledge of the type of infection prevalent in a locality and when infection is likely to strike.

An example of this is in the Guide Dogs for the Blind Association's breeding programme where, for over 25 years, early vaccination was given to the six-week-old puppy. No isolation after this early vaccination was needed. The procedure was contrary to general advice given in the 60s and 70s when puppy disease was at an acceptably low figure. Later, when parvovirus infection was widespread in the early 80s, the mortality rate of GDBA puppies was much lower than among the puppies of breeders who had kept their puppies in kennels until 12 weeks or longer, before selling them. The temperament of some breeds was also suspect, due to a longer enforced isolation after vaccination. Proper socialisation did not take place, as the new owners of such puppies were advised not to take them out until four months of age when a final parvo booster had to be given. This meant that there were no opportunities to mix with people and other dogs until an age when this, the older puppy, had already developed a fear of being handled by strangers or was suspicious of other dogs met outside the home.

DISTEMPER: Always considered the classical virus disease, it has become very rare where vaccine is used on a regular basis. From time to time distemper is seen in larger cities, where there is a stray or roaming dog population unprotected by vaccination. This may subsequently lead to infection of show, or other kennel dogs, that do not have a high level of immunity.

The virus has an incubation of seven to 21 days and infection is followed by a rise in temperature, loss of appetite, a cough and often diarrhoea. Discharges from the eyes and nose may be watery at first but often become thick mucoid with a green or creamy colour due to secondary infections. The teeth are affected when the puppy of under six

months of age is infected by the virus; enamel defects shown as brown marks last for life and are known as 'distemper teeth'.

The 'hard pad' strain seen in the 60s is now considered to be nothing more than the hyperkeratosis of the nose and footpads that occurs after all distemper infections; the name is still in use when dog illness is written or talked about. In over half of all dogs affected with distemper, damage to the nervous system will show as fits, chorea (twitching of muscles) or posterior paralysis. Old dogs may develop encephalitis (ODE) due to latent distemper virus in the nervous tissue.

The vaccines in use today are all modified live vaccines and are highly effective in preventing disease. The age for a first injection will partly depend on the maker's instruction sheet and partly on a knowledge of the amount of protection passed by the mother to the young puppies. Maternally derived immunity (MDI) might block the vaccine in the young puppy, but blood sampling of bitches during their pregnancy was used as a method of estimating how soon the puppy would respond to vaccine. The use of a first vaccine at six weeks is now becoming more widespread; this allows for the all-important early socialisation period of the puppy's development.

PARVOVIRUS: This is probably the third most important dog virus disease in Europe – the first being rabies and the second distemper – and, like distemper, it is largely preventable by the correct use of vaccination. The speed with which an infection could spread from kennel to kennel surprised many, but the disease is caused by a very tough virus that can be carried on footwear that has walked though virus-infected faeces. The virus may then persist for up to a year; it is untouched by many commonly used kennel disinfectants. The sudden death of puppies caused by damage to the heart muscle, often just after sale, is no longer seen, but the gastro-enteritis form still occurs.

The sudden illness takes the form of repeated vomiting in the first 24 hours followed by profuse, watery diarrhoea, often with a characteristic sour smell and a red-brown colour. The cause of death was often from the severe dehydration that accompanied this loss of fluid. However, once it was understood that puppies should be treated with intravenous fluids similar to the treatment of human cholera victims, the death rate fell. Fluids by mouth are sufficient in less severe cases, provided they replace the essential electrolytes. The traditional mixture of a level teaspoonful of salt and a dessert-spoonful of glucose in two pints of water has saved many lives.

Vaccination of the young puppy is recommended, although the MDI may partially block the effectiveness of the vaccine, as is seen with distemper. A live vaccine at six weeks, followed by a further dose at 12 weeks, will protect most puppies. The four-month booster is no longer in common use, but it is now more usual to see parvovirus in the recently weaned puppy or the five-month-old puppy, where immunity no longer protects that individual against infection.

HEPATITIS: This disease, produced by an adenovirus, is now quite rare but one form (CAV-2) is often associated with 'kennel cough' infection in dogs. After infection, the virus multiplies in the lymphatic system and then sets out to damage the lining of the blood vessels. It was for this reason that the cause of death was liver failure, so the name hepatitis was given as, on post mortem, the liver was seen to be very swollen and engorged with blood. Other organs are also damaged and about 70 per cent of recovered dogs are found to have kidney damage. The

eye damage known as 'blue eye' seen on recovery is not recognised in the German Shepherd but was quite common in certain other breeds. Vaccination at six and 12 weeks, using a reliable vaccine that contains the CAV-2 virus, is very effective as a prevention against this disease.

LEPTOSPIROSIS: Caused by bacteria, it differs from the previous group of viral infections as protection has to be provided by at least two doses of a killed vaccine, and a 12-monthly repeat dose of this vaccine is essential if the protection is to be maintained. The type of leptospirosis spread by rats is the most devastating to the dog and frequently results in jaundice, then death from kidney and liver failure unless early treatment with antibiotics is available.

The other serotype of leptospira that damages the dog's kidney is less often seen since vaccination and annual boosters have been regularly used. Shepherd dogs and dogs that walk and work in the country where rats may have contaminated water courses, are especially at risk. German Shepherds kept as guards in factory yards have been known to die of jaundice because of contamination by rats. Sometimes dogs kept entirely in kennels may be affected if rats cross the exercise yards and leave infected urine for the dog to sniff at or lick up.

KENNEL COUGH: As a troublesome infection that causes harsh coughing in dogs, originating from the trachea and bronchial tubes, Kennel Cough has become one of the best known diseases. Traditionally dogs became infected in boarding kennels but it has recently been suggested it should be called 'infectious bronchitis', as any dog coming within droplet infection distance of another dog coughing at a show, or in public exercise areas, may catch the illness. There are five known viral and bacterial agents that may all, or perhaps only two of them at a time, cause the disease known as kennel cough. Vaccination by nose drops of a Bordetella vaccine can be offered to give protection, and protection is often given just a week before a dog goes into kennels. The normal booster vaccine given contains protection for three other known causes of kennel cough.

The disease develops within four to seven days of infection, so it may not be seen until after a dog has just left the kennels. The deep harsh cough is often described as 'if a bone or something was stuck in the throat'. The dog coughs repeatedly. Even with treatment, coughs last for 14 days but in some dogs the cough lasts as long as six weeks. Infection may then persist in the trachea, and if the

*Photo:*
*Steph Holbrook.*

dog is a 'carrier', it may get subsequent bouts of coughing if stressed. This explains why some non-coughing dogs put into board may cause an outbreak of kennel cough. Once only a summer-time disease, Kennel Cough outbreaks now occur at any time of the year, often after a holiday period when more dogs than usual are boarded

RABIES: The virus disease is almost unknown to most UK veterinarians due to a successful quarantine policy that has kept the island free of rabies in dogs and in wild life such as foxes. The mandatory quarantine policy may not be maintained, as the six-month period of isolation does not have a strong scientific basis. The Swedish government's switch to a compulsory vaccination and identification policy for all has provided a basis for modification of the UK laws on importing dogs. In countries such as the Philippines, where rabies was widespread and causing human deaths, it was found that at least 75 per cent of the dog population had then to be compulsorily vaccinated. This included the rounding-up of all strays for vaccination and tagging, to delay the spread of this disease. The virus disease must always be rigorously controlled in animals because of the devastating effect of one human becoming infected. Rabies control measures will involve vaccinating foxes by oral vaccine if the disease enters and becomes established in the UK. Inactivated rabies vaccine is available in the UK; it has been used for many years in dogs intended for export. Elsewhere in the world, both live attenuated vaccines and inactivated vaccines are used on an annual basis.

BOOSTERS: Thanks to the development of effective canine vaccines by the pharmaceutical industry, most of the diseases described above are now uncommon in Europe and N. America. The need for an annual booster is essential to keep up a high level of immunity where killed vaccines are used, and with live virus vaccines it probably does no harm to inject repeat doses every year. It is easy to become complacent about the absence of infectious disease in German Shepherds and it is false economy to overlook the need for revaccination.

INTERNAL PARASITES
ROUNDWORMS: The most common worms in puppies and dogs up to a year of age are *Toxocara* and *Toxacaris*. Puppies with roundworms will start to pass worm eggs into the environment as early as three weeks and most eggs are released when puppies are about seven weeks of age. This is the most dangerous time for the exercise areas to be contaminated with eggs, and for any young children who play with the puppies to get the slightly sticky worm eggs on their hands. Children may lick their fingers and consequently catch *Zoonotic Toxocariasis*.

Adult dogs also pass roundworms, which have been seen emerging from the rectum of the nursing bitch that develops diarrhoea. Worms may also appear in the vomit, if the worm moves forward from the intestine into the stomach by accident.

Control of worms depends on frequent dosing of young puppies – from as early as two weeks of age and repeated every two to three weeks until they are three months old. To prevent puppies carrying worms, the pregnant bitch can be wormed from the 42nd day of pregnancy with a safe, licensed wormer such as fenbendazole. The wormer can be given daily to the bitch until the second day after all the puppies have been born. Routine worming of adults twice a year, with a combined tablet for round and tapeworms, is a good preventative measure. If there are young children in a household, even more frequent worm dosing may be advisable to reduce the risk of roundworm larvae migrating to the child and of possible subsequent eye damage.

TAPEWORMS: They are not known to kill dogs but the appearance of a wriggling segment coming through the rectum, or moving on the tail hair, is enough to deter all but the most unsqueamish dog lover. Responsible, regular worming of dogs is needed, to avoid the harm that dog worms can do to other creatures. The biggest threat is from the *Echinococcus* worm that a dog obtains if feeding from raw sheep offals. The worm is only six millimetres long but several thousand could live in one dog. If a human should swallow a segment of this worm it may move to the person's liver or lungs, in the same way as it would in the sheep. A major illness would be the unpleasant result, another example of a zoonotic infection. Foxes, too, may carry *Echinococcus* infection.

The most frequently found tapeworm is *Dipylidium caninum*. It is not a long tapeworm compared with the old-fashioned *Taenia* worms, but when segments break off they may be recognised, as they resemble grains of rice attached to the hairs of the dog's tail. The tapeworm has become more common in dogs and cats since the number of fleas has increased; the intermediate host of this worm is the flea or the louse. When dogs groom themselves they attempt to swallow any crawling insect on the skin's surface and, in this way, may become infested with tapeworms even though worming twice a year is carried out. Flea control is just as important as worming in preventing tapeworm infection. Three-monthly dosing with tablets is a good idea – less frequently if the dog is known to be away from sources of reinfection. The other tapeworms of the *Taenia* species come from dogs eating raw rabbits (*T. serialis* or *pisiformis*) or from sheep, cattle or pig offals (*T. ovis, hydatigena* or *multiceps*).

HOOKWORMS: These are less frequently found as a cause of trouble in the UK but are prevalent in other parts of the world. The hookworm does damage to the intestine by using its teeth on its lining. *Uncinaria* may be the cause of poor condition and thinness. Diarrhoea is seen as permanently soft, discoloured faeces that respond dramatically to worming. The other hookworm, *Ancylostoma*, may be found to be the reason for anaemia and weakness. Exercising dogs over grass used by wild foxes for excretion and scent marking allows the dog to reinfect itself with hookworm eggs.

OTHER INTERNAL PARASITES: *Giardia* is a parasite that occurs in dogs in kennels. It should be investigated in dogs with diarrhoea that have come through quarantine. It is a protozoal organism that likes to live in stagnant surface water; it is of especial interest because a similar strain is a cause of dysentery in humans, especially where water-borne infection is blamed for the illness. It may be necessary routinely to treat all dogs in kennels with a drug such as fenbendazole to prevent a continuing problem.

Whipworms are found in the large intestine and are identified when faeces samples are examined after mucoid dysentery affects a dog. Treatment is effective using a reliable anthelminthic. Heart worms are unknown in most parts of the UK but are a great problem in other countries. Bladder worms are only detected when urine samples are examined; they are similar to the Whipworms and fortunately are rare. Any obscure illness in a dog should require the examination of fresh faeces samples.

ECTOPARASITES
External parasites may cause intense irritation and skin diseases from scratching and rubbing. In recent years the cat flea has become by far the most common ectoparasite

of German Shepherds, but more traditional sarcoptic mange, lice and ringworm skin infections do appear from time to time. Demodectic mange may have a hereditary basis as it is seen more frequently in certain strains and litters.

FLEAS: The flea that hops may never be found in the German Shepherd's coat but its presence may be detected by the flea dirt or excreta containing dried blood. Grooming your dog over white paper or a light table top may reveal black bits that turn dark red like blood spots when moistened. Once the flea dirt is found, a closer inspection of the dog may show fleas running though the coat at skin level. At one time the fleas preferred to live in the hair down the spine towards the tail head but now they are often found in the shorter hairs of the abdomen or the neck. This may relate to the fact that cat fleas are the most commonly found variety in dogs in the UK. Such fleas prefer a softer hair structure for their 'living space'. All fleas are temporary visitors who like to feed from the dog by biting to suck blood, but in their development and egg-laying stages they may live freely off the dog thereby escaping some of the parasitic dressing put on their host's coat. Re-infestation then becomes possible and many flea treatments appear to be ineffective unless the flea in the environment is eliminated at the same time.

There is a wide range of antiparasitic sprays, washes and baths available and the German Shepherd owner may well be confused as to how and when to apply these. There is the further problem that some dogs seem able to carry a few fleas on them with very little discomfort, while others show intense irritation and will bite pieces out of themselves in an attempt to catch the single flea. A cat in the household or crossing the garden may drop flea eggs, and in a warm place they can hatch out and develop into more fleas waiting to jump onto the dog.

Flea eggs and immature larvae may lie dormant for months waiting to complete their development and become ready to bite. Adult fleas too can wait for months off an animal until able to find a host to feed from, so treating the dog is only tackling part of the problem; the kennels or the house has to be treated as well. Vacuum cleaning and easy-to-clean sleeping quarters for the dog help enormously in dealing with a flea infestation once an environmental spray has been applied. The choice of aerosol spray, medicated bath, tablet by mouth or agent that stops larval development is a wide one, and experience will show which method is most suitable for each dog affected.

LICE: These may be found in the dog's coat occasionally – especially in dog leading an outdoor life, more than the average pet dog. Lice spend their whole life on the dog and fairly close contact between dogs is necessary to spread the parasites. Large numbers of lice cause intense irritation with hair loss. Biting lice can produce anaemia when they are present in large enough numbers to remove blood continuously, at a rate similar to a bleeding ulcer. Liquid treatments applied as a total bath soak are best. Lice eggs can be transmitted from dog to dog on grooming brushes. The lice and their eggs are visible to the naked eye, and should be spotted during the normal grooming routine.

MANGE MITES: These mites cannot be seen during grooming. If they are suspected, scrapings from the skin surface are sent for examination under the microscope. The two forms of mange, *Sarcoptes* and *Demodex,* can be distinguished in this way, but bare skin patches of low-grade mange infection may at first seem similar when a dog is examined. There are a number of differences in the two forms of mange that need not be enumerated here, but one simple distinction is that sarcoptic mange is very itchy and spreads from dog to dog, while demodectic mange in the older dog usually remains as a scaly, hairless patch and, although an obvious blemish, does not cause a lot of itching. Antiparasitic baths with pyrethroids or amitraz, and topical applications of organophosphorous washes will have to be repeated, but are usually effective. Blood tests may be used for diagnosis of sarcoptic mange.

TICKS: Ticks are large enough not to be missed and can be expected in those dogs working where sheep, hedgehogs etc. leave tick eggs about. Applications of pyrethroid or other 'spot' liquids on the neck and rump will keep ticks off a dog for a month. Baths are also effective. Ticks may be removed by first soaking them in vegetable oil, then gently coaxing and lifting the tick's head away from the dog's skin.

CHEYLETIELLA: These cause surface irritation of dogs and intense itching in humans living with the dogs who happen to get bitten. The so-called 'moving dandruff' show up as white flecks on a black dog's skin, but may be more difficult to see on a light-coloured dog. Antiparasitic shampoos will kill the surface feeder but carrier dogs in kennels may show very few symptoms at all.

MALASEZZIA: This is a yeast-like surface organism that appears in dogs with low resistance to infection. A patchy coat and dull hair appearance should make the German Shepherd owner suspect the presence of yeasts in unusually large numbers. Once identified, baths and general hygiene, with improved nutrition, help the dog to overcome this problem. The yeast will also be found in the ear canal and if shown to be present on a stained smear in large numbers,

then the ear should be treated with a suitable preparation of Miconazole, Nystatin or Thiabendazole.

RINGWORM: Ringworm is found in dogs as a fungal infection of the hair. The signs of a 'ring' are not always present, and some dogs show quite a violent itchy skin response once infected. Cattle ringworm can be transmitted to country dogs. Ringworm spores can remain in the environment and in old woodwork for a long time. Diagnosis by skin tests is slow but reliable, as the 'Woods' lamp, which uses ultraviolet light, does not identify all types of ringworm. Treatment with anti-fungal washes, or the antibiotic griseofulvin, may be used to eliminate the mycotic infection.

## ACCIDENTS AND FIRST AID

A few simple procedures described here do not suggest that there are no other things that can be done as 'first aid', but in most cases the sooner the patient gets to the veterinary surgery, the better the chance of a full recovery may be. For this reason, splinting broken bones is now out of favour, and more pain may be caused in trying to tie on a splint than if the dog is quickly transported to a place where any shock and pain can be treated professionally. X-rays will better show the nature of a fracture and what is the best method of treatment.

TRAFFIC ACCIDENTS: German Shepherds, being solid dogs, seldom go underneath vehicles but they tend to get severe chest injuries if hit in front, or pelvic and limb injuries if struck on the side. Fractures of the long bones of the leg are another common result of injury with a fast-moving car. Any dog hit by a car will be distressed and because of fright and pain will tend to bite, even when its familiar owners are present to attempt to help. First, assess the injuries by noting any gaping holes and where blood is being lost. Do this before touching the dog's head. Some frightened dogs may try to run away at that point, so a lead or scarf round the neck will help to steady the dog, and a tape muzzle may have to be used before a dog is lifted into a vehicle for transport to the surgery.

A pressure bandage applied to a bleeding area is the best way of staunching blood flow, but improvisation with whatever cloth is to hand is acceptable in a life-saving situation. The dog may be breathing rapidly or gasping with 'air hunger' signs. In this case, the mouth and nostrils should be wiped free of dried blood or saliva to help unblock the airway. If you suspect a spinal injury, slide a board under the dog before picking it up. Otherwise, a blanket is the best way of allowing two or more persons to pick up an injured dog without aggravating the injuries.

CHOKING AND VOMITING: Try to find out the cause of any sudden attack. Grass awns may enter the throat and airways in the summer months, and at any time of year a dog that has been playing ball or stick retrieval games may get an obstruction at the back of the throat. Even a fine bamboo cane may become wedged across the upper molar teeth. In the case of one gundog that had been out shooting all day, a length of cane was retrieved from the upper part of the oesophagus the same evening. Poisonous substances may cause retching and vomiting; and thirsty dogs have been known to drink from toilet bowls and so unsuspectingly drinking bleach and other cleaning substances.

Having initially looked for a foreign body, your first aid measures should be aimed at providing as good an air supply as possible. If there is any blistering or soreness of the lips or tongue, use honey or salad oil to coat the inflamed surfaces. A vomiting dog should be prevented from drinking water and regurgitating it as fast as it is swallowed. Ice cubes in a dish left to melt may help the dog, as it will drink the iced water more slowly.

COLLAPSE AND UNCONSCIOUSNESS: As in the road accident, assess the dog before touching to determine the cause of the incident, so that appropriate first aid can be given. The dog running in a field on a warm day may have had a circulatory collapse; the dog convulsing may be throwing an epileptic fit. The elderly dog found semi-conscious in the morning after voiding urine and faeces may have had a 'stroke' or vestibular disease. Each condition in turn will need different treatment, but, as a general rule, pull the tongue forward to ensure there is an airway to the lungs, keep the animal cool and avoid unnecessary noise and commotion. Look for any drugs or poisons that a dog may have swallowed, gently feel the left side for gas distending the abdomen, and check the pupils of the eyes and their response to a bright light. The veterinary surgeon will be better able to deal with the situation if a timetable of events, and any contributing factors, can be given to him in a concise manner and, of course, veterinary help is required as quickly as possible.

WASP AND BEE STINGS: Stings occur more often in the late summer. If stung, the foot usually swells rapidly or, if the dog has caught a wasp in its mouth, the side of the face swells up and the eye may become partly shut. Vinegar is a traditional remedy to apply to the sting area. If an antihistamine tablet is available, this can be given to the dog immediately to stop further swelling. Biting flies cause swellings on the body and may be the cause of the 'hot spots' or acute moist eczemas that German Shepherds can suffer from. Calamine lotions cool the skin but the dog should be discouraged from attacking its own skin, because, if licked, calamine causes vomiting.

SHOCK: This occurs to a greater or lesser extent with nearly all accidents. Keep the patient warm, wrapping a blanket, coat or wool garment around the body of the dog. Unless you have reasons to think an anaesthetic will be given, or other contra-indications exist such as throat damage, offer fluids by mouth in small quantities. Oral rehydration solutions can be obtained from the veterinary surgeon and a packet should be kept in every emergency first aid kit. As an alternative, a solution of half a teaspoon of salt and half a teaspoon of bicarbonate of soda dissolved in a litre of water may be given, a few dessert-spoonfuls at a time.

## SKIN DISEASES
Fleas are probably still the most common problem; the next most frequent in German Shepherds are auto-immune diseases. Flea bites may not be obvious, especially in a dense-coated breed. Once a dog becomes sensitised to the proteins injected by the flea when it first bites, any subsequent contact with flea saliva may bring on an itchy rash, even though no live fleas are found on the dog. The various other causes of parasitic skin disease have already been outlined on external parasites.

OTHER PRURITIC SKIN CONDITIONS: Anal sac irritation will cause a dog to nibble at the hair around the tail base, or it may cause licking and nibbling anywhere around the hindquarters. The glands may be so impacted that they cannot be emptied out during the dog's normal straining to pass faeces. An infected lining of one or both sacs may also be the cause of irritation, and this can often be detected by a fruity odour to the sac's contents or, at its worst, a smell like rotten meat.

Bacterial dermatoses result from multiplication of skin bacteria such as *Staph. intermedius*. Red blotches and ring-like marks around a central pustule are most clearly seen when the hairless areas of the abdomen are inspected. Skin swabs may be used to identify the bacteria present, and this information can be used then to choose the most appropriate antibiotic for the infection causing the irritation. A particular problem in the German Shepherd breed is anal furunculosis. The skin bacteria eat into the flesh around the anus causing oozing from tunnels and interconnecting ulcers. The infections do not always respond to normal antibiotic usage; and extensive surgical excision, often followed by cryosurgery may have to be given on more than one occasion before a cure can be obtained. In hot climate countries, German Shepherds have been docked as a way of treating anal furunculosis, but such drastic measures are not to be encouraged.

HAIR LOSS AND ALOPECIA: A German Shepherd's coat is normally shed twice a year, but sometimes the growth of new hair is delayed and the coat appears thin and lifeless and, if it is groomed excessively, bare patches develop. Investigations into the possibility of thyroid disease may be needed when there is a failure of hair to grow. Other hormonal skin disease may cause symmetrical hair loss in the flanks of a bitch, or bare tail-head areas (stud tail) in some dogs. Feminisation of the older male dog will have hair loss as one of the signs of a Sertoli cell tumour. Veterinary advice should be sought.

## DIGESTIVE SYSTEM DISORDERS
SICKNESS AND DIARRHOEA: Occasional sickness is not a cause for concern in the younger dog. The dog is adapted to feeding from a wide range of different foods,

*Photo: Steph Hobrook.*

and part of a protection against food poisoning is the ability to reject unsuitable foods by returning them from the stomach by reflex vomiting. If there is a yellow coloration to the vomit, it means that the bile from the liver, which normally passes into the small intestine after leaving the bile duct, has, for some reason, been passed forward to enter the stomach. The bitter bile acids will cause reflex vomiting as soon as they reach the stomach wall, and will be sicked up, together with any food left in the stomach.

Bacterial infections, such as those of *Salmonella* and *Campylobacter* can only be detected by the culture of faeces. The recognition of the importance of strains of *E. coli* as a cause of dog diarrhoea is an interesting development; renewed interest in this organism that was, at one time, thought to be harmless, is accompanied by the human deaths from the 0157 strain in cooked and raw meat.

Repeated sickness, starting off with recognisable food followed by slime, or food followed by mucus alone, is a more serious sign. It may be associated with obstructions due to a foreign body, or to infection such as pyometra or hepatitis. Some outbreaks of diarrhoea will start with food being vomited, as this will stimulate the intestine. As soon as food enters the small intestine, the stomach empties itself reflexly, by vomiting any food remaining within the stomach. Sometimes a reversal of the normal flow of food will cause the appearance of a faecal vomit.

Diarrhoea is the passage of frequent loose or unformed faeces: it is associated with infections and irritation of the intestine. The rapid transit of food taken in by mouth means that water cannot be absorbed by the large intestine, and soft or runny stools result from the incomplete digestion and water reabsorption. When blood is present it may appear as streaks from the large intestine. If blackish and foul-smelling, it means that the blood has come from the small intestine and has been subjected to some of the digestive fluids. The condition of blood in the faeces is then known as dysentery.

Chronic diarrhoea is a problem where the looseness of faeces lasts more than 48 hours. It may be associated with malabsorption, where the lining of the intestine is incapable of absorbing digested food. There are other diseases such as food intolerances, bacterial overgrowth, lymphoid and other tumours that may cause maldigestion, where there is some failure of the digestive juices to break down the food. Other causes are exocrine pancreatic insufficiency (EPI), inflammatory bowel diseases, or any disturbance in gastric or liver function. Investigations by the veterinary surgeon will include blood tests and faecal laboratory examinations. These may be followed by X-rays or endoscope examinations.

The treatment of sickness and diarrhoea involves, firstly, withholding solid food for 24 hours, giving small quantities of replacement fluids as soon as the dog stops vomiting (proprietary electrolyte fluids are probably best), then introducing a highly digestible food (with low fat is best) in small quantities – about one third of the normal amount fed on the second day of the illness. The amount should be increased slowly until, by the fourth day, a full ration of food is given again. In the recovery period fats should be avoided, as well as milk and dairy products, because of the dog's inability to digest lactose.

GASTRIC DILATION: This disease is better known as bloat, and 'torsion' can be a problem in any of the larger breeds. It is especially associated with feeding regimes where a highly digestible food can be swallowed rapidly and, if this is followed by the drinking of large quantities of water, this contributes to the development of the bloat. Feeding immediately after strenuous exercise has been blamed too. When a dog is fed with a meal in the late afternoon or evening, there is the greater risk of the dog lying down, so that abdominal movement associated with walking or jumping up does not allow for eructation, or the dispersal of gas from the stomach. Greedy feeders that swallow air as they gulp down their food are considered at greatest risk, but it does seem associated with the flat slab-chested dogs that have large deep chests and thus loosely suspended stomachs. An enlarged spleen, as is found in some German Shepherds, may contribute to the gastric dysfunction.

The bloated stomach may rotate as a 'torsion' or volvulus, and become the gastric dilation and volvulus condition known as

GDV, which means an acute emergency. The dog needs to be rushed to the veterinary surgery for treatment of shock and for the deflation of the stomach. Affected dogs seem uncomfortable, become depressed and look at their flanks with expressions of disbelief. At first, the left side just behind the ribs is the only side to bulge; percussion with the finger tips will produce a drum-like resonance over the left ribcage edge and over the distended abdomen behind. Within a few hours both sides of the abdomen appear distended behind the ribcage, the dog becomes more uncomfortable and lies down a lot as the pain increases. The gas-filled stomach presses on the diaphragm restricting the breathing, the colour of the tongue becomes more purplish and breaths are more frequent and quite shallow. Sometime at this stage, the weight of the enlarging spleen attached to the greater curvature of the gas-filled stomach makes the stomach twist in a clockwise direction. The signs of discomfort become more noticeable as the stomach's exit to the oesophagus is pinched off by a 180-degree rotation. If a stomach tube is passed through the mouth down the oesophagus at this stage the tube can be pressed down no further than just beyond the entrance level of the oesophagus into the abdomen. No gas will pass back up the tube, even though the stomach is still tight-filled with gas.

Emergency treatment at the veterinary surgery will usually mean setting up an intravenous drip to deal with the shock. Decompression of the stomach will be attempted, possibly first by passing the stomach tube as described above or, probably more successfully, by inserting a wide-bore (18 G needle) canula at the point behind the left rib arch that shows the most distension by the gas. The finger should then be kept on the needle hub protruding through the skin, partially to hold it in place as the size of the stomach reduces, and partially to vent the gas out slowly or in 'pulses. This ensures that the blood in the veins can start to flow towards the heart again, once the abdomen size returns to normal.

Frequently a laparotomy will be necessary to empty the stomach or to provide a means of fixing the stomach to the abdominal wall so that an adhesion will make it less likely that the gas distension will again appear. A number of operation techniques are used, some involve suturing the stomach wall to a rib, while others rely on a tube to vent gas from the stomach; the aim is to have a permanent adhesion to prevent rotation of the stomach at a later date. Some veterinary surgeons believe that feeding a complete canned food diet to the dog is the best preventative available.

CONSTIPATION: This disorder usually occurs either through the dog eating too many bones whose chalky residue clogs up the rectum, or, in older male dogs, it may be associated with enlargement of the prostate gland. Occasionally a tumour inside the rectum will cause straining and apparent constipation. Treatment with oily lubricants and enemas should be followed by high-fibre diets. Soluble fibre, as found in oatmeal, is thought to add to the moist faecal

bulk and thus retain water from the large intestine lumen, so that the faeces are not bone-hard and painful to pass. Allow exercise, or place the dog in the garden 30 minutes after feeding, as this will stimulate the reflexes for normal defecation.

## BREEDING AND REPRODUCTION
There are no specific problems in the German Shepherd and both mating and whelping should proceed with the minimum of trouble (see the chapter on breeding German Shepherds).

*Photo: Steph Holbrook.*

**THE OLDER GERMAN SHEPHERD**
GERIATRIC CARE: The German Shepherd has a medium life span; ten to 12 years of age was considered a good age for a working dog but a number may be able to live to 15 years provided they avoid arthritis and injuries. The tendency is for older German Shepherds to eat less – unlike other breeds where, if the food is available, overeating leads to adiposity and will significantly shorten the dog's life. Some of the oldest dogs are the leanest dogs, so dietary control helps if you wish your dog to live longer. After about ten years of age it may be of advantage to divide the daily ration into two small feeds to help absorption and digestion; any tendency to overweight must be checked and regular weighing helps to control the dietary intake. The older dog will use up less energy in exercise and, if housed for most of the day, fewer calories will be burned up to keep the dog warm. Some reduction in calorie intake is desirable and there are special diets prepared for the older dog that are higher in fibre and lower in energy than the diet for the younger dog,

Keep a careful watch on the condition of the mouth as breath odour is one of the first signs of dental disease or of decay of food trapped between the gums and 'ledges' of tartar that may have built up on the teeth. German Shepherds may have cracked teeth from chewing bones, or iron bars, earlier in their life, and only in old age does the tooth root become infected and an abscess develop. The back upper molar teeth are often affected and an abscess will show as a swelling immediately below the eye if the carnassial tooth has infected roots. Chewing as a form of jaw exercise is a method of keeping the teeth healthy, but when there is a build-up of plaque on the tooth surface, cleaning the teeth using an ultrasonic scaler, followed by a machine polisher, is the better way of keeping a healthy mouth.

Monitor the length of your dog's nails, since less exercise and possible arthritis sometimes lead the older dog to put less weight on the affected leg and nail overgrowth occurs. Careful trimming to avoid cutting into the 'quick', or live part of the nail, will help many older Shepherds. The elbows, too, should be inspected for calluses on their outer side, as dogs that are stiff do not move as often as they might to relieve their body weight on the surface they sleep on. The skin over the outside of the elbow has little padding from fat or muscle and bone lies just underneath, so leathery skin or a callus can easily occur. In extreme cases the callus develops cracks and fissures and a bacterial infection is set up so that the surface becomes pink and oozing.

URINARY INCONTINENCE: This is one of the problems found in many older dogs. Leakage from the bladder, resulting in damp patches in the bedding overnight, may be remedied by taking up the water bowl after 7pm to prevent evening drinking. Also effective is the use of one of the sympathomimetic group of drugs to promote bladder storage. A urine sample should be examined: sometimes a mild cystitis bacterium will be found in the urine. Treatment with an appropriate antibiotic will reduce bladder sensitivity and storage will be better. If large quantities of urine are being voided day and night, then investigation of urine-concentrating powers and blood biochemistry tests are necessary, to look for major disease. Diabetes insipidus or mellitus, Cushing's disease, liver disease and nephrosis may all be first detected as the dog being 'incontinent' when left shut indoors for more than a few hours. Blood tests are necessary to distinguish many of these conditions of the older German Shepherd.

# 16 BREED ASSOCIATED DISEASES

The great popularity of certain blood lines in this breed may have led to an unexpected concentration of genetic factors; these influences can lead to good things, but occasionally to bad. The total number of the German Shepherds bred must lead to a greater prominence of hereditary diseases than in breeds where only a quite small numbers of puppies are born each year. Many diseases are thought to have a genetic basis. Some of the skin and digestive disorders probably are related to the dog's immunity level, which may become reduced from the level of a working dog bred through generations for shepherding and herding. The bleeding disorders have a known breed incidence, and severely affected dogs would not survive long enough to be used for breeding, but the carrier state allows genetic factors to miss several generations before the problem is again seen.

## INHERITED EYE CONDITIONS

CATARACT: The German Shepherd is rarely affected by blindness from retinal atrophy but there is a hereditary cataract that can be seen in the young dog, affecting both eyes. It is slowly progressive and can be detected as vacuoles at the suture lines from eight weeks of age. The eye defect is soon recognised and affected dogs and their litter mates should not be used for breeding.

OPTIC NERVE HYPOPLASIA: Another hereditary condition, this is a severe blindness seen in the younger animal that may affect one or both eyes.

BLINDNESS: Blindness of the older dog may develop in a condition known as pannus, but as an eye disease it is now quite responsive to treatment with medication, provided it is treated early enough. The blindness may start as a red patch in the corner of the eye; it is a chronic immune-mediated kerato-conjunctivitis known in Europe as Uberreiter's syndrome. Other eye defects recorded are unlikely to affect the breed, except rarely in individuals; they include Colobomata, Corneal Dystrophy, Corneal Dermoid, Multifocal Retinal Dysplasia, and a progressive retinal degeneration. Glaucoma, a condition affecting the globe of the eye that over-inflates with fluid, is known to develop in the older Shepherd and inflammation-uveitis can cause a cataract, as a further complication.

RETINAL DYSPLASIA: The disease is not generally recognised in the German Shepherd breed. When examining the eyes of some gun dogs for the better-known hereditary diseases, small marks known as 'rosettes' are seen on the highly reflective retina; sometimes folds in the retina may also be seen at the back of the eye when ophthalmoscopic examinations are conducted. Some of these folds are seen as fine grey lines that seem to be of little consequence, but sometimes larger areas of brown discoloration are seen against the bright reflective surface of the tapetal fundus – the surface of the retina. Retinal dysplasia may, later in the disease, show itself as detachments of part or all of the retina and there may be a near total loss of vision.

MULTIFOCAL RETINAL DYSPLASIA (MRD): is the sort of retina disease looked for in German Shepherds but it is infrequently seen, has no known hereditary basis and is not inspected for in the present BVA/KC certification scheme, as it has caused no eyesight problem in the breed.

THE THIRD EYELID OR MEMBRANA NICTITANS: Eversion of the cartilage of the third eyelid. The third eyelid is an important structure in the protection of the eye. It helps produce some of the fluid that lubricates and protects the eye surface; the eyelid edge can move across the eye rather like a car windscreen wiper, to remove dust or other foreign body irritants on the eye surface. Eversion refers to the rolling over of the lid due to a weakness of the cartilage that normally stiffens the third eyelid. This buckling of the third eyelid is usually seen in younger German Shepherds and, as well as being unsightly in the red area exposed, it may also lead to keratitis, or secondary conjunctivitis, by the loss of the eyelid's protective effect. It is thought to have a hereditary basis but surgical correction by removing the curved cartilage is usually very successful.

ENTROPION AND ECTROPION: The condition of entropion can be an inherited defect of the eyelid structure. Rarely seen in German Shepherds, it is as an inturning of the eyelids; there may be excessive tear formation and the overflow of tears is seen on the faces of light-coloured dogs. When entropion does appear in the breed it is often the result of an injury to the eye, such as a dog fight or some other injury to the eyelids. Once diagnosed, the severe cases will need immediate surgery to evert the eyelid edge, milder cases may be treated with lubricating eye ointments.

Ectropion is the opposite condition to entropion, involving a looseness of the eyelids with undue exposure of the pink lining of the lid, which may develop after a facial injury. Ectropion can be a hereditary disease in some breeds with loose skin on the head but in the German Shepherd it is usually the result of injury and is not inherited.

## BONE AND JOINT DISEASES WITH HEREDITARY INFLUENCES

HIP DYSPLASIA (HD): The control of Hip Dysplasia has been a major consideration in the breeding of German Shepherds, but the problem is widespread and exists in most other dog breeds. All breeds have a problem where more than five per cent of the breed are showing recognisable signs. The working guide dog is rarely disadvantaged by hip dysplasia as it does not affect the daily life of the dog – the dog walks at a slow pace, does not have to jump up and does not do agility work. Any pain or discomfort in the young dog may be associated with a rupture of the round ligament of the hip, that suddenly allows for subluxation with a short period of pain. Fractures of the edges of the acetabulum may also cause some of this pain. In the older dog, pain from the disease of osteoarthritis can develop secondary to an existing hip dysplasia. The disease of Hip Dysplasia is not entirely a hereditary one and environmental factors such as feeding and exercise – and even the position the young dog is made to sit in – all may be responsible for up to 60 per cent of the occurrence of the hip dysplasia changes as seen on X-ray.

Fortunately the extreme views once held by experts of not breeding from any dog showing any traces of hip dysplasia have been moderated with time and experience. Some of the matings of 0/0 hip score dogs have produced litters of puppies with a hip score little better than the breed average of 19. With a range of scores between 0 and 106 in the breed, there would usually seem to be little justification for attempting to breed from any stock that has an above-average score. This policy may be modified by breeding from higher-scoring bitches that may have other characteristics that could be of especial value to the breeder in a programme which is seeking a particular type of dog.

## GUIDELINES FOR HIP IMPROVEMENT

1. i) Score all stock using the BVA/KC scheme. This necessitates X-rays of all young breeding stock.
ii) As far as practical, breed only from stock with a hip score better than the breed average.
iii) Follow recommendations about feeding and exercise to avoid undue injury and stress to the growing hip joint.

2. Regularly review all inherited diseases in the dog group, e.g. in a kennels, or enquire about litter mates or parents. Expect to get evasive replies when asking others about their dogs' hip scores, as not all are low ones!

OSTEOCHONDROSIS: This is a disease with a hereditary basis seen in many large and giant breeds of dogs; it is also known as OD or OCD. The German Shepherd is more likely to suffer from elbow osteochondrosis, and the condition of an ununited anconeal process may be detected on X-ray at or just after six months. One or both elbows may be affected, as shown by a fore-limb lameness of the growing puppy. Lameness is most likely to develop between five and seven months of age; it is not severe at first but later one elbow may become so badly affected that the dog cannot fully bend its elbow, and the muscles of the shoulder on that side become thinner, causing an imbalance of the dog as it walks.

A veterinary examination will show that when the elbow is bent up, the dog pulls its foot away because of the pain, the joint capsule may become more distended and the leg feels thinner than the opposite fore leg; but over half the dogs seen have OCD in both fore legs to a greater or lesser extent. OCD can also affect the other parts of the elbow such as the medial coronoid process; osteochondritis may be found on X-ray in the medial side of the distal humerus and in joint incongruity usually seen as a 'step' in the cup shape of the elbow.

The calcification of the flexor tendons of the medial side of the elbow is also seen in some X-rays and even calcification in the tendon attachment of the Triceps to the olecranon has been associated with lameness. Dogs may show osteochondrosis in the shoulder joint as well and this seems to develop at a slightly younger age than the elbow form. Both shoulder and elbow joints of both legs should be X-rayed to be sure of a correct diagnosis. The other joint to be affected is the hock joint of the back leg.

An X-ray under general anaesthesia is necessary to view the elbow joint, with the angle between the humerus and radius being set at about 45 degrees. A screening system for elbow dysplasia has been set up similar to the hip dysplasia scheme of assessment. The X-ray position allows the anconeal process and the dorsal edge to be looked at for lines of separation and for any new bone or secondary osteophyte formation. The minimum age for scoring is 12 months. Measurements of the signs of osteoarthrosis secondary to the OCD are set at 2 mm and 4 mm height when awarding 'scores' of the joints for disease. Severely affected parents should not be used in breeding programmes. Rapid bone growth produced by some high-protein diets may make the condition worse, as the bone cartilage grows at too fast a rate to be converted into stronger bone to support a joint.

PANOSTEITIS: is one cause of sudden lameness, most often in a fore leg but sometimes the lameness will alternate from front to back legs. The lameness is sudden and severe and it might suggest that a bone has been broken but an X-ray will show no damage to the bone structure at all. Darker areas in the bone marrow region may be seen in the X-ray plate and sometimes the periosteal bone appears thickened at the site of pain. It is believed that this is an auto-immune condition, as it does not appear until six months of age and only infrequently does it cause lameness in the middle-aged or elderly dog.

Treatment involves resting the dog for a few days then giving controlled exercise until the dog eventually walks soundly again. Non-steroidal anti-inflammatory tablets can be given and severely lame dogs may benefit from corticosteroid injections.

OSTEOARTHRITIS: This condition, which limits joint movement, starts as damage to the cartilage on the joint surface, then additional bone may be laid down round the edge of the joint, possibly as a result of inflammation and an attempt to support the joint. The disease develops progressively, leading to lameness, pain, the grating feeling known as crepitus and then joint instability. The joint feels thickened from the outside and there is limited movement when the joint is bent to stretch it or flex it. If a joint is not moving, then the muscles around it weaken or atrophy so that the leg becomes wasted. X-rays should be taken to assess the degree of new bone building up around the joint. A management plan for the dog can be drawn up; pain control is the first priority in treatment. Osteoarthritis particularly arises in this breed in old age as an after-effect of osteochondrosis of the elbow and from hip dysplasia's after-effects.

CRUCIATE LIGAMENT RUPTURE: The stifle or 'knee' joint is not robustly constructed as it depends on a number of ligaments and cartilages to hold it together and give free movement. The stifle is used most in jumping and for forward propulsion. Overweight dogs that are suddenly asked to perform tasks, even as simple as jumping out of a Range Rover or estate-car rear door, may land heavily and damage the ligaments.

The cruciate ligaments are the ones crossing the centre of the stifle joint and there are two other collateral ligaments that support the sides of the joint. The knee cap, or patella, also has ligaments that run at the front of the joint and these too can fail to support the stifle joint, throwing a greater strain on the two ligaments at the centre. It is usually the front ligament in the centre of the stifle joint – the anterior cruciate ligament – that takes the greatest strain when the dog jumps or turns awkwardly and this may tear or, at the worst, completely break in half. The result is a very lame dog. Often the stifle joint is so unstable that the two bone ends that form the joint can be slid over each other; this instability is used in the 'draw forward' test.

Cruciate rupture usually happens suddenly during extreme exercise. It does not improve with enforced rest. Heavy dogs will usually require a surgical operation to repair the torn ligament. There are a number of techniques employed but most require a ligament implant inserted through or around the joint. Provided the operation is done before arthritic changes develop in the joint surface, the results are good as the joint is stabilised.

## SKIN DISORDERS WITH A POSSIBLE INHERITED BASIS

The GSD seems particularly susceptible to skin infection with *Staphylococcus intermedius*. Many dogs may scratch for a variety of reasons but bacterial dermatoses seem to be more common in this breed than in others. Allergies are common too. Housing dogs exposes them to house dust mites at an early age. In former times most large breeds of dogs were reared in outdoor kennels and frequently spent a lot of their non-working time as an adult in a kennel. Flea bites and Sarcoptic mange cause skin itch in many dogs and there is no hereditary susceptibility to either of these parasitic infections.

Anal furunculosis is a painful and unpleasant disease affecting the skin under the German Shepherd's tail; it has a variety of causes. A defect of the T lymphocyte cells of the immune system was suspected but it is probable that the bacteria in the anal region first invade the hair follicles, then cause furunculosis and deep tissue invasions. The weeping site around the anus is obvious once the tail is lifted; oozing from the surface comes also from tunnels below the skin. Anal sacs beside the rectum may also be a source of bacterial infection. Treatment may have to be prolonged and expensive, with high doses of antibiotics. Radical surgical excision, that may have to be done more than once, may be complemented by cryosurgery with the freezing of the diseased tissue.

## NERVOUS SYSTEM DISORDERS

CANINE DEGENERATIVE RADICULO-MYELOPATHY (CDRM): The older German Shepherd seems more susceptible to this than other large breeds; the reason for this is not understood. As a disease of the nerve roots of the spinal cord, signs may develop quite slowly in middle-aged to elderly Shepherds. The swaying of the hind legs that seems associated with the hips may at first be attributed to hip dysplasia. The toes begin to lose their feeling, the dog cannot place its feet in the correct spot and eventually the nails wear, and bleeding sores can be seen on the front of each toe on the back leg, as the dog fails to pick up its feet as it walks. Treatment is usually unsuccessful but in such a slow-progressing disease steroids, acupuncture and other complementary medicine treatments have been advised by various experts; some treatments will delay the final stages of the illness.

EPILEPSY OR FITS: There is an idiopathic epilepsy in the GSD breed and certain families seem more frequently involved than others. Usually the first seizure is seen before three years of age, although often signs are not seen until 10 or more years old. There are many causes of fits and some 'attacks' appear as a result of a loss of control rather than epilepsy. Anticonvulsants can be used to prevent fits but diazpam (Valium) given per rectum is the only way of medicating a large dog in the middle of a fit. Dosages of 0.5mg per Kg can be administered by dog owners in collaboration with their veterinary surgeon. Barbiturates and bromides may also be used.

GIANT AXONAL NEUROPATHY: This rare disease of German Shepherds is inherited as an autosomal recessive trait. The nerves and the spinal cord are affected. Signs are seen at 14 to 16 months of age as a progressive weakness more noticeable in the hind legs. The dog's bark may be lost or weaker than usual and there may be faecal incontinence. Dilation of the oesophagus occurs around 18 months of age with food regurgitation and sometimes inhalation pneumonia. Total paralysis of the legs is the final stage and there is no effective treatment.

## DIGESTIVE SYSTEM DISORDERS

BLOAT: The sudden accumulation of gas in the stomach will cause distress and, if left untreated, eventual death. Gastric dilation and torsion of the stomach (GDV) can be a problem in any of the larger breeds. It is especially associated with the Giant Breeds and Setters but it may be found in German Shepherds as an acute emergency. The feeding routine should be such as to avoid hungry dogs swallowing food rapidly, then being left unexercised and unobserved. The Guide Dog for the Blind Association Kennels' routine is to feed in the morning before the two work periods during the daytime so that gas cannot accumulate in the stomach when the dog is left unattended and unexercised. Any dog with a tendency to bloat will be seen at the earliest stage of discomfort. Often a silicone-based tablet can be given at this stage to stop bubbles of gas being held in the stomach. Dogs known to 'bloat' can be made to eat more slowly by supervising them and feeding them on their own, when there is no competition from other dogs stealing their food. Canned dog food seems less likely to cause bloat than some of the complete or semi-moist diets. The treatment of gastric dilation is dealt with in the previous chapter.

## DIARRHOEA FROM BACTERIAL OVERGROWTH: The condition now known as SIBO (small intestine bacterial overgrowth) is a disorder that may be the cause of persisting diarrhoea, increased appetite and weight loss. The GSD has been thought to have a low serum and mucosal level of IgA – the surface protection mechanism of the immune system. To explain it simply, it is a disorder where there are too many bacteria living in the small intestine for the dog's health. These bacteria take some of the best nutrients out of the food eaten that passes from the stomach to the small intestine. Diagnosis has to be confirmed by blood tests, then a month-long course of antibiotics together with a modified low-fat diet is usually sufficient to clear the disorder entirely. The diet may be supplemented with Vitamin B and trace elements such as are found in a number of pet health tablets available.

COPROPHAGIA: This is a habit acquired by dogs kept in kennels, since dogs adequately supervised at a time when defecation is about to occur will have little opportunity to explore the smells or the taste of recently voided faeces. The flavouring agents and palatable residues that are found in faeces after prepared foods have been apparently digested to a dog's satisfaction, must be blamed for the dog's subsequent nose investigation, then taste exploration, before ingestion of the faeces. Treatment of a behaviour pattern associated with boredom should be adopted, deterrents such as garlic, paprika and even fresh pineapple have been used to curb a dog's desire to eat faeces. Blood tests for SIBO (as above) should be taken. The habit may not be so revolting as first thought, since rabbits use the method of eating faeces taken from their own rectums as a way of further digesting cellulose for food, and many free range animals will eat faeces from herbivores left on the ground, as a way of obtaining extra Vitamin B.

EXOCRINE PANCREATIC INSUFFICIENCY (EPI): This is most often associated with the German Shepherd breed; it has a strong hereditary basis and fortunately now seems to be much less common than 20 years ago. This may be due to more accurate diagnostic tests being used and the fact that, once it was identified, litters from the same blood lines have not been bred again. One third of all cases of EPI are found in other breeds such as Labradors, Collies, Golden Retrievers and even in mixed breeds. The disease may not show up until middle age, when it shows up as a chronic diarrhoea with weight loss due to a failure in the digestive enzymes in the small intestine. The EPI blood test is used to confirm a diagnosis. The response to treatment using low-fat diets, supplements of digestive enzymes in dried pancreatic extract, combined with drugs to lower stomach acidity, is good. Unfortunately long-term treatment adds to the expense of medication.

## BREEDING AND REPRODUCTION

DYSTOCIA FROM GROSS OVERSIZE OF A PUPPY: There are no specific breeding problems associated with the German Shepherd breed. Usually the litter sizes are large in number and the relatively neatly shaped puppies are delivered by the bitch without any human aid being needed. Very large litters born may cause secondary uterine inertia with delayed birth, and it should never be assumed that a bitch has finished whelping unless a physical check has been made. If, for any reason, there are only one or two puppies carried, they will be normally shaped but can grow relatively too large for the width of the bitch's pelvic canal. Known as the 'single puppy syndrome', this problem may be seen in the older bitch whelping: reproductive failure means fewer eggs are released from the ovary for fertilisation. The single oversized puppy can present the biggest problem with a delayed birth  Any bitch over five years old mated for the first time may well develop dystocia with a dead puppy. Careful observation of the pregnancy, with scanning at four weeks, may suggest the best time for a Caesarean operation.

CRYPTORCHIDISM: Before birth the male dog's testes originate in the abdomen from a site near the kidneys, similar to that occupied by the mature bitch's ovaries. The testes normally descend from within the abdomen through the inguinal canals and can be felt in the scrotum at about 20 days after birth. Export pedigrees for dogs require a statement that both testes are present in the scrotum and it may be difficult to be certain that both testes can be felt in the scrotum of the very young puppy. Total absence of the testes (anorchia) is very rare; monorchidism implies that only one testis had developed but the most usual abnormality is unilateral cryptorchidism when one testis is retained in the abdomen and one can be felt in the scrotum.

Unilateral cryptorchid dogs are fertile and have mated bitches, but it is a polygenic inherited defect and an attempt to breed out the condition should continue by not using affected dogs for stud. A testis in the scrotum functions better because it is in a cooler situation. The problem of the testis retained within the abdomen is that the higher body temperature within the abdomen seems to stimulate the cells within the testis to produce oestrogens. The Setoli cell tumour is 13 times more common in cryptorchid males than normal-sited testis males. The other signs of the tumour are a bilateral hair loss in the older dog, a pendulous penis and the attraction of other male dogs to the cryptorchid. Anaemia may develop due to excess oestrogen production depressing the bone marrow. Castration to remove both testes is advised but occasionally a request is made to leave the one testis in the scrotum and only have the retained intra-abdominal one removed.

## HEREDITARY BLEEDING DISORDERS

HAEMOPHILIA: Blood-clotting defects may lead to weakness and anaemia through the oozing of blood, or may cause collapse and sudden death especially when a road accident or a surgical operation is followed by excessive and often uncontrollable bleeding.

The German Shepherds have been affected by hereditary bleeding disorders. The history and the clinical examination by the veterinary surgeon should be helpful in distinguishing bleeding due to clotting factor defects (hereditary) and to platelet disorders such as thrombocytopenias or anticoagulant poisons (non-hereditary). Von Willebrand's Disease is probably the best-known of the group of coagulopathies; it is especially associated with the Doberman breed. Bleeding takes place into the body cavities, lameness may be due to blood clots in the joint spaces. In the inherited forms the bleeding from the gums may be one of the first signs of the problem at the time when milk teeth are shed; lameness may be seen in the puppy at the same time.

Appropriate blood samples need to be taken before starting veterinary treatment. Screening tests that can be performed before any surgical operation include the buccal mucous membrane cutting test, as well as a blood sample collected in a bottle for analysis. The previously used nail cut test was the first one used for haemophiliac dogs, but as the test is for defects of immediate blood clotting, and is also painful unless performed in the already anaesthetised patient, it is no longer used. Plasma transfusions are considered the best method of introducing clotting factors to a bleeding patient. In cases of anticoagulant poisoning, such as warfarin, the veterinary surgeon will use Vitamin K in large and repeated doses.

# Tail-male 'bloodlines' of Sieger 1899 - 1913.

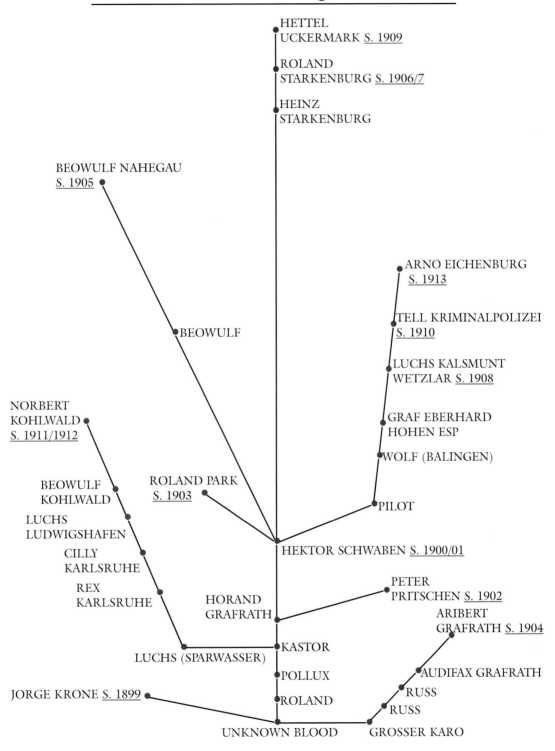

HETTEL
UCKERMARK S. 1909

ROLAND
STARKENBURG S. 1906/7

HEINZ
STARKENBURG

BEOWULF NAHEGAU
S. 1905

ARNO EICHENBURG
S. 1913

BEOWULF

TELL KRIMINALPOLIZEI
S. 1910

LUCHS KALSMUNT
WETZLAR S. 1908

NORBERT
KOHLWALD
S. 1911/1912

GRAF EBERHARD
HOHEN ESP

WOLF (BALINGEN)

BEOWULF
KOHLWALD

ROLAND PARK
S. 1903

LUCHS
LUDWIGSHAFEN

PILOT

CILLY
KARLSRUHE

HEKTOR SCHWABEN S. 1900/01

REX
KARLSRUHE

PETER
PRITSCHEN S. 1902

HORAND
GRAFRATH

ARIBERT
GRAFRATH S. 1904

LUCHS (SPARWASSER)

KASTOR

POLLUX

AUDIFAX GRAFRATH

RUSS

ROLAND

RUSS

JORGE KRONE S. 1899

UNKNOWN BLOOD

GROSSER KARO

## Tail-male 'bloodlines' of Siegerinnen 1899 - 1913.

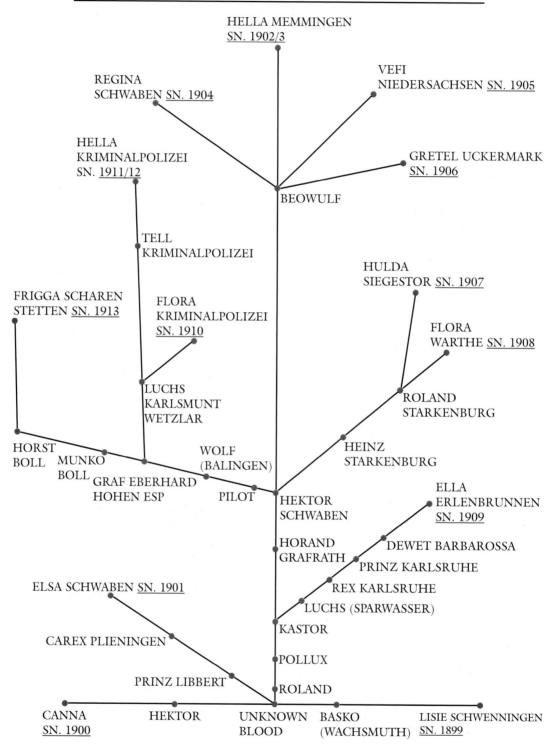

HELLA MEMMINGEN
SN. 1902/3

REGINA
SCHWABEN SN. 1904

VEFI
NIEDERSACHSEN SN. 1905

HELLA
KRIMINALPOLIZEI
SN. 1911/12

GRETEL UCKERMARK
SN. 1906

BEOWULF

TELL
KRIMINALPOLIZEI

HULDA
SIEGESTOR SN. 1907

FRIGGA SCHAREN
STETTEN SN. 1913

FLORA
KRIMINALPOLIZEI
SN. 1910

FLORA
WARTHE SN. 1908

LUCHS
KARLSMUNT
WETZLAR

ROLAND
STARKENBURG

HORST
BOLL

MUNKO
BOLL

WOLF
(BALINGEN)

HEINZ
STARKENBURG

GRAF EBERHARD
HOHEN ESP

PILOT

HEKTOR
SCHWABEN

ELLA
ERLENBRUNNEN
SN. 1909

HORAND
GRAFRATH

DEWET BARBAROSSA

PRINZ KARLSRUHE

ELSA SCHWABEN SN. 1901

REX KARLSRUHE

LUCHS (SPARWASSER)

CAREX PLIENINGEN

KASTOR

POLLUX

PRINZ LIBBERT

ROLAND

CANNA
SN. 1900

HEKTOR

UNKNOWN
BLOOD

BASKO
(WACHSMUTH)

LISIE SCHWENNINGEN
SN. 1899

# Tail-male 'bloodlines' of Leistungssieger 1906 - 1913.

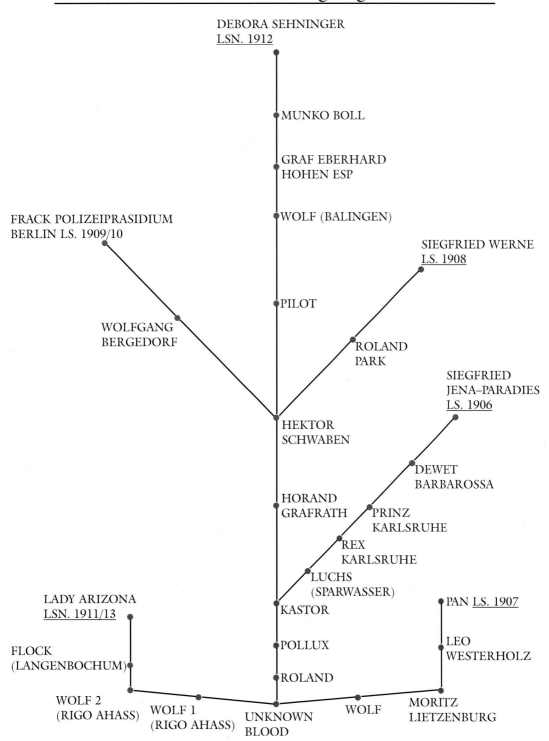

DEBORA SEHNINGER
LSN. 1912

MUNKO BOLL

GRAF EBERHARD
HOHEN ESP

WOLF (BALINGEN)

SIEGFRIED WERNE
LS. 1908

FRACK POLIZEIPRASIDIUM
BERLIN LS. 1909/10

PILOT

ROLAND
PARK

WOLFGANG
BERGEDORF

SIEGFRIED
JENA–PARADIES
LS. 1906

HEKTOR
SCHWABEN

DEWET
BARBAROSSA

HORAND
GRAFRATH

PRINZ
KARLSRUHE

REX
KARLSRUHE

LUCHS
(SPARWASSER)

LADY ARIZONA
LSN. 1911/13

KASTOR

PAN LS. 1907

FLOCK
(LANGENBOCHUM)

POLLUX

LEO
WESTERHOLZ

ROLAND

WOLF 2
(RIGO AHASS)

WOLF 1
(RIGO AHASS)

UNKNOWN
BLOOD

WOLF

MORITZ
LIETZENBURG

# Tail-male 'bloodlines' of Tending Sieger 1901 - 1913.

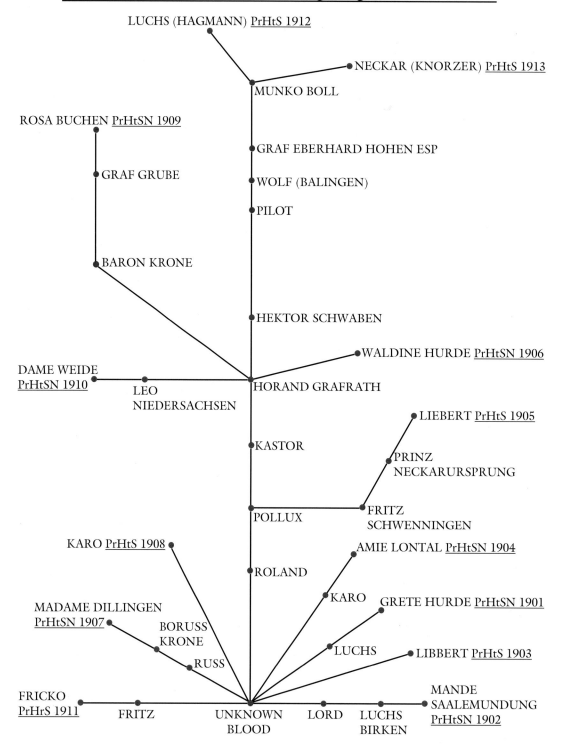

**NB: PrHtS – Preishutensieger          PrHtSN – Preishutensiegerin**